Those Who Remained

A Novel by

Zsuzsa F. Várkonyi

Translated by
Zsuzsa F. Várkonyi and Peter Czipott

English Editorial Revisions by
Patty Howell

Published by JewishGen Press
Part of JewishGen, Inc.
An Affiliate of the Museum of Jewish Heritage–
A Living Memorial to the Holocaust
36 Battery Place, New York, NY 10280

Those Who Remained

First U.S. Printing: April 2021

Original Title (Hungarian Edition):
Férfiidők lányregénye (Girl In A Man's World)
(4th ed. Budapest: Libri Kiadó, 2020)

German Edition:
Für wen du lebst: Ein Mädchenroman aus Männerzeiten
(Whom You Live For; Story of a Girl In a Time of Men)
(Konstanz: Hartung-Gorre Verlag, 2005)

Project Coordinator: Joel Alpert
Editing, Book and Cover Design: Nina Schwartz/impulsegraphics.com

Published by JewishGen Press
Part of JewishGen, Inc.
An Affiliate of the
Museum of Jewish Heritage–A Living Memorial to the Holocaust
36 Battery Place, New York, NY 10280

This is a work of fiction. Names, characters, business, events and incidents are the products of the author's imagination. Any resemblance to actual persons, living or dead, is purely coincidental.

Printed in the United States of America by Lightning Source, Inc.

Library of Congress Control Number (LCCN): 2021934306
ISBN: 978-1-954176-08-9 (paperback: 342 pages, alk. paper)

Cover Images:
Front: Actors Abigél Szőke and Károly Hajduk from the film *Those Who Remained* (*Akik maradtak*) ©2019 by Barnabás Tóth, Produced by Mónika Mécs. Production Company: Inforg-M&M Film Kft. Distributed in North America by Menemsha Films. Courtesy of the Producer.
Back: View of the Fisherman's Bastion in 1951 (Budapest).
Source PHOTO: Fortepan - ID 2223 via Wikimedia Commons.

Contents

Author's Introduction

Healing Trauma

I don't know, dear Reader, how old you are and what you have experienced in your life. Yet, as you have chosen this book to read, you must have some connection—emotionally, at least—with the ordeals that most Europeans of the 20th century endured. Suffering caused by other human beings has been dealt to most of us (and continues even today for many of us.) In this book you won't read, however, about the suffering but about the healing of those wounds. As women especially are more interested in healing than in cruelties committed, this is in that way a female story.

I was born and continue to live in Hungary, a country where both Hitler and Stalin managed to gain many industrious devotees. The social group I belong to suffered heavily in both periods of time. By writing this novel I wanted to commemorate my loved ones who bore this double storm of history with a straight back and without boasting about their wounds. Even after going through all the horrors of the Holocaust, they didn't want to teach hatred to their children, but understanding, solidarity, and love—something they developed from these extreme challenges.

During his forced labor service as a Jew, my father was in 1944 dragged to the concentration camp of Mauthausen.

He survived, returned home and became the father of us, two sisters, but disappeared once more, during a spring night in 1950, taken to a Stalinist internment camp for three years He never ever talked to us about those periods of his life. Both he and my mother wanted to avoid our coming to hate the people we were surrounded by. I am following now their intentions by not writing a single word about the horrors directly. I rather talk about the tender clinging-together during the time of permanent anxiety—my predominant experience as a child. It seems very important to me that we were able to find healing love within any social group. You will read about several beautiful *mensches* from my childhood: some of them were old, others young, some Jewish, others non-Jewish, some educated, others uneducated.

The movie based on this book was very well received internationally. I do hope that the message of this written version will also be easily understood in English: human emotions are universal, after all.

All three main characters of my story survived the Second World War completely "orphaned," and soon became fully supportive of each other: A childish, sixteen year-old girl, Klára, who even in 1948, was not willing to acknowledge the disappearance of her parents and of her whole past environment; a doctor, the son of a rabbi, who—after returning from a German concentration camp—searched for his wife and sons in vain, and kept reproaching the Almighty for letting him still be alive; and a warmhearted, weak, old aunt whose life no longer had any meaning other than having her young niece around.

The three of them help each other stand again on their own feet. Life seems to be almost normal by 1949, when the peace of their days and nights is robbed by a new wave of terror: that of Stalinism.

These were the worst years for almost every social class in Hungary. Only Stalin's death in 1953 brings some relief both to politics and to everyday life. Reparation begins for some victims early in 1956. Those rehabilitated are now allowed to accept jobs, by and large without restrictions. They also receive a compensation, although paltry, for their three or even six years spent in detention camps.

I don't want, however, to talk much about the history of Hungary. This is, after all, a novel and not a scholarly treatise. Still, I have inserted footnotes in several places where I thought these could bring beneficial context for younger, non-Hungarian readers.

In its original form, my novel showed events only up to 1950, the peak of Stalinist terror. Only a handful of diary excerpts by Klára, presented as an Epilogue, told about some later events of her life. I had to consider, however, the remarks of my Hungarian editor stating that rehabilitation for my characters could be as important as it was for my own family. That's how Chapter Four was conceived, and I am glad about it now. I hope I have been able to tell something new about the 1956 revolution: the way our people experienced it, and how I interpret the reasons for my staying in this country ever since. I am, after all, the only member of my once-big family who hasn't chosen a new country for herself and her children. The answer to why is found in Chapter Four, as well.

When I first started to work on translating this book into English, my thoughts sounded a bit strange to me in this language, although less so after finishing the German translation. This is because of something I have been aware of ever since learning these three languages: Hungarian is a "condensed" kind of language, a unique feature for people speaking Indo-European languages. But I was shocked to see, while translating my own words this time, that our encrypted/concise way of talking in Hungarian—so typical for our frightened parents' generation and completely well understood even by us, their children, is like Chinese for a German or English reader. So, I had to let go of these typical shortcuts, and make those statements broader, to be understandable to foreign ears. I was shocked to realize that the Hungarian conciseness has less to do with our grammar than with the fact that, during dictatorial times, people learned high-level skills in coded speech.

I am especially grateful to my dear American friends, Patty Howell and Peter Czipott, who did a great deal to bring my text closer to high standard American English.

One more comment on translation: small nuances of the way we address each other can tell a lot about a given relationship. As in other languages, Hungarians are inclined to call each other a handful of different nicknames, as a tender verbal stroke. I tried to keep some of them in the English text. This is especially important in the relationship between parents and their children of the postwar generation: we learn from our earliest days that our parents are vulnerable. When young Klára addresses her chosen father as " Aldó dearest", she feels the same caring as we, the postwar generation, did whenever our elder ones seemed to feel pain.

I very much hope that in reading this book, you will enjoy my story as much as my Hungarian and German readers have, and also discover some clues to the strange, sometimes whimsical reactions of your one-time war-torn family members.

Zsuzsa F. Várkonyi
Psychologist
Author

Budapest, February 3, 2021

Chapter 1

"I came over to make you happy..." *(August-November 1948)*

Klára pouted as she walked beside Olgi, who was trying to calm her down:

"He won't do you any harm. He just wanted to see you." she said. "You'll be sixteen soon! Other girls have had their periods for a long time by now! He might have some ideas how to... A decent Jewish doctor... What are you sulking about? You've seen a lot of doctors recently without being afraid of them..."

Klára knew how to annoy Olgi the most, and that was by not saying a single word.

When they entered the doctor's office, she didn't even greet him. The doctor seemed innocuous, like a cipher. Not even repulsive. Klára spied on him from underneath her eyelashes: what would this man do if she didn't respond in any way?

He moved towards her.

"My name is Aladár Körner. And yours?"

She thought about this for a while then replied dismissively, "Klára Wiener."

"Do you want to sit down?"

"No."

"Do you want your aunt to leave while we are talking?"

"No."

Klára glared at the doctor for many minutes before he gave up. He sat down by Olgi's side and didn't even bother to whisper.

"I think hormones are the smallest part of the problem here. We both know there are many reasons for this. Her body shows no signs of hormonal maturity... Klára, would you please raise your arms?

Klára obeyed grumpily. She had on a sleeveless blouse and a few orphan strands of hair straggled out.

"She's just at the start of puberty, as you can see. Let's leave her alone for the time being... Come back in six months."

"It's not the start. She's been like this for two years," Olgi whispered in despair.

"Even so, let's wait. How could her body produce hormones when she only weighs seventy-some pounds?"

• • • •

That was in August of '48. In November, Klára was again sitting on the bench in front of Dr. Körner's office, without her aunt. It was six o'clock. The doctor should be done with his patients soon, she thought. But it might take longer. Papa used to stay late with his patients, too.

One more woman was still waiting for the doctor. His assistant stepped out and said to Klára:

"Are you waiting for Dr. Körner?"

"Yes. After he's finished."

"Didn't you come for consultation?"

"No... Yes... After he's finished."

The assistant looked at Klára with impatience and pity. Then she nodded to show that she'd made her decision and disappeared behind the door. A patient left the office and the last woman went in. A minute later, the doctor opened the door.

"Oh, it's you!"

"Yes."

"Any trouble?"

"No."

"Can you wait?"

"Yes, I can."

It was half past six when the last patient left the office.

"Come in!" the doctor said.

"I don't want to go in."

"Haven't you come to see me?"

"Yes, I have."

"What's the problem with coming in, then?"

"I only want to say something. While you're out here..."

The doctor walked into the waiting room and sat down on Klára's bench.

"Aren't you going home now?" she said.

"I am. Sooner or later."

"Then I'll come with you."

Astonished, the doctor raised his eyebrows. In August she hadn't been able to shock him at all, despite her persistent efforts. So, this felt good. Like in school, where some of her teachers were sure she was retarded. Everybody can be made a fool of, she gloated.

"Does it mean you want me to change and leave with you?"

"Yeah."

The doctor nodded and disappeared. She was proud of not calling him Doctor or Sir, just accepting what he offered as if she deserved it.

The doctor came out after a few minutes, dressed for the street. He seemed suddenly much older and weaker. His movements were slower. In his white lab coat, he didn't look any older than Papa. Papa is forty-seven now. On the tenth of November. Mama had always made stuffed duck on his birthday. What's the date today?

"What did you want to say?"

Klára tried to stall for time.

"Aren't women afraid of gynecologists?"

"They don't say so."

"I don't say it, either. But I am."

"It might be the same with others...What did you want to say?"

"That I got my... period."

"That's good news!"

"It's only you who are happy about it! And my aunt, I came to make you happy. But I think it's shitty! Disgusting! Plus stomach aches... terrible..."

"Put something warm on it."

"My Mother always has a big scarf around her waist on those days. But she says it's a good thing, because that's what makes us Mothers later. I don't see any connection!"

While walking together on the street, the doctor became more and more silent, while Klára grew more sharp-tongued. She pronounced the doctor's coat ugly, really impossible, and denounced both her aunt and the school.

"You've got many faces," he mused. "Last time you seemed like a retarded child. Today when we first met, you sounded like a nice little girl. And now you seem like an annoying adolescent."

Klára laughed naughtily, "I've got even more faces!"

"That'll be enough for today!"

She became silent. The man began to regret he had put up such a hard face.

"Let's leave it for next time," he added.

"I won't come anymore."

"By the way," he said, "I've also got two faces."

"A nice one and an annoying one?"

"More or less. Which way are you going?"

"I'm just going...Where do you live? I'll accompany you. And walk back afterwards."

The doctor asked more questions. Whether she has friends—she doesn't; what kind of music she likes; does she go to movies sometimes, and so on. But it was all just empty, polite adult talk. And he asked again if she wanted to go home. To his own surprise, he finally agreed to let Klára see his place. He might have had many reasons for resisting this idea. Not only because for many years, nobody but the gas-meter reader had set foot inside. Just Klára's tiresome inscrutability would have been reason enough to say no.

• • • •

"Are you always alone here?"

"Yes. Always."

"Why do you want to send me home, then?"

"It's better alone."

"Are you lying now?"

"Yes. Always."

"Even now?"

"Even now."

"Then you're not always lying!"

"What?"

"If it were a lie that you always lie, then it's not true, of course. And if it's true that you always lie, then you are not lying now—so even in that case you do not always lie."

The man kept his eyes on her. One corner of his mouth rose. But Klára was busy with her own thoughts.

"How can a statement contradict itself? Give me a piece of paper!"

She started to draw squares, some with an X and some without, putting either minus or plus signs next to them. When the desired outcome failed to emerge, she furiously crossed out the whole design and started again. The man watched her but was not interested enough to inquire what she was doing, even though he did not understand the squares.

"What's your grade in math?" he finally asked.

"I am just about to fail."

"That must take you quite a bit of effort."

"I'm working on the same thing in other subjects, as well."

"...Is that a good goal?"

"Why should it be good? What does it mean, anyhow: 'good'?"

Without any hope of changing her, the doctor shared his next thought.

"...Before your first period, you seemed to be a gentler girl."

"But you pushed me anyway."

"No, I didn't."

"Alright, it was my aunt. But she wanted you to help with this."

"But I didn't."

"I know."

"Why did you say so, then?"

"...It felt good."

A naughty smile appeared on her face again. The doctor did not resent it—but he looked away.

"It's for your aunt's sake, by the way, that I'm asking you to go home. She hasn't had a single restful minute because of you."

"I know. Her life would be easier if I weren't here anymore either."

"...Do you want some tea?"

"Don't start feeling pity for me! That's what I hate the most! I'm fine without your tea!"

"Is there anything you don't hate?"

"No, there isn't. I hate tea, too. But you have to put something into your stomach as long as you're alive."

The doctor watched her. Wordlessly. That felt good although she was afraid that he'd try to talk her out of her ideas.

After a while, Klára gave voice to her thoughts again.

"Why are you alive?"

"...Is there any explanation for... such a thing?"

"There should be!"

"But there isn't."

Silence, then Klára again.

"It's us who came off worse, I think."

"Worse than...?"

"Than those, who... went away... I was left behind simply out of forgetfulness. You, too?"

This bald description hit him deep in his center. Adulthood disappeared from his face instantaneously. He started to nod slowly, while looking into the distance. Then he turned his back to rearrange his features. He fiddled putting on the gas for tea, and spoke with his back to her, "I just call it by another name."

"What do you call it?"

"The punishment. It's not over, yet. I still have to go on."

"What's your sin?"

"I don't know."

"I might not even have any sins. It's just like the family has gone on holiday and didn't notice that I missed the train. And the train can't turn around. My brother at least got on another train. I didn't."

Silence.

"Does he write?"

"How do you know that...?"

"What?"

"That he's able to send letters."

"Your aunt told me that he left for Palestine."

"What the hell else did she tell you? Damn!"

"Not much. I asked her if she's got any idea why you don't want to grow up."

Long pause. Then Klára asked, "And what've you concluded?"

This was the first time her voice had sounded relaxed, almost cheerful. The voice of her home, Papa's voice. But rather than answer her directly, the doctor seemed to be working on a tactful evasion.

"If you want to tell me a lie again, you'd do better to say nothing."

He smiled. It was a real smile, and nodded.

"If you don't like the taste of tea, you can drink it quite light, with a lot of sugar and lemon substitute."

"Do you add sugar to tea? Olgi won't let me. All the sugar we get in a month has to be put aside for the weekend cakes. It's her obsession that I can gain more weight from having the sugar in a cake. You can see how fat I've got! Almost eighty-five pounds! Olgi is a genius!"

"Why are you mad at her?"

"'Cause she's an idiot."

"Why?"

"Because she was born like that. My parents had seven wonderful siblings and cousins! But who's the only one left? Poor dumb Olgi!"

"Why do you call her an idiot?"

"Do you think she's ever read a serious book? She reads romance novels where you need two big handkerchiefs per page!"

"For God's sake, she's not intending to be your literature teacher—just to cook for you, to be there for you at home, and to be worried to death when you have a problem..."

"These are just mother-hen instincts! She doesn't understand anything! She didn't understand that her husband's gone, her two sons are gone and now my brother's gone! You know what she talks about the whole day? Where can you get potatoes, which day the meat will arrive in the store, and whether there are enough eggs for the Saturday cake!"

"How can you," the doctor whispered, mostly to himself.

But Klára heard him. She turned towards the window. She was angry and bitter. Why does this doctor want to take away even her little pleasures, like being angry with Olgi? Of course, she's saying ugly things—but isn't that allowed? Her eyes were burning, but she wouldn't let herself cry.

The doctor touched her lightly on her back. Klára clenched her fists.

Just don't turn around, she said to herself. But she could not resist the second touch. The man hugged her. It was Papa's gesture! Just like him! His smell is different, not as delicious as Papa's, but even so–so wonderful! Everything is all right. Now she can die in peace!

"The water's boiling," came the wake-up call.

Klára let him go with a feeling of acceptance, the way she had learned to release a good dream in the morning.

The doctor started to prepare the tea. Klára sat back on the kitchen stool. Her mouth watered as she watched the third spoon of sugar being poured into her mug.

"Do you like it with lemon substitute?" he asked.

"Don't know."

The man poured some tea into a small mug, put a little bit of sugar into it and started to grind a white tablet with a knife. He added the powder to the little portion and handed it to her. Klára sniffed it skeptically and finally tasted it.

"It's good."

The doctor dropped the rest of the tablet into Klára's big mug.

"Is lemon substitute made out of lemon?" she asked.

"No."

"I thought so. Like other things."

They drank the tea without talking. It was very good although it was so hot they could only slurp it. You shouldn't slurp, if you have good manners... but the doctor slurped it, too.

"Aren't you hungry?"

"No... never... How can somebody be called Aladár?"

"You should have asked my parents."

"And what do people call you?"

"...Doctor."

"Alright, but by name?"

"Nobody calls me by my name."

Klára thought that he might be serious. Much more so than what he had said about lying. Her discomfort showed on her face. So the doctor made the effort to change to a more easy-going tone.

"It's all the same whether the name is Aladár or Hugo," he said.

Without asking, he put some biscuits on the table. Klára waited to be offered them.

"If you dip one into the tea, it will even pick up some flavor. Are you really never hungry?"

"Sometimes I am, in the evenings. But even then I can push it aside if I want to. During the day, however, I don't eat. But I'm naturally slim."

"Was your mother slim, too?"

Long silence.

"Do you think she can't come back anymore?" Klára asked.

The man looked far away and replied with a sigh, "It's been easier for me since I accepted the way it is. If you want, though, you can keep waiting."

Klára stood up, slowly picked up her bag and went to look for her coat."

"The tea?" the doctor asked uncertainly.

She shook her head.

"I'll see you home. It's dark."

Klára shrugged her shoulders. It was too weak a protest.

They did not speak on the street. Sitting on the tram, they saw a cart loaded with potatoes and pulled by a horse. The man was relieved to have a reason for breaking the silence.

"Olgi would be happy."

Klára nodded. And she, too, offered a little present.

"She makes very good mashed potatoes. If we have butter."

"You need it for the real thing."

"Do you cook, too?"

"Sometimes, on the weekends. There's a dining service in the clinic. What I get there is enough."

"Isn't the food yucky there?"

"It's food."

"I know you want to say that we should appreciate it. I think it'd be better the other way around: not to appreciate it at all. That way we aren't held back by food either. I've managed to kick the habit pretty well by now."

Now the doctor could no longer resist opposing Klára's perennial wish to die.

"When somebody is as young as you, there are still a lot of meaningful things to do here."

Klára made a face with a disparaging sound. After a few seconds she also perceived another message behind the words.

“Does that mean you’ve earned the right to give up, but I have not?”

“I did not say so. What I meant was that you can look forward to much more joy.”

“Yes, sir. I see that. Very clearly.”

The man withdrew again.

Klára continued, “Or... if you doctors would stop curing people... that’s a solution, too. One day, sooner or later, we’ll be all gone.”

“Stop that!”

“Why? The punishment would be over much quicker.”

The man could not decide whether to take this miserable little creature back to his home or forget about her forever. After getting off the tram, Klára—just for a change—decided to “behave” again.

“And what do you do all alone in the evenings?”

By now, the doctor was afraid of her every question.

“I read... medical journals...”

As there was no new suggestion coming from Klára for collective death, he went on.

“I spend a lot of time with them, because I read German pretty slowly. But I’ve got plenty of time.”

“Do you read the *Wiener Medizinische Wochenschrift*? And the *Hungarian Journal of Internal Medicine*?”

The doctor looked at her, amazed.

"Papa... my father subscribed to these, and to the *Révue Médicale Français*. But those got lost. Only the *Wochenschrift* and the *Journal* got saved. Papa always makes the joke that the *Wiener Medizinische Wochenschrift* is named after him—because our name is Wiener! I don't know where the *Révues* have gone. Such things shouldn't have been stolen by the Arrow Cross gang.[1] It was smart of Olgi to let our apartment be locked after she found my brother and me in the Red Cross House. In that way she saved what had not been stolen."

"I did not know your father was a doctor."

"There are still many prisoners of war, aren't there?"

The man hadn't felt so tired for a long time.

"We don't know how many. But there must be some."[2]

"There are, aren't there?"

"Yes."

They arrived at Olgi's place.

"That's where I live," Klára said.

"Good night, then. Next time, however, you should let Olgi know when you want to stay out so late."

"She doesn't fight with me about that anymore."

"That still doesn't make it easier for her."

Klára did not move. Her face lost its confident mask, as well as its characteristic defiance. She looked at the man's face and then at the asphalt under her feet.

1. *Name of the Hungarian Fascist Party.*
2. *As far as the general public was informed, all prisoners of war had been released from the Soviet Union by the summer of 1948.*

"Could you...?"

"What?"

"Could you..." She looked at her shoe: "...Could you... once more... like in the kitchen... give me a hug?"

No less embarrassed than she was, the man obeyed. While Klára was taking several deep breaths as if getting oxygen after a long time, he also got caught by the feeling of holding her and started to tremble. Frightened by his own reaction, he withdrew and asked, "Can I also... ask you for something... in return?"

"For what?"

"That you eat lunch. I have lunch, too..."

Klára wished she could hide under the skin of the doctor. She had finally come up with an idea where to hide! She had a hard time remembering ever having felt so good! She gave a huge sigh and asked in a pretend-mean voice, "Do you mean tomorrow?"

"No," the man replied with a smile. "I mean every day."

"For just a single hug?" Klára flirted happily. She may have been ten when she had last responded to someone in this way.

"For two... or... we can still bargain. Now you go. I'll wait until you get up the stairs."

"How do you know we live upstairs?"

"You looked up when we arrived, maybe to check if the lights were on up there."

• • • •

Sweet Mama, dear Papa!

Yesterday I went to see the doctor I told you about in that stupid gynecology place. I just wanted to tell him that I got my period. I thought he would be glad. He wasn't really. He is just like Laci Weltheim, whom you called a "sad ass," Papa. He probably wasn't this sad before the war. I guess he's not really an ass, either. But Papa, you called Laci one, even though he also was smart. The Doc said there are still many prisoners of war. And the radio also said that there are still many wounded Hungarians in hospitals in Sweden and Holland. Papa, may I use the Wochenschrifts*? I'll take good care of them!*

. . . .

To Olgi's surprise, Klára spent most of the rest of the week at home. In the mornings she left for school. On some days she returned well before lunchtime, without any conceivable explanation—like she had before—but she spent the rest of the day in her room instead of wandering around town.

She must be busy with straightening up her parent's things again, Olgi thought. There was some truth in it. Klára also asked her for some money, but not much. After disappearing with her four Forints,[3] she was soon back, holding something wrapped in her hand. It looked like a long, thin book. Olgi had learned not to ask. But, altogether, Klára seemed much more tolerable than usual. The typewriter in her room was tapping away until late. Where had this child learned to type? That's why she had been desperate to save that gadget. She must have bought the paper for it yesterday, Olgi thought. Where else could

3. *In those years, you could buy approximately 2 pounds (1 kg) of bread for this sum.*

those big sheets have come from? And she is eating a bit more. On Saturday she had said she would like some caraway soup.

Olgi could not believe her ears. She thickened the soup quite a lot and risked Klára's complaining about too much fat. But Klára ate a full plate of it with all the toasted croutons. Olgi did not dare to show her joy, knowing that would make Klára refuse the soup.

. . . .

Monday at six, Klára was again sitting on the bench in front of Dr. Körner's office. She clutched an elegant, old-fashioned leather briefcase in her hand. The assistant looked carefully at her and gave a nod in response to Klára's silence, to show she knew what Klára wanted. When the next patient left the consulting room, the doctor stepped out, too.

"Hmm?" he smiled.

"I've brought you something... When you're finished."

"There are still three ladies waiting."

"I know. I'll wait out here."

The doctor did not move.

"What did you bring?"

"I'll show you later. It might be... not as good... I can wait."

"A surprise?"

"Yes. But you might not find it... useful. I just brought it."

"Show me a little bit?"

"Later, when you have time."

"Alright," he replied and went back to his office.

Before the door was closed with the last patient behind it, the doctor stuck his head out again. "Very soon now..."

Klára gave a nod. It was almost seven o'clock when the doctor finally stepped out in his ugly, old man's coat.

"How old are you?" she asked.

Oh, my God, she is starting again! An hour ago, she still seemed like a pleasant child.

"About forty-two."

"My Papa is forty-seven now. But he was also forty-two when I last saw him. Have you never had children?"

"What did you bring along? You promised to show it to me."

Klára could accept his answer, because this wasn't just a stupid adult evasion but was meant seriously, like his comment about nobody calling him by name. Mama always warned her not to make anybody talk about painful things. Olgi has never heard of that rule, of course. She could keep silent by now, but only because Klára's tantrums had taught her to.

"I went through Papa's journals. And translated the tables of contents of the *Zeitschrifts* for you. I also kept the original titles, so you can compare them. If you tell me which article is of interest for you, I'll translate it. I've got nothing better to do anyway. And I translated one article as a test. I just don't know... in some places... if it's all right. I checked in the dictionary when I got stuck, but it did not help much. I always put a question mark after such sentences, so that you don't think I'm stupid."

"I don't think that."

"I was taught translating by Mama. She always says I've got ears for languages like an ape. Apes are supposed to have good ears. Don't they? We talked with our grandparents in German... and Papa and Mama were very proud of me translating the whole *Max und Moritz* into French for my little sister. But that translation got lost, too. And little Juti died. She died. I saw her."

The man started to tremble again.

"It's very cold," he said. "Why don't we sit in a café? I could look at your translations in there."

"Shall we get sugar with the coffee?"

"Sure."

And so they went into the Café Savoy. The man broke the silence after a while. "Have you had lunch?"

"Today?"

"Today and the other days."

Klára counted on her fingers: "Three times. But not today."

"Why not?"

"I wasn't at home."

"Did you tell Olgi?"

"I only said I didn't know when I'll be home."

The waiter soon appeared at their little round table: "Would you like coffee substitute or black coffee?"

"Coffee substitute" the doctor replied.

"I don't want any coffee substitute! Then I won't drink anything!"

"But black coffee is very strong."

"I don't care! I don't want any substitute for anything anymore! Not even lemon substitute."

"Bring us two black coffees, please. Do you have milk? And cakes?"

"Mignon?" she asked with sparkling eyes.

"We've got mignons, too. What kind would you like?"

"Go to the counter and choose." the doctor suggested. When Klára was already on her way, he added, "choose two cakes!"

"But I don't know which ones you like!"

"I meant two for yourself. Alright, choose one for me, too. Any kind."

Klára looked almost like a happy child when she came back. "I got chocolate and also a fruit one for me and a chocolate one for you. Is that all right? But they will cost three thirty all together."

"No problem."

"Do you have plenty of money?"

The doctor made a face as if to say: It all depends.

Klára suddenly realized that adults call this topic "improper." She tried to fix it.

"I can pay for them, too."

"Let me invite you to be my guest," the doctor smiled. "So that I get a chance to spend my heaps of money."

"I didn't mean it...But we have so little money. Olgi knits scarves and does needlework for sale. She gets her widow's pension and my orphan's allowance. All in all, it's good that Olgi is there. Without her I would now be sitting in the Jewish orphanage where Mama and Papa would not find me if... How many children live there?"

"A hundred and fourteen now," he said.

"How do you know?"

Coffee and cakes arrived at the best possible time. Klára instantly forgot about the orphanage and the doctor's suspicious familiarity with that information. When the delicious cakes were all gone, he inquired about her translations. Klára insisted that the waiter wipe off the table first. The leather briefcase must stay clean. It belongs to Papa. It mustn't get stained! The doctor started to read, lifting his eyebrows and opening his eyes wide.

"Hey, kid... you should do this... later, professionally. Your Hungarian is also beautiful."

He was thinking about Klára's uneven speech, sometimes so plain, at other times so exacting. She reminded him of a boat without ballast.

"I read a lot. That's the key, Mama says. That's how she phrased it."

"And Olgi says that you're out and about a lot! But if you read so much, you must be at home a lot, too..."

"No. I mainly read during classes. And also in the afternoon, in the lobby of the movie theater... Sometimes I get a pretzel from the pretzel guy."

The man sighed again.

"And what sort of books do you read?"

"Well, whatever I could save from our library. But unfortunately, I've already read all the good things. I finish a book every other day... Well, I might learn to like the others later... Thomas Mann is best! Not so much in Hungarian, but he's beautiful in German. At some places I've even figured out, how I'd have translated them...not the way they are in the book... Have you ever cared to read some Thomas Mann?"

. . . .

The man sat down in the kitchen with Klára's briefcase. He put some old newspaper under it. He wasn't really interested in the content of the translation, but was surprised to see some elegant linguistic solutions—along with a few silly attempts, of course. He spent long minutes deliberating over which article to have Klára translate, one with clear connection to gynecology. Otherwise—as suspicious as she is—she would doubt the sincerity of his interest. He could bet on it... Okay, but how could he spark some interest in her schoolwork? Is she going to flunk in German and Hungarian, too? Considering her many aristocratic mannerisms, what kind of life would she face if she failed to graduate?

When he realized he'd been fantasizing about Klára's future for half an hour, he angrily pulled out his chess set, as he usually did on his worst nights. This was the perfect exercise to replace the missing souls around him. The trembling came on several times while he played. He was glad that in the last year or two he'd only trembled at home, out of sight of witnesses. But this girl had triggered it often. For the first time in many years, he imagined how wonderful it would be to bathe in a full tub of water. His muscles might relax there. But, alas, only five gallons of water fit in his washtub, and that made for only five inches of water in the bathtub... Nevertheless, he filled the pot and lit the gas under it. Although on Mondays, he usually only washed in the basin, to keep the gas bill low.

The doorbell rang. It was half past nine! Could it be another broken water pipe? That was why the neighbors rang so late last time. Klára stood in the doorway. Her face was more strained than ever.

"What happened?"

"Can I stay here?"

"What's wrong?... Here, come on in."

"I'm not going to go back to Olgi..." she sobbed.

She gave no useful information for a long while. Nor did the doctor try to push her. First he just tried to comfort her, then he made her a tea with a lot of sugar but no lemon substitute, and a buttered bread. There wasn't anything else at home, anyway. To his surprise, Klára accepted everything. Then, slowly, the picture came into focus.

"She saw us from the window today, when we arrived... and how you hugged me...,She said she's had enough... That until today, she thought I was an unhappy child... but she is not willing to raise a whore..."

She really is no flaming genius, he thought, Klára was right about that.

"And that she can't take any more... If I really hate her that much, she said, it would be better for me, too, if I left... She can't do anything more for me, than she's done... This week she saw me 'in much better shape'... because I was at home all week... And she was glad because she thought I was happier with her than before. But, well, if I want to take up with men, she can't just sit and watch..."

"Do you have a telephone?" sighed the man. "What's your number?"

"I won't go home!"

"You don't have to go home... if you don't want to... But we have to appease Olgi too."

"She must be perfectly all right by now! ...Or... she'll say that I should go home, after all... If you kick me out, I'll go to the waiting room of the train station to sleep! There I can really become a slut. There are lots of guys there. Full of men..."

The doctor was silent for a while; then he asked:

"Don't you want to take a bath? I just began to heat the water. There isn't much, but this is how I usually bathe."

"...Us too," replied Klára in a hoarse baritone.

"Then I'll wash the tub for you..."

"But don't call Olgi!" yet another helpless sigh.

Then a new idea struck him. "But I'm the reason you got into trouble!"

"You're not at fault! I was the one who asked you to hug me!"

"Fine, but I, for my part, agreed to it... for four lunches a week."

Klára was thinking again. Then she sounded out a new thought:

"Why is someone... who's scared to be alone... called a whore?"

The man rested his eyes on Klára.

"Can I call her up, if I promise you that you can stay here, no matter what she says?"

"No, because you're going to feel sorry for her, and you'll try to reconcile us, I know. Don't call her, please."

"And how about if *you* called her?"

"No..."

"Alright, I'll wash the tub and bring the water in for you. Meanwhile you think hard, too... Let's find a solution that's good for you and good for her as well."

Klára regained an even keel. Even Mama would have been proud of her next thought:

"But wasn't that bath water meant for you?"

"I'll put up another potful."

"We don't take a bath every day... because it costs too much. But in the old days, we used to bathe every evening. We had a water heater back then."

"Us, too."

The use of the plural made Klára think about the man's family. Still, she'd rather not ask about them anymore. As if, finally, Mama were standing at her side and, with a smile and a wink from below, she were saying "My little girl, you know... we don't ask questions about things like that."

The bathwater was ready. The man set out a towel, and a huge, nightshirt-like piece of clothing made of white linen, stamped "Saint Stephen's Hospital Maternity Ward." Before she closed the bathroom door, Klára called out:

"Promise you won't call her while I'm bathing?"

"Well, this was our deal, right?"

Doc's bathwater pot is a lot bigger than Olgi's. They couldn't carry in this much water. Klára slid down as far as she could in the tub, and the water covered her almost entirely. For the first time in many years, it occurred to her that you could also lie on your stomach in the bathwater.

Long ago, she and Gyuri always "went swimming" in the tub! She wondered if Gyuri was also hairy "down there" now? And suddenly she flashed on what Papa looked like naked. She'd see him that way sometimes. It was fascinating and a little scary too. One night when she and Mama were whispering to each other before their goodnight kiss, Mama said it's not scary, because it also has to do with love. Klára was sure that Mama was telling the truth, so she was not interested in more details.

. . . .

"Well now, have you been thinking about it?" asked the man, when Klára emerged from the bathroom in her oversize shirt, with an embarrassed smile on her face. But Doc didn't seem to find anything odd about her outfit.

"About Olgi? Actually, no..."

"Although we agreed you would, right?"

"Yeah... alright... then go ahead and call her. But I won't go home!"

"Okay. Give me the number."

The man didn't dial right away, but wrote down Olgi's number first.

"Can't you remember six digits?" asked Klára, in a voice actually more pitiful than disparaging.

Doc didn't react. As if he were tired. Klára eavesdropped on the conversation for a while:

"Good evening, this is Aladár Körner speaking. Your little girl is here with me..."

Long silence.

"I don't know, why me..."

Silence.

"You can be sure, Olgi dear, it wasn't my idea..."

It seemed to be Olgi's turn again.

"Of course, I understand... This period seems to be a difficult one, as well..."

Doc sighs again and again.

"That was me... I know it may look misleading, but... you don't need to worry about her because of me... Even if I lacked common decency, I don't belong to that category anymore... if you understand what I mean... But my decency is still functioning."

Olgi spoke again, while Klára was waiting for his next reaction.

"For her... I can't discuss that right now..."

Klára felt safe enough now to offer him some more lip again.

"Oh, just go ahead... feel free...."

The man didn't react. He kept listening to Olgi. He sighed deeply, and closed his eyes from time to time, like someone who needs a respite.

"Well, I have no idea what to do about the neighbors... If you could come to my office tomorrow morning..."

Klára had left the scene by now, knowing that they had moved beyond the danger zone. It's Doc who should have to struggle with Olgi, since this was his dream. She was already browsing the books on his bookshelves when the man hung up the phone and sighed once more, deeply. But he didn't report on the conversation, so Klára resorted to scrutinizing his facial expression.

"Okay, to sleep... I made your bed over there. We have to be up early tomorrow. You have to go home for your satchel."

"It's not a must. I could skip the day... They'll kick me out soon, anyway..."

Oh Lord, don't give me any more assignments, the doctor begged silently. But he suppressed his impatience and stepped aside from the proffered topic of dispute.

"I'm going to go wash up, and then I'll turn out the light. You can sleep soon."

Klára was alarmed by the impenetrable look on his face. She was surprised at how quickly the doctor discovered how to restrain her and bring her into line. Olgi had not figured it out to this day. Papa used to say at such times: "Well, my little lady, now you can change the record on your gramophone for a nicer one! I can cause trouble too, but I don't choose to amuse you in that way..."

. . . .

Doc came out of the bathroom in ugly striped pajamas, turned off the light, and crawled into his bed, in the corner opposite to Klára's divan.

"If you don't want me, I can leave."

"Good night."

"Are you angry now?"

"No, just tired..."

"And if you weren't lying?"

"Good night."

The man tossed and turned in his bed a long time, puzzling about what to say to Olgi in the morning. He was sure she'd come around. She's truly pretty limited. Fine, she didn't seem a genius even before, but today! Worrying about what the neighbors would think! Who cares about the neighbors? ...And what could be done about school or, rather, about Klára?...

...who wasn't tossing and turning in *her* bed, because she was listening. She was waiting to hear the deep, slow breaths from over there. If he snored, like Olgi, she would be able tell for sure when he fell asleep. At home, meaning, at Olgi's place, Klára would turn on the small reading lamp after Olgi fell asleep and read awhile, if she hadn't finished the book during the day. Sometimes she'd fall asleep reading, but by morning, the light would be turned off. At least Olgi didn't growl about this.

There was no snoring here, but the breath sounds had become reassuring. Klára sat up. She could see quite well in the dim light coming through the curtains. Doc didn't move. Klára put her feet on the floor. She wanted to watch him as he was sleeping turned toward the wall. It's too bad that his breathing sounds were coming from so far away. She had moved into Olgi's room at night, after Gyuri left, because she couldn't sleep without hearing the sound of somebody's breathing.

She stood up. No change from over there. She took a couple of steps: no squeaks from the floor. She could keep walking. Slowly. This guy is asleep. She reached the bed, still no change. She leaned down to hear the breathing better. In a minute she leaned even closer to sniff his pajama jacket. Papa smells better. She'd already noticed this when hugging the Doc. Still, it was a nice uncle's smell. Yes, Uncle Elmer had this smell.

Getting tired from bending over this way, she knelt by the bedside. But from this vantage point, all she could see was his back. She leaned her elbows onto the wooden bed frame, so she could lean in over him better. How far away he is...two feet, at least. Then she put her arms in farther, onto the mattress. And very slowly she pulled her feet up after. There she lay beside him. He's not waking up! Unbelievable! He must be asleep, he's not moving. She began to feel chilled. Why hadn't she brought over her blanket...she can't freeze to death! She began to lift Doc's blanket very cautiously. And she was already under it. Another success. Working up her courage, she conformed to the man's S-curve and leaned against Doc's back with her arms.

Suddenly she felt the man's trembling. Good God, he's not sleeping! Horrified, she pulled away and also started to tremble about being caught moving over here. The man turned towards her. Then he slowly extended the arm he was lying on, as if he wanted to build a bridge for Klára, who cautiously began to crawl closer. She carefully considered where to stop, then crossed her arms and leaned them against the man's chest. After a few more seconds' thought, she hid her head in her hands, as though she weren't even there.

"The person who's afraid to be alone... is no whore... I'm afraid, too..." the man whispered.

No more discussion. They slept till morning, without waking up. Except that Aldó couldn't move his arm when he tried to turn. Klára had clutched the sleeve of his pajamas tight in her fist.

• • • •

The fact that they overslept made the start of the next day surprisingly easy. The doctor hadn't overslept in several years. He used to lie awake before dawn, waiting for the time when getting up would finally make sense. This haste now gave a false impression, as if nothing could be more natural than getting out of bed from next to a prepubescent frog weighing less than eighty pounds— albeit one with weighty issues.

As far as the rest of the day was concerned, he had not one bit less difficulty with Klára than the previous night. He wanted her to go home, change clothes, make up with Olgi, then go to school at eight, and stay there until the end of the classes.

Well, at first Klára wanted to accomplish zero percent of those assignments. Given that it was quarter to seven, this was really no small task, but on the other hand, he was unable to accompany her himself, since he had morning office hours.

"Fine, then, just go in whenever you get there..."

"If I go in, I've got to go for the whole school day now, because Olgi isn't allowed to write an excuse for just some classes. Should I miss just one more hour without an excuse, the headmistress said, 'I'll be kicked out. They put up with enough from me even without that.' Also, that other children lived through the whole war, too, yet they don't cause as much trouble, 'not even combined...' she said."

"Because you behave like a spiny, prickly hedgehog... And what if *I* wrote your excuse?"

"Only parents may write one... for those who have them... in other words, Olgi."

"As a doctor, I can certify that you were at an examination."

"But I don't want a gynecological excuse, 'cause they'll make fun of me."

"Fine, we'll ask then for a stamp from the ear doctor. He's right next door."

"But Olgi will argue with me..."

"No, she won't! Go ahead, and get dressed... Wait, I'll bring out my shaving kit."

"But I want to watch you as you lather up!"

At this point, her voice was that of a five-year-old.

"Some other time! Now, young lady, you will get dressed, and quickly."

Klára sadly watched as the shaving soap, the lathering brush, the Gillette, the hand mirror and the razor receded, and then closed the bathroom door with a feeling of defeat. Meanwhile, the man had to put on the water for tea, find out from Klára how many buttered breads he should pack for her mid-morning snack, and check whether her shoes, thoroughly soaked from yesterday, had gotten dry on the radiator.

The man suddenly became aware that he was bustling about with these tasks, there are things to do, there is a meaning, there is a kid here, an ordinary cheeky kid.

• • • •

Sweet Mama, dear Papa!

We have math now, so I'm writing in a hurry. Although I know Mr. Bokor would never take my diary away. Olgi almost threw me out, but I knew she wouldn't. It's just that Doc walked me home last night and Olgi thought that "some guy" hugged me at the front gate and that I'd become a slut.

I managed not to break down and cry, and I ran away to Doc. He doesn't talk much, but he's nice. I slept at his place and he called Olgi to tell her not to worry. I'm sure he had children, but he doesn't talk about it. I'd love to live with him over there until you come home! Olgi isn't mad any more, but now she's the sad one. Someone's always sad! But I'm not, now. It's just that I feel a little sorry for Olgi.

. . . .

At eleven o'clock, just as the doctor finished with a patient, he saw with surprise that there were no more patient records in the in-box. It's rare to have any free minute during office hours but it was perfect for him that way.

"Nobody?"

"Yes, there is," replied his assistant. "An older woman is waiting outside, but she wanted to wait her turn until all the patients had left. She's been sitting out there since half past eight."

The doctor knew that this was Olgi. He'd been waiting for her anxiously, but now he was scared, nonetheless.

"Should I call her? I can leave while..." offered the assistant.

It was Olgi. Her eyes were red from crying. She seemed even older than last August. How old might she be? Her tears didn't stop flowing while she was speaking, but she was completely calm, like someone who'd given up on everything.

"I can't give her anything else... I'm a much simpler person... I know this isn't what she needs... They never liked us all that much... They were always nice to us, but... we didn't have as much schooling... I can't even help Klára with her classwork...

"Her father, poor man, was my nephew; he fulfilled his promise... I was looking for my other sister's grandchildren in the Red Cross house, when I stumbled across Klára and Gyuri... I had thought that Bandi and his family... that they had managed to flee abroad... I took the children home... and at first everything went okay.

"Klára was constantly reminding her brother to study hard and keep his things in order, because if their parents returned, they had to find everything in its place... Of course, I knew... but I didn't tell her... Life with her turned into hell only after her brother left. I mourned for him, too, when he left... and for my sons, and for my husband... and tonight for Klára-baby. That's how her parents nicknamed her. She was such a sweet little girl!"

Keep talking, keep explaining, begged the doctor silently. Just don't make me have to speak up. And Olgi continued, indeed:

"If you took her... it would be better for her, for sure. Not for me, but for her. Klára isn't happy with me... If the Eternal One wants to take this child from me too, I can do nothing. That's the way life goes..."

By now it became clear that the doctor wanted to speak. But he couldn't. Olgi placed her bony little hand on the man's arm.

"Of course I know that I can trust in you... And she's a smart girl... you'll see... Well, she's somewhat immature and hotheaded, but she has brains... With less brains, she'd have adjusted to... to... by now."

"Klára... needs... both of us."

This worked. Going on felt much easier.

"If she were to lose you, dear Olgi, that would be another horrendous loss for her. Even I can tell that she needs... somebody like a father, too. She keeps saying Papa would say this, Papa used to do that... I can't be as optimistic and cheerful a father to her as she'd like... but I might be better than nothing. I never had a daughter... But, well, I'll learn. And maybe I could learn with her... to help her catch up, where she's lagging."

Olgi's tears stopped.

"Would you learn with her?"

"It won't be easy, because she's very stubborn, you know... But when my office hours are in the morning, I could work with her after school. I don't have any other business... except I go to the orphanage every Thursday afternoon. But I can reschedule that for some morning hours."

"Does this mean I could keep her?"

The doctor suddenly realized that his mind had already put Klára into his life, into his apartment, into his days. But this is just his desire, he thought, it can't really happen.

Olgi's life is filled only with Klára—the same way his life would only have her. He couldn't rob her.

The other solution—to contest every day about whose solitude will be eased by this little devil today—would also be ridiculous! He was starting to ponder how to work it out when Klára's image flashed across his mind.

"I won't take her away, for sure... but I don't think this depends on you, dear Olgi, or on me. It strikes me that Klára decides everything here."

Olgi nodded vigorously, with the joy of recognizing the truth. The man added shortly:

"But we'll find out."

"Please forgive me for saying such silly things last night... I do sometimes... I was just so confused..."

The doctor smiled, while an odd thought struck Olgi in her great relief. She had no idea she had brought up one of the hardest possible questions.

"Haven't you found a suitable child for yourself at the orphanage?"

She saw instantly from his face how wrong her question must be. The man stood up, went to the window and stared out. Olgi's fear grew. The scene resembled the silence before Klára's terrifying explosions. But the doctor didn't explode.

"One can't raise a small child alone while working... Not even a bigger one like Klára... Did she get to school on time?"

"Well, she set off."

"We had a deal."

. . . .

The doctor's relief was disturbed on his return home, when he realized that Olgi had left without reaching any clear agreement with him. When could he see Klára again? Soon he felt relieved, thinking of Klára's ways: She'll come anyway, even without permission, if she wants to. And there's no doubt that she wants to.

Still, they would have to make a deal, to make sure it fit Olgi, too. Could it work to have Klára in the afternoons on the days he had morning appointments, and return her the following morning? And maybe Saturday... Elderly people feel safe with regular schedules. He could help Klára with her schoolwork. On other days he could prepare himself for their next time together, also by studying the schoolbooks she would leave behind from time to time. Olgi's phone number was on the table, but the doctor did his best to resist the temptation to call. The doorbell rang at six. Finally.

"Olgi said I could stay here tonight, if I wanted. True, she was a little sad, but I told her that I'd live with her, too. And she sent some semolina pudding for you. I promised to call her when I got here, to let her know if I could stay."

"Then go ahead and call her."

"I brought my satchel, and Olgi packed some fresh underwear, too. I told her I had a nightshirt here, so I don't need one of mine. I told her how awful it looks! But it's okay... it's funny."

Now she was talking like a ten-year-old, right down to the inflections. And she was surprisingly friendly to Olgi on the phone.

"I'll come home tomorrow after school, since he has afternoon office hours anyway... Don't cry..."

The man asked Klára for the receiver with unaccustomed insistence. Finally, he got it, and said:

"My dear Olgi, I was thinking about how best to organize her studies... I haven't talked it over with Klára yet, but she might be here on Tuesdays and Thursdays, and on the other days she could study at home, alone... Well, of course... I'll discuss it with her as well... And she said you were kind enough to send me some pudding. Thank you very much. I haven't eaten that in a very long time...I'm sure it's delicious."

• • • •

They had a nice evening. Klára happily agreed with Doc's proposal for the weekly schedule. It had been so long since anything had actually gone the way she wished. The unexpected easy victory buttered her right up. She didn't make a single unpleasant remark, or ask a discomfiting question, all evening.

They shared the semolina pudding, and Klára ate a large portion. Olgi had even included a small jar of apricot jam to spread on it. After finishing their snack, the man suggested calling Olgi again, to let her know of the unanimous agreement on the plan and of the pudding's success. Olgi was pleased, and she asked for the doctor's phone number. She wouldn't bother him much, she said, it just feels good to know that she can reach Klára when feeling very lonely.

After a brief perusal, Klára took a book from the shelf and curled up with it on the sofa. It was Antal Szerb's *Journey by Moonlight*.[4] Might such a book be too mature for her? The doctor meditated a while, then dismissed the thought. Such a life is too mature for her as well, yet nobody censors that... He sat in his armchair and pretended to read something, while actually monitoring the girl.

"Are you done with your schoolwork?"

"What kind of schoolwork?"

"I'm thinking of tomorrow's classes, in the first place."

"I paid attention in geography, so I don't need to study that. In Hungarian, nothing I write is any good for the teacher, anyway... And math... I haven't understood a single word of math for a long time already... German... in German I'm not willing to analyze such a stupid poem for her..."

A sigh. I can't cope with that, the doctor thought. It had been Ilona who had helped with the boys' studies, when needed. Then he upbraided himself: this is not the time for self-pity. You have to act.

"Give me your math book..."

"But I don't want to study math now!"

"I just want to see what you're studying," he replied, with a fatigue often generated by Klára's outbursts starting with "No" or "But."

4. *Antal Szerb was one of the most popular writers in the 1920s-30s. He died during a forced march in 1945 in West-Hungary. (Original title of the novel mentioned here: Utas és holdvilág).*

Although Klára's face didn't show any defiance, she remained still. And she asked: "What should I call you?... You don't have a name."

The man left her alone with her self-inflicted task and waited for the outcome.

"Can I call you Aldó?"

"Call me what?"

"Aldó."

"Why 'Aldó'?"

The reply came slowly, but it came, and it didn't even start ominously:

"I have a cousin. His name is Bódog... like 'boldog.' Isn't it funny that somebody is named 'Glad,' but the L is missing? And his mom wasn't 'gad' about his name—Papa made this joke; he'd make a joke out of everything—because she had wanted to name him Felix. That's the same name in French, from félicité. But Uncle Imre wanted to give him a Hungarian name. "'Cause we're Hungarians." And when Bódog was a little baby, they didn't know what nickname to use. I was little, too, and I named him Boldó. And ever since, that's what everyone calls him...I don't know where he is now... But you could be Aldó."

A long, peaceful silence followed. Klára wasn't reading either, just pretending. Then she spoke in her well-known, sulky tone.

"You didn't even look at my translations..."

"Oh yes I did!" said Aldó and was glad to be so well prepared. "I've even chosen the article!"

"Really?"

"Really. Because this one must have important gynecological content as well."

"Which one??"

"The title is..."

Klára jumped up: "Where's Papa's folder?"

"In the kitchen... but I put a newspaper under it."

Klára ran and brought the case. Aldó read the table of contents line by line, looking for the article.

"What's the title?"

"*Zusammenhänge von Hormonstörungen und ulceralen Erkrankungen.*"[5]

How lousy his German pronunciation is, she thought, but only said to him:

"This should be at the bottom of a page... Here it is! I'll translate it for you. It'll be done very soon... From seventeen to twenty-three, that's just seven pages! Is it urgent?"

To his astonishment, something akin to humor popped up in Aldó. Humor had not been a forte of his, even in old days. He wasn't aware this was actually Klára's sense of humor, or even more like Papa's. Without being aware of it, he wanted to resemble him, for Klára's sake.

"I want you to tackle it without delay—as soon as you are done with your homework!"

5. *The Relationship between hormonal disorders and ulceral diseases.*

Later in the evening, Aldó prepared the bath for Klára. And he boiled water also for himself. Klára will be reading anyway, while he is in the bathroom. He took out a clean pair of pajamas from the wardrobe. After his bath, he told her goodnight.

"But... can I come over there... if I'm scared?"

"...Of course you can. But I'm right nearby, so you don't have to be scared."

"But what if I still am?"

They turned off the light. After a couple of minutes, Klára set off. This time she took her blanket and pillow. Her place was ready.

. . . .

Around midnight, Aldó carefully climbed over Klára and went to the bathroom.

A moment later he heard her shouting:

"Aldó!"

He tried to finish his business before responding, lest his shouts be overheard by the neighbors, but she shouted again at once, even more frantically.

"Just a sec!" he called back.

He emerged from the bathroom.

"Here I am."

Klára was furious:

"You should wake me up if you're gonna leave!"

"You want me to wake you when I go to pee?"

"Yes!... 'Cause why weren't you here?"

"Fine," said Aldó after a sigh—the moment he understood. He's familiar with a hundred modes of rousing up. This would just be the hundred and first one.

Suddenly, Klára began to giggle. Impossible to follow!

"Now what?"

"...Papa would say that he wasn't here because he couldn't manage to be in and out at the same time."

"He is perfectly right!" said Aldó, stroking her hair. Then, with quick movements of his hand, he encouraged her to scoot her blanket and pillow toward the wall, so he could sleep on the outside. Then he asked her:

"Does Olgi also wake you up at night when...?"

"She shuffles. I can hear that by myself."

The next morning they awoke on time. Aldó kept offering Klára the use of the bathroom. She seemed to hesitate.

"But you won't shave out here while I am there, right?"

"...The lather?"

"Yeah."

With excited pleasure, Klára sat down in her oversized nightshirt on the laundry hamper's lid and watched as Aldó prepared the shaving foam.

"Your brush has such a pretty handle..."

"This is from the old days."

"I figured."

Aldó lathered his face as Klára, visibly happy, watched silently. After a few minutes she spoke up, a little embarrassed:

"Put a dab on my nose..."

Aldó dabbed. Klára looked at herself in the mirror. She giggled.

"If we were good, we always got a dab..."

• • • •

Aldó waited until Klára left for school and then looked at the list of teachers he'd obtained the night before, counting the Jewish names he noticed. Then he memorized their names by subject. There's a Becher and a Wiesmann. And Harsányi is likely to be Jewish as well. He planned to begin with them. One morning might not even be enough to speak with all of them, if they had ongoing classes.

He had an uncertain feeling of discomfort, as if being afraid of some bad surprise. The background story he'd devised seemed to be all right: Olgi had asked him, as a friend of the family, to help find out what might be done to motivate Klára. He knew that he couldn't promise anything in advance. All he could do was survey the terrain. But the undertaking quickly found its lucky star—well, not right away.

Mrs. Vidák: Chemistry and biology. Hair pulled tight in a big bun, completely unapproachable. She'll certainly flunk Klára! If a performance like hers weren't rewarded with an F, what on earth would it take to flunk anybody? And is this the goal? Aldó wondered silently. A student who doesn't answer questions when called, for weeks on end, has no business being in high school.

High school's not compulsory, you know... Does she ever speak up? Sometimes. Then she knows the answer. She did get a C on one assignment, but the others are all F's, because she hands in a blank sheet of paper. She hides novels under her desk and reads during the whole class. The headmistress told me, unfortunately, not to take Klára's books away. School's not for acting out your moodiness. I won't put up with prima donnas. Too bad that the headmistress doesn't share my point of view.

Becher and Wiesmann didn't even show up. József Bokor: Math and physics. A big bear with a big mustache. According to his impression, Klára must be very intelligent, but a hard case. She must have been emotionally badly damaged during the war. He can't tell how far behind Klára is lagging because she isn't willing to tell him. Should she cooperate, he'd gladly include her in his small tutoring group. Aldó was so grateful for Mr. Bokor's offer that he promised to try talking Klára into this.

In the meantime Mrs. Becher arrived. Nervousness is written all over her. Why did her colleague say she had not shown up yet? She'd been in a meeting since seven-thirty! Klára? Oh yes, she won't flunk her in Hungarian or in German, because she is really knowledgeable. But she's a queer fish, and that's unacceptable. Yes, she's given her several F's because she hands in impossible things: she ridicules some honorable poets and writes parodies in lieu of the assigned essays...

Also, not long ago, when she herself had accidentally written something wrong on the blackboard, Klára had gone up to the board and, without a word, crossed it out and corrected it... She's fishing for serious trouble if she keeps this up. She could try to have a lower profile... Haven't we already had enough trouble in this country? ...One should not stand out constantly! Couldn't you influence her, Mr. Körner?

While waiting to nab the next teacher, Aldó prepared notes, lest he confuse the details later.

Jolán Gerecsey: Music and choral singing, tall and thin, as dry as an accounting teacher. Klára does accomplish the bare minimum, and she's given up expecting more from her. Even though she once noticed that Klára could play the piano a bit. It's a pity that she lacks any ambition.

Mrs. Wiesmann: History and geography. Sad-eyed, intelligent, a tiny build.

"If Klára gets a personalized assignment at the level of a university course, she performs wonderfully. Most of the time, I give her such challenges. But even in this respect, she's unpredictable. I'll try to find out exactly what makes her perform, and what does not...

She is interested in everything up to the previous century, as long as the subject isn't war. But she loses interest as soon as we get to the twentieth century. That's all right, she'll get past it sooner or later. For some time, I have given the class two or three different topics to work on simultaneously, and let Klára sit with the group whose topic fits her interests most.

I have no problem with her, but you should be aware that there are some who would stop at nothing to see her expelled. She irritates them. We had many difficult children in forty-five, forty-six... But the kids all shaped up... or fell by the wayside. Klára's not improving. On the contrary, she's walking around here like a living rebuke. And the... well, the others... they are very sensitive to this... Most of my colleagues have a very tough time with her..."

"Whose goodwill do you think she needs the most now?"

"I'm not supposed to tell you things like that..."

"Aside from Mrs. Vidák, whom would it be important for me to see?"

"Next year Russian will be introduced as the compulsory foreign language, taught by Mrs. Harsányi. She's their gym teacher now. She regards it as very important that everybody be equal here. Klára has to understand this... She must fall into the exercise line. You know what I mean..."

"I do. I'll speak to Mrs. Harsányi. And to the child as well."

"And do go see the headmistress... she's good... it's good to talk things over with her, as well."

He hadn't considered this before, although it could be crucial, since it was precisely the headmistress who had threatened Klára with being kicked out. Mrs. Somogyi. In contrast to Aldó's expectations, the heavy-set, reserved, fortyish woman made an engaging impression as soon as he stepped into her office. True, according to Mrs. Vidák, that she's the one who defends Klára's reading stories under the table. In a terse but soft way, she offered a seat to Aldó:

"We have quite a few students of Jewish origin. We pay close attention to them. None of our teachers have been involved before..."

Isn't this issue taboo?

"But the other kids calmed down since... somehow... they work, and they want to live... Not long ago, Klára ran out in the middle of class, in such a state that we feared she'd end up under a streetcar... After this episode, I directed her teachers to leave her alone. Should they have any problem with her, they have to talk to me.. She has a younger brother... is he doing any better?"

"Her brother's no longer here..."

"Did he die?"

"No. He emigrated... with a group."

"To Palestine?"

Aldó nodded.

"When?"

"At least a year ago."

"I can't grasp that... How could two orphan siblings go their separate ways? That's unusual..."

Aldó was cornered. But he found a shorthand way to say what he wanted:

"Klára's waiting for her parents."

"For the past three years?"

"...Four. Five."

"This is awful!"

Aldó fell silent, just as he had at Olgi's. The headmistress waited.

"Should our secretary make us a coffee?"

Aldó nodded. The coffee arrived quickly. Swallowing actually helped Aldó. By this point, he trusted this woman fully. An unusual feeling for him.

"Klára said that you'd expel her if she had one more unexcused absence from a class..."

"Oh, I only said that because I know that this is the one single thing that's important to her: that she attends our prestigious high school. She would never risk losing this. I thought this warning would make her disappear less often in the morning hours. And if she's here, more of the material will stick, willy-nilly...

After all, she should be able to pass the graduation exams. More than one of her teachers thinks that she's extraordinarily intelligent. She was a straight-A student at her prewar school: I saw her report card... Each time I see her, I get a different impression of her. And, well, her physical condition is pretty worrisome, too... Recently, we've often gotten free milk for the undernourished, but she won't drink any... As though she didn't want to face puberty... I'm no expert in these things..."

"She's started to eat a bit more, recently."

"Are you a relative of this girl?"

"Klára treats me like one...She loved her father deeply. He was a doctor, too."

"In that case, you can surely influence her. Doctor, what if you told her to study for her parents' sake?"

Aldó shook his head at length.

"I won't do that... Even if it's terrible to be confronted with the truth, she, too, will have to get past it at some point. I can't play into her delusion—the same way that I can't push her into this insight... Nonetheless, it will be easier once you are past it. Not better, just easier. Everything will be hollow. But you can fall asleep at least. And, for her, perhaps...eventually...her life can perhaps even be filled...by something better."

Now it was the headmistress who fell silent, and it was Aldó who tried to encourage her:

"I'll do my best to make her study seriously...She should, I think, make a real effort in Mrs. Vidák's classes..."

"Yes. That'd be appropriate. By the way, those are the two subjects lying closest to her father's profession."

"Why, that hadn't even occurred to me," Aldó said happily.

The headmistress ushered him out. At the banister, she said one more thing:

"I don't know how much longer I'll remain as headmistress. If there is a changing of the guard, look me up. It'll be known for sure... And you can find Mrs. Harsányi in the exercise room on the ground floor."

. . . .

Aldó washed the bed linens on Friday evening. This involved boiling them with liquid soap in the bathwater pot. He didn't bother to scrub or wring the laundry the way women did in the washtub, but, well, things get clean enough this way. And—the main point—the laundry cleaned itself: all you had to do was rinse it out in the bathtub. At most, he'd scrub his shirt collars, but only if he really had to.

While the clothes boiled, he attempted to repair the sag in the middle of the sofa. Of course, kids usually didn't get backaches from this sort of thing, but it's really not healthy to sleep like that. And Klára has to get used to sleeping in her own bed, sooner or later. He took out a bunch of old towels and pillowcases and, making ever wider layers, filled in the crater, so that none of the layers' edges would dig into her. When he was satisfied with his artistry, he took out a torn blanket that was, in any case, too small to be of any use, and applied it like a tourniquet around the filling. He was able to tension it pretty well on both sides. All that was left was to cut a remnant piece of upholstery to cover the ugly mess.

His heart jumped happily at the unexpected ringing of the doorbell. But this is Olgi's day, he suddenly realized; so who could have arrived? It was Klára.

"I'm done with the translation!" she announced.

"Very well, my little Hedgie, but why did you leave Olgi so late? What time will you get home?"

"...She said I could sleep here tonight."

"Nothing doing! We had a deal! Today is Friday!"

"But she said it's okay..."

"And was she very happy?"

"...Not really..."

"You forced her to give in, didn't you?"

"I only said I wanted to bring you the translation. And that as long as I was here, I'd stay... But you're not even happy..."

"The fact that I'm happy to see you is not enough reason for you to be here... Understand this: Olgi needs you too!"

Klára was dumbfounded by this formulation. She knew this was the case, but she had never yet heard it said out loud. Slowly and sadly she said:

"Should I go home now, then?"

Aldó's heart almost broke but, since this was the moment he first succeeded in mounting the horse called Fatherhood, he would not dismount willingly.

"Let's call Olgi first, then we'll look at the translation carefully, and afterwards I'll walk you home. Besides, I'm in the middle of stuffing this cruddy sofa...you know, where it's caved in...so you wouldn't be able to sleep on it tonight, anyhow."

"And tomorrow?..."

"Well, we haven't decided about the weekend, yet..."

After a minute of hesitation, worried, Aldó asked: She hadn't told Olgi about crawling into his bed during the night, right? (They both knew that this didn't happen during the night, but just after a few minutes after retiring to separate beds the proper way.) Klára's glance asked: do you think I'm a complete idiot?

But, well, if she understood perfectly, how absurd this would appear to anyone else—how could she have been so certain that Aldó would be that precise, single other adult person on the planet, who needed this cuddling just for the sake of cuddling? That he would happily accept the offer just for his own survival? Like any newborn who has lost the safety of its boundaries, and only has its own tiny fist to trust, agrees to accept the substitute being offered, even though it realizes it's been hoodwinked... because it is desperate to be touched.

Klára's mute response did reassure Aldó, and he regained his self-confidence and asked Klára to phone home. He was listening meanwhile.

"Olgi, Aldó says that I should come home, if you want me to. Well, I guess, it'd be better for you, if I came home... um, well, I'm coming home... soon. Aldó will walk me home."

My God, she's talking like an eight-year-old! She, who can deduce the paradox of self-contradictory statements, who compares Thomas Mann's prose with its Hungarian translation, who can describe the experience of being left behind by a large family, and who translates articles from medical journals!

"Because I forgot that on Friday... but Olgi, on Saturday... Alright, I'll hand it over. Aldó, Olgi wants to talk to you."

"Think nothing of it, Olgi dear. This is what we'd agreed on. Klára understands, too, that without her honoring the bargain, the whole agreement won't work. She has to be as trustworthy as the grownups... Well... I'd love to... But are you sure I won't be a bother?... What time should I come over? And what can I bring along?... Of course I will... Anyway, I'll figure it out myself... Alright, now Klára and I will have a look at her translation, and then we'll head out."

• • • •

Klára was already working on her third translation for Aldó, often choosing his place for the job. From the standpoint of the translation, this was beneficial: Klára asked many insightful questions. She quickly learned to recognize words of Latin origin. For those, she didn't need to find Hungarian expressions, since Hungarian doctors used the same Latin words.

She quickly developed a sense for their Hungarian declination. Sometimes she'd still ask for help. Once she pointed out to Aldó that "visceral" could not only be "viszcerális" in Hungarian, but also "zsigeri." as she found out when—for no good reason—she decided to look it up in the dictionary. If that's the case, then in her opinion it would be better to use the proper Hungarian word.

And she asked Aldó for a new blank notebook. The next day, he saw in the title block the words "German-Hungarian-Latin Dictionary." He glanced at it. It was a proper trilingual concordance, with eight expressions lined up so far. Aldó insisted that she leave the typewriter at home, to avoid having her come over under this pretext and leave poor Olgi alone even on "her days." Klára could write by hand, if she wanted to carry on the translation over here, and then type it at home.

Despite seeing her joy in translating, Aldó would have preferred that Klára concentrate more on her homework. He raised the issue at every opportunity, and asked leading questions, but they just bounced off Klára.

"Let's see how you're doing in math..."

"I have no idea, it bores me. I didn't get it even last year."

"With your brain, it would be no big deal to come up to speed...Let's take a look and see how much of it you understand, and then start from there. I've already looked over nearly the whole book. It's really not that awful."

"Aldó, drop it! I don't want to. I'm translating."

"Come off it already, don't be so stubborn! You can't stand it if you don't pick something up as easily as languages, literature and history, am I right? That you might even have to work at something a little?"

"How do you know that history..."

"Oh, it's just a for-instance... Hedgie, we did promise Olgi that we'd study! Come on, let's sit down and look at the ma..."

"No! What the hell should I count for?"

Aldó hadn't heard this tone of voice from her for quite some time. He didn't realize that children struggling with their disappeared ones refuse to count, and he got furious at his own ineffectiveness.

"Then I won't ask you for any more translations either!"

They didn't speak to each other for hours, just spying on each other for signs of surrender. Aldó won, just as he was about to yield the front. It's just that Klára started to get hungry. And since it still happened that she was unable to distinguish among her different unmet needs, now all she felt was that she wanted something from Aldó. She closed the book of short stories that she hadn't been reading for hours, excavated her math book from her satchel, went over to Aldó and slammed the book down in front of him:

"Then go ahead!..."

Aldó smiled at her, as if asking forgiveness. It was not his intention to defeat her, just reach the point of...Does there have to be a loser in everything?

"Come on, let's talk first."

And as he had decided, with some difficulty, during their hours of silence, he revealed to Klára that two weeks ago he'd been to her school. That there was an opportunity for extra tutoring, but if she didn't want it, she could study math with him. That she ought to taunt Mrs. Vidák by writing a few essays for her that would merit an indisputable A+, just to watch her squirm. That in Hungarian, she should... and, and...

Klára snorted every time Aldó seemed not to share her opinion of a particular teacher, and she listened, wide-eyed and grinning, whenever Aldó expressed solidarity with her. On the whole, she seemed satisfied. After musing a while, she asked him:

"And you went there because of me?"

"...No," Aldó grinned, "because of little Johnny next door!"

"That's not what I meant... And did you say to them you're my dad?"

"No."

"...Okay. I don't want them to think I'd been lying. What I said was that my papa is a prisoner of war."

Aldó was meditating about this new acknowledgment about her father, when Klára shifted gears, unexpectedly fast: "Can we eat?"

"Let's eat."

• • • •

They had just finished dinner when the phone rang.

"Olgi, for sure..." said Klára, already running to the phone. Aldó let her get it, since she seemed happy.

"...It's for you," she said, disappointed, and held out the receiver.

Klára thought that Aldó had nobody in his life, except for her. And this would've been so nice. But she could quickly tell that the phone call was okay. "Alright, Monday morning I'll be in anyhow... So much progress, already? Of course, I have time... Well, I'd rather be there on my three free morning days. And on those days I could go back after six again... Really? That's great. How many are there still?... And how many families have made a firm offer?"

. . . .

"Who was that?"

"His name is Gyula Barta. He is responsible for the adoption of children in the two orphanages. But we try to find a family for every child, at least for Hanukkah. We succeeded last year, and these families ended up adopting many of the children... Well, it happens that some return a child, but more and more of them may stay on."

Aldó waited for Klára's reaction. It had occurred to him more than once, that sooner or later Klára would learn that he assisted at the two orphanages. Even so, he was unprepared for her question:

"And do you... bring home a child too?"

"Me? No."

Klára stared at the ground. Aldó thought he needed to say something more:

“I’m not a family... I can’t cook properly. And I don’t observe Hanukkah any more.”

Klára still didn’t look up.

“In our family, grandpa and grandma used to observe it. Hanukkah and Passover...But we are not religious. You aren’t either, are you?”

“Not any more.”

“Do you believe in God?”

“...I don’t know.”

“Are you mad at Him?”

Aldó nodded.

“I don’t believe. So I can’t even be mad at Him.”

Aldó understood the point, though it didn’t seem to lead anywhere. But Klára was already taking the next turn:

“Then who should I be mad at?”

This came as a relief to Aldó. He smiled:

“You seem to use poor Olgi for that sort of thing.”

“Not me!” said Klára ruefully—and she was already smiling too.

Mama often says this sort of thing. And she, too, says it the same way, without anger. This always makes Klára feel that it’s her own task to set matters right.

She had more questions about the orphanage. How many children still lack families? Could there be kids there whose real parents are still searching but don’t know to look for them there? And what happens if a kid doesn't like his new parents? She'd never go to strangers...

Aldó smiled inside: this must mean that he's not a stranger to her. He asked whether she'd like to play Merels. He'd bought the game a week ago, and when they first played it, Hedgie beat him at every turn. He'll teach her to play chess!

The game changed Klára's mood quite a lot. She began to tell stories about her classmates. Now, for the first time. Most of them, of course, are idiots. But Agnes Feldmann is very smart, no matter how the other girls mock her. Well, it's true, she's tongue-tied. But she'll speak up when it's just the two of them, and she's lost her mom somewhere, too. And her dad keeps fighting with Agi about everything. They used to be very wealthy, but they lost all their possessions.

Also, another girl, Ica Lakatos, was really happy when Klára made fun of two idiots from the class who always called Ica a slut.

"And I think that's why she gave me three Starking apples as a present—her folks are greengrocers—I brought you one of them, you know. The biggest one, because Olgi's and my stomachs are smaller."

. . . .

Dear Mama and Papa!

Just imagine: Aldó went to school and the teachers could see that I have someone else besides Olgi! I'm sure they said all sorts of bad things about me, but I bet Aldó defended me. He wants me to study properly, like I used to. We even fought about it yesterday, but then we made up, because Aldó loves me and I love him very much, too. You don't mind, right? And besides, I don't mind studying if it makes him happy. You used to be always happy too. It's just that I feel much more like translating now, because he has nobody else to help him either.

. . . .

The volunteers acquired so many potential families that sifting through them by Hanukkah seemed to be almost impossible. Interviewing the candidates had been Aldó's job since last year. If a couple matched the requirements, they could go and see the children and choose. But that part of the process would be settled by someone else. Should, Aldó, however, find anything alarming in their behavior, he'd send them to his colleague, the psychiatrist János Csillag, who would—in most cases—justify Aldó's suspicion. Again and again, it took János by surprise what a sensitive ear for hysteria Aldó had. They agree fully that children should not go to families that are severely out of balance.

. . . .

Gyula Barta, head physician—and general factotum, by his inclination—of the orphanage, had requested that Aldó do this job in the summer of forty-seven. Aldó had just dropped in to pay his monthly contribution. He was able to save three or four hundred Forints every month that he donated to the orphanage. Gyula noticed him at the cashier and invited him into his office. They hadn't seen each other for a long time. Aldó had always felt miserable simply being close to Gyula. This wasn't Gyula's fault, however.

"How is work going?"

"It's perfect. It makes me feel like I'm functioning normally again, and makes the daytime quite tolerable."

"You're working for an outpatient clinic, aren't you?"

"Yes. There are no childbirths there. Otherwise, I couldn't cope."

"Do you really think so?"

"I'm not really sure of anything anymore, but I think so. I can't look children in the eyes. And least of all, those of a newborn."

"Are you still alone?"

"Yes."

"Are you sure that's best?"

"... I can't imagine anybody... at my side."

"Well, there are so many decent women who are lonely. Meeting opportunities have been organized recently."

"Gyula, what did you want to talk about with me?"

"Alright, I get it, I'm no matchmaker! But one has to learn to live with the way it is! To construct life from what we've got! We all have to do that."

"I am pursuing that course, too... My brain just doesn't seem to work."

"And how about doing some work for us?"

"I wouldn't dare."

"Aladár, have you had any... since..."

"No. But if you had even one such episode, you'd think better of tempting the devil."

"Aladár... I also got scared, when it happened to you... but I think it could have happened to any of us. I used to have long weeks in the camp when I'd hear voices and see figures in the evening. Even later, back at home, many of us often felt that our eyes were deceiving us when put to the test."

"Nice wording. But putting it into a professional context, you can talk about a proper hallucination. I don't want to work with children. You can ask me for anything else... but... I never want to see the face of my son on any child again."

The familiar trembling took hold of him.

. . . .

He suddenly saw himself in the summer of '45 coming out empty-handed from the last room of the bigger boys and wandering around in the big dormitory hall of the little ones. The boys were looking for his glance while he passed all of them by: That's not him, that isn't, either. He was already checking the last row of beds. There were hardly any faces he hadn't seen yet.

On the next to last bed, a little boy, lying motionless. He is not interested in the bony man with his wooden face; he won't look up; he just lies there with his eyes almost closed. His eyebrows are shaped like the new moon, his eyes show enough to reveal they are dark brown, his nostrils are narrow, his lips fleshy... István dear! My little one! István! It's me, Daddy! Don't you recognize me? István looks shocked at Aladár. He doesn't recognize him. Because there is no István anymore.

Gyula took him by the arm and led him into his office.

"But he is my little son! You should tell him... Isn't he?"

"His name is Andris Wechsler. He was brought to us from the South, from Pécs."

Gyula was overcome by a sudden feeling of guilt now and switched the topic:

"How about doing the adoption paperwork? There are a lot of them recently."

"I could do that. Of course. I think. I'll try, at least."

. . . .

That's how it started for Aldó in '47 and, soon after, the task of interviewing foster parent candidates. It's now his second year in this role for Hanukkah preparations. And Passover also brings a lot of work to be done for more adoptions. The number of children living in their Houses keeps decreasing. It'll go under a hundred, soon. Two volunteers had started to reconnoiter around the provinces, although there is hardly anyone who had returned there from the camps. Half a million Jews disappeared from the country, for sure. In Gyula's opinion, it might even be more.

The days went by quickly. There were three weeks left before Hanukkah. Even if Aldó were to go to the House every day, he couldn't finish the interviews all by himself.

"Isn't Thursday not suitable at all? Not even Tuesday?" Gyula asked in an unusually impatient voice. "Of course! All anybody cares about now is taking care of his own business. Our issue is not so important anymore! Most of them have gotten beyond their mourning, their doubts and their guilty feelings by now; and they live happily and well! Financial contributions have decreased, as well. Everybody already has ideas about what to spend their money on! Last month for the first time our per capita donations didn't increase... on the contrary."

"On these two days, I actually have somebody to take care of. Is that so bad? But on all other days I am available... whenever I'm needed... Concerning contributions, yes, last time I also brought eighty Forints less. But... I found a girl... or she found me... She used to be anorexic when we first met. So I buy her whatever she feels like eating. And we spend Tuesday and Thursday afternoons together. I admit it's good for me, too, no selflessness here. She won't let me help with her schoolwork yet, but I hope the time will come. She's being taken care of by her grandmother's sister."

"Oh, then it must have been her who picked up the phone last time! That's good news, however."

"I think so, too. It's not easy. She can cause at least as much trouble as two boys. But... it's very good... for me... that it's not a boy."

"Of course. Then... shall I do these two afternoons?

"I'll check with her what she'd think about this."

"Couldn't you bring her along? She might get along well here. How old is she?"

"Sixteen. But a twelve year-old mouse would make a more robust impression. She might feel okay here playing with the other girls. I'll have to talk to her first. I'd like to spend the coming Tuesday with her, anyway. She doesn't tolerate anything unexpected very well.

. . . .

For the next Tuesday, they planned to go and buy new shoes for Klára. Olgi wanted to pay ("That's what we get the orphan's allowance for," she said), but Aldó won the battle: he received a Christmas bonus—what else could he spend that money on?

The shopping went well. Aldó hadn't ever seen Klára caring much about her looks before—her only inclination was to criticize his clothing. Olgi didn't mind not participating in the excursion. Still he thought, shopping with a young girl was anything but easy.

Klára instantly headed toward the children's department of the store. Of course, her feet were small, too. She soon fell in love with a pair of brown and yellow shoes. Most shoes were just one color: "They're so boring." she explained. This pair really looked nice and matched Klára's childish style.

"But do you have enough money?"

"Yes, I do. But tell me, Hedgie, didn't Olgi want winter shoes for you instead?"

"These *are* winter shoes! Just not lacing boots! But I don't like those. Look, they're warm! The leather is quite thick." Aldó had always preferred to withdraw from such disputes. Come to think of it, Olgi hadn't specified boots, either. These sporty ones were nicer, indeed. Klára could wear the old ones whenever snow was expected. They had recently been repaired by the shoemaker and wouldn't get wet inside anymore.

Returning to Aldó's place, Klára walked around happily in her new possessions. Aren't they pretty? Juli Szendrei will envy her for them! And all the others will like them. Except, of course, those ridiculous "ladies" in the class... But who cares about them!

Aldó waited for the moment when he could start talking about the Hanukkah campaign. He mentioned again, how important it was to see as many candidates as possible, so most children could find a family for Hanukkah, at least. Klára was listening with the same apprehension as when the topic had come up last time.

"But I don't want us to miss each other for three weeks now... How about doing your homework alone on Tuesday and Thursday, and then coming to the orphanage, where you could..."

"No! I won't go to the orphanage! No! No! I'm not an orphan! No! No! No!"

She yelled louder and louder. She screamed hysterically: " No! No!...."

Aldó tried to embrace her, but she squatted on the floor like a fetus. Her back... only bones... Nothing but 'No!' could be heard, until it slowly subsided. Aldó lifted the whining bundle of flesh from the floor, sat down in the armchair, and held her on his lap. When the voice became quieter, he was sure that something helpful had happened. The muscles of his Hedgehog kept relaxing, while her tears were peacefully dripping onto his shirt. She had overcome something; she had left behind a realm that can only be identified when looking back. A realm they both knew by now.

Chapter 2

"Heal us, Eternal Father, and we will be healed."
(Refoenu, Adonai, venerofee.)

(December 1948-December 1949)

The next day, Aldó worked at the orphanage in the morning hours and went from there directly to his office. His assistant, Elvira—by now knowing her way around Aldó's small number of people—waited for him with the news: Olgi had called. She asked if Aldó could come to see them after his office hours because Klára had been sent home from school with a high fever.

He picked up the phone. A hundred and two? Any pain? Did she call the pediatrician? What time did he promise to come? She should change her compress frequently and give her lukewarm tea to drink. Also, he would like to be called after the doctor was finished. He wants to consult with him. Now Klára wanted to talk to him. Her voice was unusually thin.

"You will come over, won't you? You'll be here soon, right? The compress is awful!"

"Yes, but it helps. Be a good girl and follow Olgi's orders!"

Klára continued with her complaints, while Aldó did his best to calm her down.

"We can't predict whether or not he will give you a shot, but it would only take half a minute... Of course, I'll come as soon as I can... I will be there around six-thirty."

After finishing with two more patients, Aldó dialed again.

"Hasn't he shown up yet? Call him again. A hundred and three? It's time to make a cooling bath for her... Yes, definitely, even if she is defiant. The bell? Great!"

Olgi called back fifteen minutes later.

"He has just given a prescription for Kalmopyrin. He says the compress should reduce her fever. It's probably just a cold, he says. And he didn't let me call you to talk to him. It's not necessary, he said, and he has no time for... He also asked me why I bothered him instead of a doctor for adults, since Klára is no longer a child."

After seeing two more patients, Elvira asked for Aldó's permission to leave for the greengrocer's. They have lemons! And her colleague from the Otology department is holding a place for her in line, too.

Aldó didn't mind this idea right now: if Elvira leaves, he could take a break without a bad conscience. He took out his wrinkled notebook and picked up the phone. He called old acquaintances, one after the other, asking the same question: do they know anything about Pista Seilmann? He should have returned from the camp. At the fourth attempt, Aldó finally got Pista's number. An elderly woman with a pleasant voice answered the phone. It wasn't Anna Seilmann. But Pista was alive and would be available in an hour or so! Could he please call Aladár Körner at this number before six, or the other number after six-thirty?

Elvira returned, full of enthusiasm. She explained that, while she was waiting in line, it occurred to her how helpful it might be if Aldó brought some lemon to the sick girl today. And the sales clerk—who is, of course, not allowed to sell more than a pound to any client—was kind enough to smuggle a third pound into Elvira and her friend's paper bags. His Hedgie will be so happy to have the real thing, Aldó thought. He was also glad about seeing Elvira develop an almost human face. It's not what she looked like before.

At five o'clock, Aldó called Olgi again: he is trying to find a decent pediatrician, he reported. Did she fall asleep? That's good. Of course, he'll hurry up. This was the first day Aldó felt he had too many patients. At five-thirty, Elvira handed over the receiver:

"Doctor Seilmann is looking for you, Doctor."

• • • •

Around seven o'clock, Aldó and Pista Seilmann sat together by Klára's bedside. Pista had grown pretty old-looking, although he might not even be sixty yet. His smiling at children, however, hadn't changed in the least. Olgi was puttering around them. Klára spoke very little, mainly because of her constant coughing. Her voice now was surprisingly weak, and this was touching. Her sparkling, dark green eyes combined with this new weakness were those of an ageless child. Nevertheless, she did not seem unhappy. Aldó had been prepared for her to resist the idea of a second doctor but that hadn't even happened.

"I'd like to listen to your breathing." Pista said, "Would you take off your gown?"

"But... then... you should turn away, Aldó"

“I will.”

Olgi made a dismissive smile about this request, risking Klára’s resentment. Klára noticed it, but in reprisal she used a softer weapon than usual:

“Well... alright... but Aldó is not the doctor now!”

“Yes, of course, my Hedgie, it’s true.”

Pista Seilmann’s examination was as thorough as always. He’d always tell the children every step in advance. Aldó learned this habit as a young doctor from Pista, while seeing him treat his own sons. Ever since, he, too, explains everything in advance to his patients. Elvira used to smile about it in an uppity way at first but today she speaks of it almost proudly: “That’s why three times as many patients ask for Doctor Körner than his colleague from the other shift.”

“Does it hurt when you breathe deeply?”

“A little bit, back there.”

“Anywhere else?”

“No.”

“What did you eat today?”

“She didn’t want to eat anything for lunch...” Olgi complained.

“Did you eat your mid-morning snack?” Aldó asked.

“No. It’s still in my satchel.”

“How much did she drink?” Pista asked Olgi.

“Two or three glasses of tea...”

"That's not enough. She should drink a full mug of tea every other hour. Otherwise, she will dehydrate. We must do everything to prevent her from having to go to the hospital."

"I won't go to the hospital!"

"If you follow instructions, your chances for a home recovery will be much better," Pista explained. "First of all, your fever must come down as soon as possible. You know: cold compresses or a cooling bath, if needed. These are not pleasant, but they're tolerable. Also, I brought some suppositories for you."

"I hate those, too!"

"Listen, Hedgie dear, those things are not invented for our entertainment," Aldó intervened, "but for our assistance... You will get a special reward at the end, okay?"

"What kind of reward?"

"Well... how about mignons?"

"I don't feel like eating mignons right now..."

She even had to laugh at her own remark. A coughing fit lasting several minutes followed on the heels of her laughter.

"Second," Pista went on, "you have to drink a lot. May I examine your belly a bit, too?"

"Aldó..."

"I'm turning away."

• • • •

The night was still worrisome. Klára's fever did not change. Although she didn't have any nightmares, her constant moaning, and unresponsiveness to anyone while awake, alarmed both Aldó and Olgi. A cooling bath was prepared for her before midnight and also around dawn. Aldó carried her into the bathroom and, fighting her stern words, kept her in the water as long as he could stand the sounds of her rebellion.

Lemonade was the only thing that made Klára happy. By drinking one glass of tea, she earned the right for a lemonade next. With lots of sugar. After swallowing wrong, she could hardly stop coughing. Alarmed, Aldó hit her on her back, while watching her face and breathing. Then he laid her back down and stroked her forehead with a wet cloth. In a few minutes, Klára seemed to be asleep again.

Aldó left the room. Olgi followed him, after hearing the kitchen door creak. He must be hungry, she thought. But the kitchen was dark, illuminated only by some light coming in from the street. Aldó stood there with his back toward the door, slightly swaying his bowed head. Olgi recognized his murmured prayer: Refoenu, Adonai, venerofee: Heal us, Father Eternal, and we will be healed. She did not know, however, the next prayer: Pnei elai vechoneni ki yochid veoni oni... Turn to me and have mercy upon me, for I am lonely and poor.

Olgi closed the door silently and withdrew. What a gift to have this dear man here... Finally, she doesn't have to cope with everything all alone. Not even with the prayer! What a difference it makes when the prayer is offered by a man! It's their job! Her voice has never mattered, just that of her three men. It was their voice that the Lord really heard... as long as He heard anything at all. Why did Klára say that Aldó didn't believe in God?

. . . .

Klára was sleeping peacefully by the time Aldó left for home to wash up and change. Before leaving, he explained to Olgi that he would come back after two o'clock for only a short while, because in the afternoon he has to be at the orphanage. She should make a light, salty soup for Klára, portion out the two remaining lemons as well as possible and be careful not to cover her too warmly. Olgi listened eagerly to Aldó's every word. She had brought up two children without needing instructions for nursing the sick. But recently, there was nothing she missed more in life than being told by somebody what to do...

Aldó called already at nine to speak with Klára.

"Well... I'm fine."

"It doesn't sound quite so."

"Yes, it does."

"What's wrong, Hedgie?"

"Nothing."

"Go ahead!"

"...Because you didn't wake me up!"

"Why should I have awakened you? I was glad you were sleeping!"

Silence.

"Sleeping is crucial to quick healing."

No answer. What else could he say? Nevertheless, Klára must be much better if she was back to her usual sulky ways.

"Would you have awakened me if I were sick and finally fell asleep?"

"... I wouldn't have left you that way, for sure."

Now it was Aldó's turn to be silent. His Adam's apple moved as he swallowed hard.

"I know," he said, "you are wiser. You know better about what's important. Are you mad at me?"

"Well... not anymore."

"And how about those mignons?"

"Later... tomorrow... for sure. But they'll keep well, if you bring them today."

• • • •

At half past two, Aldó arrived with a bag of apples, eggs and mignons. He found a pile of prewar satirical magazines at Klára's bedside, part of Olgi's onetime collection. Klára's fever had gone down a bit, and she was eating the soup Olgi had made for her.

Yesterday's alarming weakness had turned into mere weariness by now. She even welcomed Olgi's "mother-hen instincts."

Aldó had been feeling uneasy all morning whenever he thought of the possible reaction to his afternoon program in the orphanage. To his great surprise, it was Klára who brought up the topic:

“How many families will you talk with today?”

“Four or five.”

“Do they know by now what kind of child they want to get?”

“Some do.”

“And what if the child turns out different? Or if they find they don’t like it? A child can’t just be handed back that way... After she... he... has entered into the spirit of... belonging...”

Aldó was aware of just what they were talking about.

“This Hanukkah visit, and more visits later, can help them learn about each other more, before ‘entering the spirit of belonging.’”

“Is the child also allowed to say No?”

“Of course. She... or he is the most important one.”

“But who would she have, then?”

“She will find somebody else later. Many children know exactly whom they need.”

“That’s true.”

“It is, indeed. Now I have to go, Hedgie. I’ll be back some time after eight. If you’re asleep, I’ll wake you up.”

Klára reached her arms out for Aldó. This was their first kiss ever.

. . . .

Around nine o’clock, Olgi received him with the news that Doctor Seilmann had visited once again. There was nothing wrong, they didn't call him, he just came to see Klára. He was satisfied with the improvement and didn't want to take any money.

Klára winked at Aldó cheerfully from her bed. Her fever was down to a hundred! Aldó also had good news: Gyula Barta had volunteered to replace him in the parent interviews tomorrow.

"Why? Because I told him that you are sick."

"Where does he know me from?"

"I've spoken to him about you."

"Really? What?"

"That he could hardly ever meet a more lovable hedgehog."

"Stop kidding! Really, what?"

By now, Aldó was really tired. In old days, in the Childbirth Center, he had always managed to keep on working with no difficulty after a sleepless night. But now he had difficulty keeping up the pace.

"How about talking about this tomorrow?"

Klára had not yet learned to tell the difference between Aldó's being tired from the day and getting tired of a dead-end discussion. Actually, she had only experienced the latter up until now. Often.

"What was wrong with my question this time?"

"Nothing, my Hedgie, I am simply tired. I won't stay too long today. I want to go to bed. I'll be back tomorrow morning. I can stay with you all the way till noon."

"Don't go home! You can sleep here, too!"

Olgi asked him to stay most respectfully, Aldó resisted, though not convincingly, and Klára had the victory. Olgi took out a pair of men's pajamas— precisely ironed and folded—from a drawer that had been locked up for years. She left to make the bed for Aldó, who headed for the bathroom.

The two available couches were in the children's room. One of them had belonged to Klára in the last few years. She would only cuddle up and read there during the day since her brother, Gyuri had gone, while she slept in Olgi's double bed. The other couch had been Klára's. Since neither had been used at night for years, Olgi suddenly remembered their former usual set-up: her Ervin's bed was in the corner, while Peter had slept close to the window. They even did this in their adult years, whenever returning home for a weekend.

"Olgi!" Klára shouted in a new, chirpy tone. She didn't get an answer for several long seconds, so she kept on shouting. "But... if that's so, I would rather move to..."

Olgi appeared in the doorway. When Klára set eyes upon her, she cut off her reverie.

"What are you saying, Sweetheart?" Olgi asked.

"Nothing, Olgi dear, don't be sad... You should have a mignon too. You said Aldó brought a lot of them."

. . . .

Next morning, Klára announced that she was hungry. Could she have some hot chocolate? Aldó left for the store to see if cocoa powder was available. Chances were slim. Meanwhile Klára asked Olgi to make her bed in the children's room "because it's easier to show Aldó Papa's journals and books from there."

Those were squeezed into the bottom of the dresser and the bottom drawer of Gyuri's bed. Novels were piled on top of her dresser and continued on top of Olgi's dresser. Dictionaries and the typewriter were on Klára's desk.

Last week, she'd been busy putting paper strips as bookmarks in those pages of the journals where there was an article having to do with gynecology. Those marked issues stood in a separate pile on the floor. Now, Klára began to arrange and rearrange her treasures—Olgi didn't succeed in sending her back to bed, even though she still had some fever.

After a while, Klára felt hungry again. Where is Aldó so long? She went to the window and kept watching the street, despite Olgi's offer to take over the sentry job herself. Klára refused to drink tea with sugar or eat any buttered bread. She became more and more fractious, and yanked off the morning dress Olgi tried to make her wear down from her shoulders. She was close to crying.

Half an hour later, Aldó arrived, of course. He had known that Klára would be mad. Still, he didn't want to give up his place in line: lemons again! He hadn't intended to go to a greengrocer at all but noticed the long line on the other side of the street while looking for a third grocery store with a chance of having cocoa powder. And over there, it was actually available.

It also occurred to him that Olgi might not have any milk at home—he was right—but he didn't have a milk can. Olgi hadn't thought of it, either. But he was lucky in this respect also: bottled milk was also available. He hadn't bought bottled milk since the war, not even milk in cans very often.

"You are such an idiot not to tell..." Klára said while opening the door.

Olgi looked at her with outrage. She became even more embarrassed when Aldó put the paper bag with lemons, the ice-cold bottle of milk and the cocoa powder into her hands. Klára went back to her bed, dramatically. She planned to keep up her performance for a while, but noticed suddenly that Aldó had pressed himself up against the radiator.

"Is it very cold outdoors?" she asked with a guilty conscience, probably instilled into her by Mama. Yes, she is the one who has to take appeasing steps now.

"Yes, pretty much."

"Olgi told me it's only fifteen degrees out there."

"Maybe. Anyway, we're lucky that you don't have to go out today."

Well, the issue didn't seem resolved to her, yet. She still had to appease him, she saw that clearly. The same way that Papa wouldn't have tolerated any bullshit. When any of his children ever went beyond a certain limit, they'd recognize this by seeing Papa suddenly behave in a gruesomely correct manner. Like a stranger. Aldó had the same trick in his repertoire.

"If I'd known you were standing in a line, I wouldn't have been so upset."

"Of course."

Gosh, that still didn't do it!

"What a pity that you can't put the telephone in your pocket and call home from anywhere far away."

Now, finally, Aldó smiled vaguely at this funny idea. But Klára wasn't smiling. She stayed silent for a while, turned toward the wall, and said:

"If you disappeared, too, I wouldn't want to live any longer."

Olgi brought them mugs of hot chocolate with perfect timing.

. . . .

Later in the morning, Klára announced an appetite for "Bird Milk with floating islands." Olgi was happy to cook, cool and serve it. Both ladies insisted on Aldó's eating everything Klára did. She asked him to move the big armchair to where her piles of journals were waiting for them. Aldó made a niche for her in the armchair.

They read the titles of the articles Klára had selected so he could decide which ones interested him. Priorities should also be determined based upon urgency. Aldó was game for that, too, although meanwhile, he was thinking constantly about how Klára might return this favor: when would she sit down with him and study math? Would she be willing to go through the curriculum in chemistry? Ever since their "big quarrel," he hadn't recovered his courage to talk about schoolwork. It was sheer luck that he suddenly saw a marked article that was suitable for launching his attack:

"Oh, this one should be very important! But there is too much chemistry involved... I don't think you could handle that."

Spying on her from the corner of his eye, he saw her take the bait, and soon the well-known resolute defiance appeared on her face. With a winner's confidence, he decided to raise his bet:

"Just drop it!"

"No! Whatever I want, I can understand! Do you think... like that idiot Vidák, that I'm stupid?"

"Well, then nothing should stop you doing it," Aldó grinned.

"It won't, you can bet on it!"

"Besides... this one would be my top priority."

"Don't worry! Aldó...bring me a chocolate mignon from the kitchen... please."

The mignon arrived soon and found Klára digging into the bottom of her wardrobe.

"Why aren't you in your niche, at least? You still should have bed rest."

"I can't find my chemistry book from last year! Although it must be here somewhere..."

• • • •

Klára asked Aldó to bring the book she had been about to read over from his place tonight. He shouldn't do any shopping, please, just be here again as soon as possible.

Also, he should bring along his shaving kit, because shaving is the only reason to go home anyway, now.

"Why are you looking at me this way?" she asked, scared.

Aldó kept silent for a while. By the time he gave his answer, however, he was confident and calm. Klára's Papa might have been sending him useful hints.

"Hedgie dear... I won't move in here with you. But I won't disappear, either. I'll always tell you where I am. I'll do my best to be on time. Should I be late, you only have to remember that the war is over. There are no reasons other than just long lines, slow, jammed streetcars, or more patients in the clinic than usual. I will not disappear. I promise."

. . . .

Dearest Mama, Papa, Grandma, Grandpa, Juti, wherever you are!

Imagine, Aldó will come here for Hanukkah! It will be a real Hanukkah with a man attending, too! But I miss you all so much. I am crying right now. Olgi also cried with joy about Aldó's coming. I can tell just seeing Aldó's face when he would like to cry, too, if he weren't a man. I always start joking then so he'll cheer up.

I don't want to be a man because then I wouldn't be allowed to cry either.

. . . .

On Tuesdays, the two of them studied math and physics, while on Thursdays chemistry and biology were on their schedule. The breakthrough hadn't been achieved just by

Klára's sudden appeasement, not even by her impressively quick mind, but rather by Aldó's success in shifting her attitude at a crucial point. In the old days, he would never have dreamed of cynically inciting his children to rebel against their teachers. But with Klára, that was the clue. It might be the same with his sons, should they—with all the losses Klára had suffered—be standing here now, lonely, hungry for any recognition.

"Vidák wouldn't reward whatever I write her anyway... Even if I handed in a paper with no mistakes at all, I would get a C from her, at best."

"Who cares about Vidák? I would be proud of you, if you were just familiar with the Periodic Table. The whole thing is a logical game! Like one made just for you! Vidák's only job is to let you pass in chemistry and biology. Once you've passed, you'll be eligible for your graduation exams, and after that you finally can start studying what you are really interested in."

Since Klára was listening with genuine attention, Aldó went on:

"You don't need to like Mrs. Vidák. And you shouldn't expect her to like you, either. She can't even grasp what a person you are. But never mind, she's a completely insignificant human being in your life."

Alas, should Aldó's parents hear this! "Show respect to everybody for his knowledge!" "Do everything to your best ability!" "Whatever is worth doing is worth doing well!" Poor father, blessed be your name.

The home tutoring didn't follow the exact curriculum, because Klára mainly was interested in a survey of facts.

Details only gained importance to her after she could fit them into the system. She mused a long time about equations:

“Look, Aldó! 4 HCl + O_2 —> 2 H_2O + 2 Cl_2. You see?”

“Yes, I see. It’s all right, isn’t it?”

“First...” she started in a reciting voice, “they used to live in families... the hydrogens and the chlorines. There were four of them. Later, the oxygen invaded and robbed the families of their hydrogens... they turned into water and leaked away. Only the chlorines stayed behind and now they cuddle up with each other in pairs.”

Aldó’s gaze stiffened. He nodded abruptly, just enough not to be impolite, and left for the bathroom. Klára sensed that Aldó hadn’t left to go pee. Frightened, she watched the door closing behind him. She was waiting... she might be wrong.

“Aldó!” she shouted after a while.

No answer.

“Aldó!”

“Just a minute,” came the weak reply.

She chose to wait a bit again.

“Aldó... is it because of the chlorine?”

“Coming... soon.”

Klára pressed her ear against the door. The water was running in the tub. No other noises. Yes, it must be because of the chlorine... Why is she pushing him? If it’s better for Aldó now in there... She can’t stand it either when Olgi won't leave her alone with her bad mood. But she just wants to comfort him now! ...Is this what Olgi wants to do, then?... Anyway, he should come out first.

"I only want... to give you a hug... but... if you don't feel like... yet... you can stay."

Aldó was grateful for her permission. He kept to himself for two or three more minutes. This was "unpleasant but tolerable" for her, as Pista Seilmann put it when talking about a cooling bath. She sat down on the floor, close to the door of the bathroom, leaning her back against the wall. The noise of running water soon stopped, and finally the door opened. Klára stood up and went to him with open, embracing arms, the first time ever. Aldó let himself be hugged for a minute before he lifted his arms and hugged her the usual way: Klára holding her arms in front of her chest and leaning against his. Soon he found the words:

"Are we the chlorines?"

"Yeah. And we really did find each other."

Aldó was surprised to see Klára outdistancing him in their mourning. True, children heal quicker. Once they've started.

"Only you knew what to do, while I did not," he said while still fondling her hair. Klára cuddled up tight to him.

"That's true... but you allowed it."

"A great mercy!" he smiled at last. "We men believe that there is no better solution than enduring."

• • • •

Being off duty, Aldó would await Klára every second Saturday in front of the school. They'd go home—to Olgi—together to have the Sabbath lunch there. All in all, Monday was the only day of the week when they didn't see each other. Klára kept coming Tuesday afternoons and Aldó would see her off Wednesday mornings at the streetcar stop. On Thursdays, she would come again, and next morning they'd set off together, Klára heading to school, Aldó to the orphanage.

On Saturdays, they'd spend time together from noon till evening. Sometimes they would even have an activity to do together on Sunday, accompanied by Olgi, since "it's her day." So Monday was easy to endure. They talked on the phone, anyway. Also, Monday was Aldó's shopping day. He'd buy almost everything for the week, so he could offer Klára something special for dinner on Tuesday, make hot chocolate for her breakfast and put something rich into her mid-morning snack.

. . . .

My dear Diary!

Today—just by chance, really—I overheard Aldó and Olgi chatting in the kitchen. You have to know that Olgi often grumbles, asking why I won't greet Aldó. (I don't greet her, either, but she doesn't mention that.) Aldó said to Olgi that, in his opinion, I do that because I want to pretend that we haven't ever been separated before, and that by not saying goodbye before leaving, I'm denying the upcoming separation! He's pretty sure about this because I do greet others who are less important, he said.

That's true, by the way. She can't think as complicated as that, Olgi replied, but is willing to believe Aldó's point. I feel sorry for Olgi whenever she thinks of herself as stupid. She is really not very smart. But she is a good person. Aldó likes her too. (I think this case shouldn't make her feel stupid, anyway. It hadn't occurred to me, either, that this is the reason, although I am anything but stupid. In my opinion.)

. . . .

Aldó had some friends from the old days who used to invite him from time to time for Saturday lunch, as a mitzvah. He preferred to see those families where the good deed seemed to be reciprocal. The Freuds, for instance. This couple had fought their way home, but all three of their children had perished. Aldó had been the doctor assisting at the birth of their two younger ones.

Compared with the general mood of the Freuds, Aldó made a cheerful impression. That's why the Freuds were the only ones Aldó sometimes called without waiting to be invited. In the first months after the war, Aldó and Mishi would play chess after lunch while Betty would sew by their side, often sighing deeply.

At some point, it came up, just by chance, how much Betty used to like playing Rummy as a young girl. So, playing cards soon became part of their afternoon ritual. The men didn't find it much more boring than playing chess. They, too, offered this to Betty as a mitzvah. While playing cards, Aldó sometimes mused: It's good that Ilona didn't live to see this. He will endure somehow as long as he must, but he wouldn't expect this from her. The full bookcases—reaching to the ceiling—seemed like décor left behind from the past. Nobody was interested anymore in what the wise ones and the poets had to say.

In the fall of '47, Aldó had come up with the idea that Betty could teach needlework to the girls of the orphanage. Betty was so well read that she could have taught almost anything to the children. Yet it took until January to get her to agree. She was trembling the whole way there. Aldó didn't admit to her that he, too, only had the courage to enter the girls' house. The Freuds had had a daughter as well as two sons.

Some of the girls, however, received Betty so gently that, after half an hour, Aldó felt okay about leaving her with them. After settling his business in the office, he returned and saw—for a minute—the happy radiance of the old days on Betty's face.

Last year, after Passover, the couple had finally adopted two sisters whom they adored despite constant worries. Since they had brought the children home, Aldó declined their invitations. He just called sometimes to find out if they were all right.

In March, he decided to tell them about Hedgie. Betty invited them over instantly. Aldó was afraid of the plan at first. He kept explaining how unpredictably Hedgie might behave. And that she had only "buried" her parents just recently, so the notion of the orphanage might evoke bad feelings in her. Besides, he wanted to prevent Hedgie from using her barbs against the girls.

"Our girls are very likable and understanding," Betty boasted. "Everything will be all right! Just bring her!"

"But I know how worried Mishi is about them."

"It's less pathological now," Betty laughed.

Aldó would have also liked to boast about all the wonderful qualities Hedgie had. But he said only:

"I can't remember how old your kids are."

"Panni is nine, Jutka is thirteen by now. And yours?"

Aldó felt good about this definition of Hedgie: "She's turned sixteen. But don't expect this from her. She can be anything between five and seventy. And her looks are... mostly twelve."

"Oh, we know that well, too. Our girls are just about to find the way back to their real age."

"With Hedgie... it happened just the other way around. In December, when she first began to calm down, she suddenly turned into a little child. She is still often that way. She seldom resembles a teenage girl... her awkwardness, maybe, sometimes... but less and less. And, thank God, that terrible bitterness one finds in some elderly people is about to disappear in her, too.

Except for the few inescapable words he had exchanged with Elvira and Gyula Barta, this was the first time he had talked about Hedgie to anybody. Well, he hardly had anyone to talk to. He would see a few old acquaintances, one or two families a month, when invited to Sunday lunch—not Saturday anymore, because Saturdays belonged to Olgi now.

This conversation with Betty finally sounded like those he used to have in the old days, when he would chat as a "normal" father with other "normal" parents about their children. Times when he hadn't yet realized that having children was no self-explanatory gift of life. Now he started to talk to Betty about Hedgie's obsession for literature, about the translations, and also about her family.

Betty and he ended up with a compromise plan: Aldó would bring Hedgie next Saturday, pretending they'd just chanced to drop in for a short time. They would see how the girls got along with each other.

"What's her real name?" Betty asked.

"She's Klára. Everyone else calls her that. But for me, she is Hedgie."

. . . .

Klára kept cross-examining Aldó about the Freuds' children. She had been mostly interested in their numbers. This was new.

"If they've been with their new parents for one year by now, then they must have spent three years in the orphanage."

Aldó kept silent. Klára went on with her counting.

"If the little one is nine now, she must be born in thirty-nine or forty."

"Yes."

"Little Juti was also born in thirty-nine..."

Good God, Aldó thought terrified, one of the girls is also called Jutka! Which one, what did Betty say? No good can come out of this!

Klára was quicker in noticing Aldó's worry than he was in finding anything reassuring to say to her. She tactfully switched topics.

"What grade is the older one in?"

"She is thirteen, so she must be in..."

"...in the seventh grade. I hated to be in the seventh... after the war. The only good thing was to have the boys' school just next door. Gyuri and I were waiting every day for each other at the gate."

Whenever they discussed a topic like that, Klára would cuddle up to Aldó on the couch and let herself be hugged. Aldó's listening was always so nice, so silent, as if offering her the whole space... While Olgi would keep interrupting!

"Did the Freuds also have children before?"

"They did."

After a longish silence he added:

"Three."

Klára just nodded and put one arm around Aldó's waist. She hadn't asked a question like this since November. Before November she had lived as though anesthetized, so anything could easily slip through her lips. She didn't know anything more about Aldó than what Olgi had told her: that he had never had a daughter.

. . . .

Klára entered the Freuds' apartment glued to Aldó. When a chair was offered to her, Aldó—seeing her hesitation—shepherded her further, to the couch where they could sit at each other's side. The whole family was very friendly. Small talk about school and the upcoming Spring holiday began while Betty brought the cakes. And also some raspberry soda. Made from real raspberry! Klára nodded politely: yes, everything tastes very good.

The younger sister, Panni, soon discovered Klára's brown-and-yellow shoes. She ran into her room and came back in a hurry, showing off her new shoes.

"You've got very nice shoes," said Klára in an encouraging, motherly voice Aldó had never heard before. Panni seemed to be the only one Klára was willing to look in the eyes, at this point. Panni sat down at her side.

"Shall I show you my new skirt, too?" she asked. "Mami made it! And another one for Jutka. Jutka, may I show your skirt to Hedgie, too?"

Klára was surprised to be called Hedgie by anyone other than Aldó. But Betty had instructed her girls for days about how to receive their guest. Mishi was just about to suggest a visit in the children's room. (He never had the right sense of timing, least so when he had sent their children to "their aunt's safe, hidden place" where, as it turned out, nobody survived.) And, in fact, Klára didn't move at all while Panni began the next delivery from her room. Unexpectedly, Jutka wanted to put her little sister in her place:

"Panni, boasting is not appropriate!"

"Oh, I'm glad to see the skirts," Klára replied. "My little sister also used to love showing off her new treasures!"

Her expression became quite grown-up, like that of a big sister who is ready to support and please the little one. The way she praised the skirts was a kind of demonstration—addressed to Jutka—of how to do that. Meanwhile, the girls caught Klára's previous sentence about her sister. They stared at her, quite still, for seconds, and then realized: there is nothing to be asked here.

"Well, alright, then," Jutka said leniently and pulled her sister close.

"See?" Panni replied in a triumphant voice.

Klára looked away and slid back next to Aldó who put an arm around her shoulders. Now, Mishi's sense of timing happened to work well:

"Aladár told us that you like Thomas Mann very much," he said.

Distrustfully, Klára tried to figure out what Mishi was fishing for.

"Is it true?"

She nodded her approval.

"In that case, here is a surprise for you."

Klára was still nestled at Aldó's ribs.

"A recent book by Thomas Mann."

"Which one?"

"*Doctor Faustus*. It first came out two years ago, but last year it was also published in Hungarian. We got a copy of the German edition as a present just recently. Am I right about your reading German as well?

Klára nodded again.

"You may have it for a while—if you are really such a big Thomas Mann fan."

"Although it's not light reading..." Betty intervened half-heartedly, since it wasn't her intention to discourage Klára.

"Nor are the other ones," Klára replied. "My Mom said I will really understand them only after finishing high school. But I do already understand them!" Then she turned to Aldó: "Maybe, not everything the way... I should... I read *Tonio Kröger* recently again, and there were parts where I found it different now... But that's okay, isn't it?"

"Sure."

"Any more cake?"

"Yes, please. My grandma would bake this cake sometimes, too. Right, Aldó?"

"Yes, she did."

Panni was bored by the dull topics and tried to regain Klára's attention. She could show Hedgie her books, she thought, if that's what appealed to Hedgie anyway. She took her guest's hand and pulled her toward the children's room. But Klára wanted to check Jutka's face first. And she got her permission in the form of a benevolent smile. So the three girls disappeared with unexpected ease into the other room.

There was silence in the living room. Betty made an attempt to contradict Aldó's worried, deep sigh:

"She's a special child..."

"Special for me, but what do you mean by that?"

"I don't really know. I just feel it. She really doesn't have any apparent age... While ours would rather drastically switch between being three and being thirty years old...

back and forth... both of them. But Hedgie... with her... it's her expression, rather than her behavior, that tells where she stands right now. And she switches so quickly, it's impossible to follow. Isn't it, Mishi?"

"It's certainly different. But even in our case... first we couldn't imagine learning to follow those... switches... Still, we managed to learn! It's the same with Hedgie, for sure."

"Yes," Aldó replied. "I can follow her changes by now... but I see her as much more damaged than your kids."

"Well... siblings are a great support. Only children are a much harder case. I could see that in the orphanage, as well," Betty mused.

"Her aunt told me that life only became unbearable after her brother left for Palestine. He sends letters from time to time, but Hedgie won't respond. Just Olgi."

"Is Olgi the aunt or the grandma?"

"Hedgie has been calling her 'aunt' up until now, but Olgi is actually her father's aunt. This was the first time I ever heard her honor Olgi with the title of 'Grandma.'"

Later, Aldó talked about his new experience with a daughter. Both the joys and difficulties are so different than with a son. But he felt quite comfortable with it by now.

"Once I used to think that someone who was both a child and a woman would just overwhelm me. But Hedgie has never taken advantage of me. And also, she makes so many sweet gestures a boy never would. Nevertheless, her nickname derives from the fact that—at first—that was the zoological species she resembled the most. Today, I would probably give her a different nickname."

Mishi and Betty were laughing. They started their story about Jutka, the older girl: She had calmed down miraculously ever since Betty realized why she had turned into a screaming baby after the adoption. She had been only eight when left behind by the parents, and since then, Panni had clutched at her like a newborn. So Jutka hadn't been allowed to live like a little girl of her own age. Now, after finally having parents again, she wanted to make up for the missed years, and to be heard. Whenever Jutka burst out whining, Betty had started putting her on her lap. Such scenes now occurred only once or twice a week, instead of several times daily.

Surprisingly to all of them, Betty mentioned that talking about their dead ones had also become part of their life. Although crying was inevitable every time, they told each other something crucial by doing this. Mishi rose from his chair impatiently and went to the window while Betty added, for Aldó:

"Well, we can't take too much of this at one time, of course..."

"I am not even as far along as that... But Hedgie is, as you could see. When I first saw her, in November, she was talking about her parents as if they were still alive. That's what she thought at that time. And this way, it was easy. Later, in December, when she finally did... grasp it... I thought she would never mention them again. But she does! You could see. As if they were living inside her. I can see every day how she draws nourishment from them. She is the only real believer among us, I think. Although she has never been taught to believe. She has simply found her belief.

A chat about the Jewish community was launched, and Mishi came back to his armchair. Jutka soon emerged from the children's room and sat down by Mishi's side. Meanwhile, she was watching the door of her room, as if she wanted to tell a secret.

"What would you like to say, my girl?"

"Papi," Jutka began, somewhat embarrassed. "If Hedgie could visit us from time to time, she could also have something like sisters. But Panni wouldn't leave with her, would she?"

• • • •

On their way home, Klára asked question after question, less about the children and more about the couple. She liked Betty more.

"Betty's the smarter one, isn't she?"

"...Maybe. I've never thought of them this way. But yes."

Klára kept musing for a while, then—staring into a shop window—she just said:

"Mama's name is Anna."

"That's a beautiful name."

"And... whenever Papa was upset about something, Mama never lost her temper. She'd say to us: 'Just keep calm! He'll cool off soon. We'll wait it out!' Isn't Betty like this, too?"

Suddenly, a male voice shouted from across the street: "Aladár!" A slim, bald man, about Aldó's age, waved vehemently.

"My cousin, Tamás," Aldó explained while returning the wave.

Tamás run over to them instantly. He shot a quick glance at Klára and began spluttering:

"Hi, little lady! Aladár, have you heard that apartments can be claimed? The same size you used to have!"

"This is Klára, my foster child..."

"Hello!... You're in a flophouse rather than an apartment now, aren't you?"

"I have a one-room apartment allotted. It's big enough for me."

"What a meshuga you are, Aladár... once again. Well, excuse me, little lady, otherwise he's a very smart man but... Aladár, go and see Robert Weinmann in the Jewish Community office. He'll explain what to do. Will you promise to do that?"

"I often go to the office whenever I've to arrange things for the orphanage... It's just very unlikely that big flats would be given away while the authorities are placing co-tenants into every single empty room."

"Aladár, you're hopeless! Reparation money should be coming, too. As soon as I get more news about it, I'll call you. And then, it's only up to you if you ruin your chances or not... Aladár! You don't seem to grasp the importance of things like that! Or... do you simply prefer to keep suffering?"

Two sharp lines appeared around Aldó's mouth, unknown to Klára before.

"I am interested in every form of reparation, as soon as the package includes the promise that our families can return. That'd be the time for you to call! I'll be standing in the line with this child in the very first row. We'll have two different registration numbers."

Tamás might have left soon even without this lecture. He gave the impression that running was his basic speed. When the departing figure got tiny, Klára comforted Aldó's silence:

"Never mind! Forget about him! Papa also had a niece like that who acted like she knew everything. And she also regarded everybody stupid. Papa called her Little Miss Know-it-all."

. . . .

On another Saturday, Aldó again waited for Klára in front of the school.

"She was so 'charitable' today that she gave me a B!" Klára announced.

"Mrs. Vidák? That's perfect for us! Was it chemistry?"

"No, biology. And she said in a... well, in such a... what's it called... way: 'Your common sense seems to be returning finally.' I hate her!"

"You may. We are not studying for her sake. Just don't talk back!"

Not long ago, Aldó noticed the ease with which he now rebelled against norms—norms that he used to respect totally—if it pertained to Klára. When he'd pinched the first bundle of cotton wool from the clinic in December, he'd felt like a common thief. By now, he would walk out with some without further consideration. Well, only at moments when Elvira couldn't see it. In the old days, nothing could have justified his taking anything this way.

He couldn't even have explained it to himself that cotton wool was not available in the drugstores and that Klára was still kicking so violently against this biological predestination that at least she should be spared having to deal with the monthly cloths. If she got enough pampering and painkiller at these times, she would calm down, at least by the third day. Anyway, cotton wool is something she deserves, wherever it might come from. The same way her resentment is all right whenever a teacher puts her down.

Recently, Aldó has started to ask a new question of the world: "Is it really us, yet again, who have to keep to the rules? Never the others?" There were no such questions for him in the old days: The teacher was the teacher, and property was property.

"However, I don't like you to say 'what's-it-called...' You have such a beautiful vocabulary!"

"I just couldn't recall how to say 'superiorité' in Hungarian. And Mama said, I should never mix German or French words into my speech, because people get irritated by that and start abusing us Jews."

"We really have to be careful not to provoke that. But you can speak to me any way you want. It's very important that we find the missing words and enrich your vocabulary for translations this way, too. Supérieur means condescending or uppity. Alright? ...And, I also have good news! Elvira's neighbor is a French teacher! My idea was that you mustn't lose your French either. Do you feel like taking lessons in French?"

"Yes, I do! Is she a real French person?"

"No, she is Hungarian but was brought up in France."

"She mustn't have a strange accent... that wouldn't be the real thing." And she added with some newly learned modesty: "If she was brought up over there, she might have authentic pronunciation. The key is to hear French as a child from a real French person. As I did."

Aldó suppressed a smile and kept listening.

"We used to have Charlotte. As long as she lived with us, everything was beautiful. Poor Charlotte had a limp. Because a motorcycle had hit her when she was twelve on her way to the school. All the bones in her leg had been broken. And she was told she'd never be married because of her limp.

She cried bitterly 'cause she wouldn't be able to have children then, either. Later, she studied to be a teacher but the children ridiculed her because of her leg. And she almost wanted to die by the time she heard that we were looking for a French governess and she came to Hungary. We really loved her very much!"

Klára was suddenly seized with laughter:

"I started to limp one day and my parents were scared about what was wrong with my leg. I told them that I only wanted to 'walk French.' I thought every French person walked like that... But I wasn't stupid, just young. I was only four... Charlotte was so sweet! She'd called me Clairette.

Clairette is actually a pink wine. What's its name in Hungarian?"

"Rosé, I suppose. But that's not a Hungarian word, either."

"...And she returned home in 1943, because Papa had told her he would understand it if she wanted to leave.[6] It was hard for her, too, to leave us after seven years. Still, she left. And Papa was soon drafted into the forced labor service."

Aldó stared into a great distance. Klára brought him back:

"How old is she?"

"Who?"

"Elvira's French teacher."

"I haven't asked. But I can ask her on Monday."

. . . .

Klára set out with enthusiasm to meet Mrs. Venczel who asked her—in Hungarian—how long she had studied French and if she was studying it in school, as well. She also asked her to read aloud and announced that any foreign language should be mastered at the conscious level.

Klára felt uneasy. Why was it all right for Charlotte to speak with her the way they did? Why was it such a joy to read novels together and discuss them for long hours afterwards?

"What grade are you attending now? Seventh?"

6. *It had nothing to do with Charlotte's choice. In those years Jews were not allowed to have any employees anymore. Klára's parents, however, kept it a secret from their children.*

"I go to high school, in the tenth grade."

"You?"

"...Yes."

She had never ever experienced anything other than compassion and caring whenever adults hinted at her scrawny build. And she had even gained weight recently!

While reading aloud, Mrs. Venczel's pronunciation turned out to be more or less acceptable to Klára. She heard no Hungarian taint in it but found it somewhat strange and affected. She didn't know, of course, what kind of dialect hers was, because she also didn't know that Charlotte's wasn't the only possible French pronunciation. Mrs. Venczel stopped Klára's reading:

"Now put the story into the future tense!"

Klára looked surprised: If something happened once in the past, you can't pretend to expect it to happen in the future, she thought. Still, she started to tell the story in the future tense, by heart.

"Stop improvising! Look at the text and go from sentence to sentence!"

Klára knit her eyebrows: what the hell is this good for? They used to learn English this way in her old school, because they had been just beginners, but why in French?

"I am told that you want to take language lessons. And I can see that you possess no grammatical awareness at all."

Perfectly true. She could, however, happily live without that. What's this whole thing good for? ...Alright, she could survive it the same way she is surviving Mrs. Vidák. But it would be utter nonsense for Aldó to pay this witch extra money!

After finally freeing herself from Mrs. Venczel, Klára wondered if she had met her a year ago whether she'd have slammed the door on her right away. Yet, she also remembered how hollow she had felt after doing that kind of thing: even if she had managed to escape, she had nowhere to run back for comfort.

. . . .

Mama! This awful Mrs. Venczel is just like Strebiczky used to be at the swimming club. Can you remember him throwing me into the pool and saying that it would make me fearless? I thought I would drown while he just kept laughing. And you asked him nicely to just teach me swimming technique, and you would take care of my character yourself.

He got offended and said that the only people who didn't trust him are such Jewish hussies. And Papa said you shouldn't bring me there anymore, so we didn't. I won't go to Mrs. Venczel anymore either! She seems like an antisemite, or simply an idiot. Do my looks say I'm Jewish? I'll ask Aldó about it. But will he accept my not going to French lessons anymore? He only wanted to make me happy, I know. But I am not happy about this.

. . . .

"I have some bad news for you, Hedgie! Mrs. Venczel is also Jewish."

"What??"

"Did you think all Jews were pleasant people?" Aldó asked with a laugh.

"No... but..."

"There are nasty people everywhere... Anyway, grammar is just logic and you like logic. You might be asked about it on an exam some time. Still, if you don't want to... this is not compulsory," Aldó explained. Klára felt a bit relieved.

"But won't Elvira be mad at me, if I don't go through with this?"

Elvira's story about Mrs. Venczel occurred to Aldó suddenly: The lady had kept her doormat as clean as if she wanted to eat her breakfast on it. She even keeps a wet cloth on top of it, and—if it's muddy outside from rain—she'd put an extra cloth in front of the door. Well, this should've made him realize that Mrs. Venczel wouldn't be a favorite of Klára's.

"I don't think so," he replied.

"Aren't you mad at me, either?"

"No."

"But I can see!"

"The only thing annoying me here is that this doesn't solve the issue! ...Is she very nasty?"

Klára was confident by now that she could count on Aldó's support. She smiled:

"Like Vidák... almost."

Aldó uttered a sigh and went on reading his newspaper.

"Aldó, read a book instead!"

"Why?"

"You always get in a bad mood after reading the newspaper."

"The problem may not lie in the reading... Well, Hedgie dear, you go on with your homework!"

And indeed, Klára obeyed this time. After finishing her tasks, she closed her physics book with a bang, relieved, and climbed up on the couch—where Aldó was reading on his stomach—to get the next book she was planning to read down from the shelf. She just had socks on, and, momentarily losing her balance, happened to step on Aldó's back.

"Oh, that's nice! Step on it again!" he moaned.

She thought she had caused him pain.

"Really?"

"Really."

"Won't it hurt?"

"No, it's great!"

Incredible! Well, he should get it if he wants, Klára thought, and gripped the shelf with one hand to avoid putting her whole weight on him. She trod his back up and down several times. This ceremony became the pampering in Aldó's life. Whenever he was tired or in a bad mood, Klára instantly volunteered to walk on his back. If she were mad at Aldó, she'd threaten to withhold this service. And with that having been said, they'd have a good excuse for laughing.

Now the phone rang. Aldó's responses made it clear that the call was a nuisance for him. After putting down the receiver, he grinned at her:

"Hedgie, be prepared! Gini the Terrible will soon drop in!"

"Who is she?"

"A member of the extended family, not a relative of mine... she's supposedly just dropping by to say thank you for something. I have no idea why this call couldn't do the job..."

"How can a family member not be a relative?"

"The sister-in-law of my sister-in-law is no relative to me anymore."

This was the first time—since meeting Tamás Know-it-all—Klára had heard about any family member of Aldó's. And she was glad that he mentioned it with such ease. But soon she started to think about something different:

"Isn't the sister-in-law of one's sister-in-law the same person?"

"Not necessarily. Because the chain of in-laws can be any length, as long as brothers and sisters exist. Gini, for instance, was the sister of the husband of the sister... of my wife."

"And what does she want to thank you for?"

"We used to have some household items I don't want to own anymore. And I offered them to her."

Gini really didn't make the impression of being related to Aldó in any substantial way. After entering the apartment, she immediately covered Aldó's and Klára's face with lipstick and saliva. Then—for a change—she opened her mouth to talk, but that didn't make the situation any better.

"Ali, dearest, we are rrrreally very grateful for your gift! You can't have the faintest idea of how much you've helped us with those things! We haven't even had a decent plate since the war... nothing! Your dinner set is just beautiful! And the glasses, too..."

"You're welcome, Gini dear... And how are you doing?"

"Miserably, of course! We got bombed out. We have nothing! You might have heard that I married Karcsi's business partner... He even has a nicer temperament than poor Karcsi used to have. But we've been displaced into the boondocks. We live in a slum, along a dirt road, surrounded by ignorant peasants. We have to sit on the streetcar for two hours every day! We don't even have a decent dress... not even the girls...

"Oh, Ali dear, it occurred to me just now what Veronka told me when packing your dishes at her place: That they put many things into your own cellar when you moved in... Many old things... which are... aren't they... unfortunately... not needed anymore... Ilona's clothes."

"I don't know. Veronka and her husband arranged everything in my cellar, too. I'd rather not touch it."

"I am ready to have a look at it by myself if..."

Paralyzed, Klára watched Aldó's face. But Mama's command from '44 ('Keep quiet whenever strangers enter the house!') stopped her from interfering by saying to Gini: "Leave Aldó alone! He doesn't want that!"

"Gini, dear," Aldó brought himself to say, "I'll let you know whenever I put things straight there."

"It's not a problem if they are not straight..."

Klára was thinking that she would certainly throttle the person who wanted to take Mama's and Papa's things. Although in their case, there were not even any clothes left behind. Those had been stolen by the time Klára first re-entered their apartment. The only treasures she could save were books, photo albums and the typewriter. Now she finally found the courage to speak, though with caution:

"How old are your daughters, Aunt Gini?"

"Well, they are big girls by now! Seventeen and twenty-one."

"I'll turn seventeen soon, too."

The reception of the news wasn't much warmer than at Mrs. Venczel's.

"You must be a late bloomer, my dear. My girls already need to dress ladylike."

Aldó exploited the thought quite skillfully:

"Klára will need to, also. I'd like to save things for her..."

"Alright! I haven't said a word, okay? Although Ilona had so many beautiful dresses... My girls could have got some of them, I thought. Aunt Rose used to be so fond of them, too."

Aldó stood up from his chair, inhaling deeply. And that made Gini finally understand his answer. She also stood up. Aldó made an attempt to bring the scene back to normal.

"Would you like to drink a coffee or tea?"

"No, thank you. I don't want to disturb you any longer."

She surveyed the flat with her eyes:

"Well, your apartment isn't the same as it used to be, either... but at least you can live downtown. You're so lucky!"

"This word hadn't occurred to me, until now."

. . . .

The next Saturday, they were invited to the Seilmanns'. Klára wanted to know about their family set-up in advance, too. One of 'Uncle Pista's' daughters was saved with her children and husband, but the other daughter and her mother were deported to a camp and never returned. Nevertheless, Klára found the report too scary after a few sentences.

"But Uncle Pista was very nice to me," she interrupted Aldó. "Where's he working?"

"In a hospital, in Pediatrics."

"He must have a bad opinion about his hospital."

"Why?"

"Can't you remember? When I was sick, he said, we should avoid taking me to the hospital by all means."

"True! But being in a hospital is always worse than being at home, isn't it?"

"Yes, it is. But I can remember his grimace...He had a reason for saying so."

Aldó could easily imagine that Klára would observe things like that—even with high fever—more sensitively than he did.

. . . .

Pista and his new wife, Margit, were the only hosts, yet Klára had a very nice time there. Margit was an unusual phenomenon in that world, full of energy and optimism. She gladly showed Klára all the family pictures her son kept sending from America. Klára was eager to hear all the details proving that those living so far away are getting along just fine. Aunt Margit could even attest to this with her photos. While the two of them were busy with the pictures, Pista—somewhat bashfully—showed Aldó the letter that very son had sent to thank him for being there for his mother.

Margit suggested playing the board game she'd owned for a long time: Quiz-questions in the realm of literary and language education were to be answered in one minute each, measured by a small hourglass. Klára proved to be a real master! Aldó was so proud that he couldn't help shouting out loud after some brilliant answer of hers. She had never heard him be louder than a soft indoor volume, and her own pride made her almost do backflips.

When seeing her guests out, Aunt Margit asked if they would come again. Klára replied immediately:

"When can we come next?"

. . . .

The Freuds also sent another invitation that made Klára happy. Life resembled the old days more and more. She had friends again! It was so nice to go someplace with Aldó and be expected there. Olgi and Klára also visited two other families from time to time. They were relatives of Olgi's husband. But the time there—even if they were happy to see a child—was spent mostly with the typical, repetitive deep sighs of old people.

Klára had only one friend of her own: Emmi, whom she had first met in the Jewish Ghetto, in '44. Emmi might be about Mama's age. Her husband had never returned; they never had children; Emmi was now teaching piano. She kept inviting Klára and her brother after the war, whenever she happened to obtain some precious food.

Since Gyuri had left, however, Klára had accepted Emmi's invitation only once, because she found out after her visit that Emmi had called Olgi to say how worried she was about her. Olgi took those words as an accusation and cried bitterly. At that time, Klára wasn't concerned about Olgi's crying, but she was always upset when talked about behind her back.

Well, she might give Emmi a call sometime again. She might introduce Aldó, too... After all, it was Emmi who had wanted to take her and Gyuri home after the liberation of the Ghetto. But Klára had chosen the Red Cross House instead, hoping to be found there more easily by their parents. The parents never came. Only Olgi had emerged suddenly one day, the last day before children were taken to the orphanages.

• • • •

Klára made excited preparations for her next visit to the Freuds. Neither Aldó nor Olgi had ever seen her planning her outfit in advance. She also asked Aldó if he could buy her a new pair of knee-length socks: those white ones with white embroidery that her classmate, Juli Szendrei, also had.

The whole Freud family received them like old friends, with great joy. Klára returned *Doctor Faustus* to Mishi. Then the kids went into the children's room—not even Betty's cakes appealed to them much; only the almond cakes that Klára and Aldó bought had won their brief attention.

Aldó started to tell his news from the last month: how happy he is to see Klára's sudden change regarding school; what great grades she is now earning; how wonderfully she performed at the Seilmanns', and so on. He also reported about their failure to find a good French teacher. Mishi agreed completely with Klára: these teachers today don't have the faintest idea how much caring and attention these children need!

It happens with them, too, that one of the children returns home crying. And he, of course, goes to see the teacher in question immediately—even if, in Betty's opinion, these school visits of his do more harm than good... Well, Hedgie won't cry in front of others, but this doesn't work well either, because the teachers resent her edgy ways, too.

The two men went to check on the children. Hedgie and Panni were sitting on the floor, playing cards, while Jutka was reading a book on her bed. Mishi disapproved of the scene and said:

"Children, why don't you play something all three of you could do?"

"Jutka thinks Go Fish is boring, but Hedgie is willing to play with me," Panni explained.

Although Mishi wasn't happy with Jutka's glance, not having any better idea, he left them. And he started to boast to Aldó about the pretty gifts the children had made for Betty's birthday. Later, he told of his invitation to be a high school literature teacher. He would be able to return to his original job, and also enjoy having more free time for his children. But... recently, even teachers have to undergo a political interview before getting hired and he...

"You stupid idiot!"

"You're the idiot!"

"She's MY sister!"

All three adults jumped up and ran toward the children's room.

There were more unintelligible abuses coming, while all three kids burst into tears. Klára ran out of the room:

"I want to go home!"

Aldó ran after her into the hallway. The door was locked but Hedgie didn't touch the bundle of keys hanging in the lock, just squatted on her heels in the corner. Aldó knelt down to her. Mishi's voice came from the room: "How can you treat your guest like this?" Jutka's sobbing reply: "Silly high school girl!" Betty interfered: "Come on, my baby, tell me!"

"I want to go home!"

"What happened, Hedgie, dearest?"

"I want to go home!"

Mishi—and Panni, sobbing with fear—approached them. Aldó waved them away. Hedgie was still sobbing, but as soon as she let Aldó set her on his lap, he felt easier: This must be the same crying as in December. The two were still quiet when Betty emerged. Aldó waved her away, too. Betty complied.

"My little baby... why don't you tell..." he whispered.

Klára soon found the words, although her sobbing made it difficult to understand:

"I also... have... a brother... just not here."

. . . .

April 11, 1949

Today I signed Olgi's letter to Gyuri. Although lately he doesn't write anything else about me, just "Greetings to my sister." Why is he the one who's mad, when he's the one who's left us? Well, anyway, I signed it. He can't have it easy, all alone there, either.

I also read his last letter. He's got some friends now, and that family he lives with. Although they often have tantrums, something of the sort we always hated! It might be just like it used to be at Aunt Manci's place, where Mama and we always fled from quickly. Next time, I might write him to leave the room when they start their scenes. He really wants to get his French visa at last. Will we ever see each other again?

. . . .

It was early June; the weather was beautiful; and school was ending soon. After their Saturday lunch, Aldó lay down, as usual, on Klára's bed to have a nap, while Klára was washing the dishes. This, too, was Aldó's idea "to let Olgi have an easier day sometimes." he explained, although his main point was to make Klára get used to household chores—an ambition seemingly missing from both her parents and Olgi. She was, by the way, quite good at sewing, having learned it from her grandmother—the reason why she knew these special expressions only in German.

Ironing and cleaning were also jobs she actually liked. Still, she tended to gloss a small surface to its best shine, rather than clean a room systematically. She gladly helped at Aldó's place, choosing her tasks herself and doing those thoroughly. Ironing shirts, for instance, turned into a job she wouldn't let be taken away from her anymore. Her only request for repayment was to be praised for every single well-ironed shirt.

"You will look beautiful in this!" she commented sometimes in the tone of a five-year old playing house. Then, she might condemn the next shirt heatedly for its old-fashioned style, and demand that it be discarded.

There was, however, no way to counter Olgi's determination. That's why dishwashing on Saturdays became the only chore Klára would do at home, and then only thanks to Aldó's presence. After Aldó would awake from the peaceful dreams of his nap, they'd only choose their afternoon activity according to the weather. They often took Olgi with them. Not today, because Olgi was suffering from knee pains. Klára would've liked to go to a movie, but Aldó insisted—in an unusual way—on his own plan to have a walk with her on Margaret Island. Klára thought he didn't have the money for movie tickets and gave up tactfully.

• • • •

On the island, she started to talk about the private English lessons of her school friend, Ági Feldmann. Ági had studied English for three years now, while Klára had studied it for only one. In the second year, when she might have continued with English, Jews were forbidden from attending that school anymore. Ági's idea was that Klára could join her in her private class—provided that she could make up for the missing instruction. This solution could even make the costs of the tutoring lower for both of them. Of course, Klára would check out Ági's teacher first to avoid bumping into a second Mrs. Venczel! If the teacher were all right, Klára could make up over the summer what she'd missed and start taking classes in the fall.

"That's a great plan!" Aldó said with enthusiasm.

"And... could you pay for the tutoring?"

"Yes, I could."

"I haven't asked how much..."

"This is very useful, anyway. We'll tighten our belt a bit, you know, the orphanage..."

"I know."

"Would you really study in the summer, all by yourself?"

"Aldó! Don't you believe me that I can learn whatever I want to?"

"I love your modesty!" he laughed. "Then go ahead!"

"Well... alright, it's hard with the pronunciation, I know. But I can listen to the BBC and..."

A huge sigh. Klára was pretty good by now at interpreting Aldó's different sighs but this one wasn't clear to her. She looked at him puzzled. Aldó waved by his hand to show that they should sit down on the next bench.

“Hedgie dear, I want to discuss something with you. That’s why I wanted to come here.”

“Why here?”

“It’s better if nobody can hear us... Now that you mentioned the BBC... Well... you were right when you said that I always get into a bad mood when reading the newspaper... You must know, too... the world has turned difficult, recently.”

“Where?”

“Here, in this country.”

“Again?”

“Let’s hope it’ll be different this time. But you yourself told me that your new headmistress asked about your parents’ professions.”

“Are Jews going to be persecuted again?”

“No, I don’t think so.”

Aldó embraces Klára’s shoulder. How can he keep her calm while bringing home to her the need for caution, as well?

“They’re searching for ‘enemies’ again. Till now, it looked like they were only attacking the wealthy class. But recently they started to hunt down their own people and...”

“Who are ‘they’?”

“The communists.”

“Harsányi, our gym teacher, is a communist, she said. She was made Director, just last week.”

A grimace, with tightly closed lips, appears on Aldó’s face.

“Hedgie, dear… from now on… you watch out. Don’t tell anybody your opinions, don’t tell stories about us, and don’t tease any adults, okay? Do you promise?”

Klára suddenly turns as old—very old—as she used to be five years ago.

“Because we’ll be displaced, then? …When the Arrow Cross gang came, we had to keep silent, too. We weren’t allowed to know about anything or anybody, either.”

Good God, how to ease her dread? Still, she has to be aware of the new situation.

“Listen, my little one! We are most likely not interesting to them. We only have to keep quiet to avoid becoming interesting! We’ll only be declared enemies if we behave toward them with hostility. Don’t say that Mrs. Harsányi or any other teachers are idiots, or that you were better off in your old school. Don’t speak about ‘good old things’ or ‘the good old days’. And altogether, keep your opinions to yourself—about anything. Don’t even make faces… Your English lessons shouldn’t be mentioned, either.”

Klára keeps silent. Aldó tries to cheer her up.

“Last year, you had no difficulty pretending to be stupid if you disliked a teacher! Do the same now when being asked about your opinion!”

Klára says not a word.

“Hedgie, my little girl... this may soon pass... But it’ll be better from now on if you pretend you’re part of the furniture.”

“I can keep quiet,” she says and her face looks as apathetic as it did a year ago.

“My sweet little one... tell me or Olgi whatever you want to say, but nobody else!”

Klára waits a while and then she asks:

“And to Ági Feldmann?”

“To her... you can say whatever... But first of all you should tell her to watch out for her mouth, too.”

“She won’t talk to anybody in school. Just to me. She is also Jewish.”

“I know.”

“How do you know?”

“It’s a Jewish name.”

“Is mine also Jewish?”

“Yes.”

“And yours?”

“Mine, too... But the problem is precisely that Harsányi, your new Director, is Jewish as well.”

Klára turns white as a sheet.

“Are the communists Jewish?”

“There are some among them.”

“But... we aren’t communists, aren’t we?”

"No."

"Isn't every communist a Jew?"

"No, I told you."

Aldó looks worried at her devastated face. He forces himself finally to simulate some light-heartedness and says:

"Just to make us completely confused about the rules of the game..."

Klára cuddles up to him and murmurs something. Aldó fails to notice when she actually starts to cry.

"What did you say, dear?"

"I want to go home."

"We all do."

. . . .

Sunday morning Olgi called: Klára doesn't feel well and would like Aldó to come over. No fever. But she'd asked Olgi to call.

Aldó was prepared for that. He was pondering for long hours in the night about how to ease Klára's dread; how he could spend some time with her today. He also decided to go and see Mrs. Somogyi, the former headmistress of the school on Monday and ask her for some points for Klára to go by.

"I'll be there soon. Does she have any pain?"

"Was there no other way than... to tell her...?" Olgi whispered.

"It had to be done, Olgi dear. I'll set off soon."

. . . .

Aldó sat by Klára's bedside. Olgi bustled around them. She was sure that all the troubles would be blown away by Aldó's arrival. Everything would be the same as it was in December. Her task would only be to cook delicious meals or bring a compress from time to time.

Aldó's impression was quite different. That disease before Hanukkah was just a pleasure drive, a kind of compensation for her previous journey in the inferno. But now they still had to face many things. He decided to throw Hedgie over this precipice, whatever it might cost. Where did his confidence come from— maybe from the simple fact that it was needed?

Aldó was sure that Klára wanted to be alone with him. He asked Olgi to cook bird-milk with floating islands once again. Although Klára wasn't fond of this idea—she complained about her stomach—Aldó insisted on it. When the two of them were left alone, he asked some more, insignificant questions about her well-being while both of them were aware these were not their topic for the day.

"Well... Hedgie... I'd like to tell you a few things about history..."

"No need to..."

"You do like to understand things, though."

"There is nothing to understand here. I don't want to go to school! I don't want to go any place!"

"Sure you do! This is not like '44! You don't need to do anything other than be cautious what you're talking about."

"I don't want to be cautious... I don't want anything! Last year, I would've been ready to die, too... I did not only because of Olgi... And now I'd have the courage again."

"You get out of bed, right now then, and go to the bathroom! We'll go somewhere."

"I won't go! ...Where?"

"Don't know yet. Someplace where we can have a nice time. We'll find out."

"...Would you... be sad, if I died?"

"...No. I would slap your face!"

Even in her distress, Klára couldn't help but laugh.

"Now you go to the bathroom!"

She didn't move. It felt good, very good, to have Aldó at her side. His agitation felt good too. A lot like Papa used to be. But he doesn't understand something. She has to put it a different way to make it clear to him.

"I don't want that once again," she started in a calm voice that soon turned into crying: "I couldn't bear having to be so afraid again. I don't WANT to bear it!"

Motionless, Aldó watched her for a while then he started to speak very quietly:

"Let me tell you then... that I talked to the Eternal for three years after the war only to blame Him furiously again and again for having left me alive. I talked to Him with terrible disrespect... But since I have you, I say thanks to Him every night and ask Him to forgive me. He knew His reasons for keeping me alive. Only if you are all alone, is life so hard. But if you have somebody to live for, everything becomes much easier."

Klára turned her palm into Aldó's hand, which had been resting on hers for several minutes:

"I love you, too, very much... You won't be taken away by the communists, will you?"

"They have no reason to. I'm a physician, I heal people and I'm not interested in politics."

"They can't take Olgi either, can they?"

"They're not interested in old grandmas!"

"And in children?"

"Not them, either. But you are not going to be a child for much longer. So, you'll take care of yourself, as well as of me, by being cautious... Well, my little one, get ready and we can start to discuss our operational plan!"

"What kind of operational plan?"

"I will tell you what I've devised. But eat your breakfast first."

. . . .

Ági Feldmann's English tutor, Mrs. Mestrovich, made a pretty schoolmarm-ish first impression on Klára. Still, her calmness and kindness quickly won Klára over. Her remark during their first meeting—showing concern that Klára's knowledge of French might cast a shadow on her English—sounded belittling to Klára at first, but she was wrong.

Later, Mrs. Mestrovich asked her about how to put this or that English sentence into French or German, and was clearly proud of having such an erudite student. That being the case, Klára was soon happy about seeing her weekly, even in the summer. Mrs. Mestrovich was also glad to meet Klára's need for more homework. At the end of July, she confidentially told Aldó that Klára would not only make up for Ági's head start by September, but—being a hundred times as talented as Ági—she should, by no means, be held back for long at Ági's leisurely pace of learning. Aldó was proud to be able to educate his girl, although he was afraid that Mrs. Mestrovich's prognosis might harm Klára's only friendship. He must watch out and discuss this issue with Klára.

Another big event of the summer was Aldó's birthday. It was back in the spring when Klára looked at an old certificate lying on Aldó's desk. She was just curious about the old picture of him ('How beautiful his face used to be!') but she also noticed his date of birth. It was unique: the seventh of the seventh month in nineteen-seven! Why did he say last fall that he was already forty-two, when he is just turning forty-two this summer?

In May, she filched his shabby, old cardigan that he had called his one-time favorite—for two days, and brought it home. Olgi copied the pattern and the size, and the two of them went from store to store, until they got the very same yarn. For weeks, Olgi was busy with manufacturing her piece of art during every free minute.

. . . .

Dearest Papa!

I organized everything in your leather folder as a special gift for Aldó, for his birthday. He can use your folder now, can't he? I bought black and colored pencils (those serious ones, made for grown-ups) plus paper and envelopes, and an eraser.

You don't mind, do you? I will always love you as much as I used to, but I also love Aldó very much. And he was very glad to see the cardigan Olgi made for him. And I also saved money for two handkerchiefs. He was happy and sad at the same time. But Olgi and I did our best so he didn't get really sad. I told him that our birthday parties used to be different but this is okay now also because this way nobody is left alone.

. . . .

What made Aldó even happier during the summer was home canning. Ever since his earliest boyhood, he was crazy about this ceremony. Even at the age of four or five, he couldn't be dragged out of the kitchen on canning days. He would sob bitterly for hours after coming home from school as a first-grader, and hearing the news that cherries had been canned in the morning. From that time on, his mother and her help, Mrs. Mayer, did their best to spare him from any more injustice of that sort. Ali was—even as a high school boy—willing to get up at five to accompany Mrs. Mayer to the farmer's market, just to be part of the event, at least as a deliverer. His declared reason was that Mrs. Mayer couldn't carry so much heavy stuff anymore. Fortunately, most fruits have the decency to grow ripe during the summer holidays. Keeping the story in mind, Ilona had also done her best to schedule this peaceful event on Ali's off-duty days whenever possible. She liked his childish ways.

On seeing the freshly filled jars of sour cherry jam on Olgi's kitchen table one Saturday, Aldó was instantly beset by the plaintive bitterness of his early childhood, followed soon by that bitterness beyond anyone's help anymore. He hadn't seen summer fruit canning for six years, and had given up all hope of seeing it again.

"Why didn't you tell me to help you with the fruit? I'd be glad to go to the market with you any time," he complained to Olgi.

And indeed, next time with the apricots, the apples, and the tomatoes, everything happened the way he wished. He could even use the old tomato-grinder! Tracking down plums at the best time of the season became his task exclusively. He walked through the market every morning, checked the prices, and consulted Olgi later on the phone to find out if she'd vote for buying now or if she preferred to keep waiting for the prices to go down further. Olgi knew by now that Aldó always must be included in this big event.

. . . .

Fall arrived with unpleasant, wet weather, and Olgi frequently had pain in her knees. Klára decided to do the shopping herself more and more. Whenever it wasn't Aldó's day, she'd be waiting for Olgi's shopping list. Carrying was less of a problem than climbing the stairs up to the fourth floor, Olgi said. The elevator had been out of order since the war. She even learned to trust Klára with buying meat, although she had regarded it as the most delicate task of a housewife. However, Uncle Braun never cheated Klára—on the contrary: he always gave her the best-looking chicken giblets, maybe to give her a chance to earn praise from her aunt. After buying meat, Klára crossed the street and went to the grocery, recently renamed 'Central Food Supply'.

While waiting for her turn at the counter, she kept looking at the bun of hair on the lady standing just in front of her in the line. She could be Olgi's age, she thought, but Olgi's hairstyle is never done so nicely. Grandma used to have this kind of hairdo and nice dresses.

A young man emerged from somewhere and did his best to persuade the lady with the nice bun to let him be served first. After a moment of hesitation, the lady gave in:

"If you're really only buying bread and butter, then go ahead!"

Klára's alarm went off instantly: These are no Hungarian R-sounds!

It's as if she were French! She peeked forward to see the face of the lady—but this wasn't too enlightening. The lady noticed her move and, after considering for an instant, she gave her a smile. Flustered, Klára pulled back to her place, although her excitement hadn't ceased. Hungarians don't smile, she thought, only at babies at most. It will be the lady's turn, soon! She can't let her walk out! Klára leaned over, quite close to the knot of hair, and asked:

"Vous êtes française?"[7]

No answer. She has to pretend, then, not to have said a word. But the lady bent down to her basket on the floor, coming closer to Klára this way, and whispered:

"N'en parlons pas ici."[8]

7. *Are you French?*

8. *We shouldn't talk here.*

Klára blinked happily and the lady returned her gesture. The young man with his bread and butter left. Now the lady handed over her ration card for white flour and asked for some other items as well. The two checked each other's face once more. What next? She has to do her shopping, while the lady would leave!

"Well... then I'll show you where the drugstore is," the lady said with her rolling R's and waited until Klára finished with her list.

They headed toward the exit, with Klára following the bun like a magnet.

"Haven't you been told at home not to talk with strangers?" the lady asked in French again.

Klára looked astonished: that prohibition can't possibly apply to a lady like this one! She has never been wrong on such issues! A second later, she suddenly could imagine being wrong. Aldó once gave a longish lecture about stool pigeons but at that point, Klára stopped listening to him. Her confidence in her own insight into human nature was wavering for the first time ever. Even her logical thinking was switched off at this moment, given that it wasn't the older lady, but she herself who made the first step!

"I only figured that you are not Hungarian..." she started her excuse, also in French. As if language could provide shelter against evil...

"It's all right... No problem... Just be careful with others. By the way, I am not French, but Austrian. My governess was French and I've always been laughed at, back at home, for not having learned the Austrian R-sound. And later, I married a Hungarian. And where does your French come from?"

Klára was close to crying when she realized that this awful caution—confirmed even by the lady—made it impossible to say things, even to people who seem like you. She was silent a while, but then she found something safe to say, since it was mutual:

"We also had a French governess..."

"One from the south of France, as your pronunciation reveals."

"Maybe," Klára replied while knowing exactly that Charlotte had been brought up in Bourg-en-Bresse, close to Lyon. Nowadays, she often studied this region on the map.

The lady sensed the cause of Klára's withdrawal.

"You know, my girl, this is not our world now. We have to watch out carefully what impression we make. Nobody and nothing is welcome from abroad. Actually, the same is true for people from here.

"I know."

"The most harmful thing about it is that in this way we teach you, the children, not to trust anybody."

"That's true."

"My grandchildren, at least, managed to leave for Austria. Life is no paradise there, either, but speaking out is allowed."

Klára wished she could talk about Gyuri's leaving, but she didn't.

"And why did Madame not join them?"

Now it was the lady's turn to be quiet. She stood there, still, with a gloomy expression.

"You don't need to talk about it!" Klára backed down.

The lady looked at her with a gentle smile. Yes, it was like Grandma's smile. She regained her confidence completely, and said with a mischievous smile, while anticipating the joy of surprising:

"Aber mit meinen Großeltern haben wir deutsch gesprochen."[9]

The lady stopped again, her lips opened for a new smile, and she spoke in Hungarian the first time since they were on the street:

"What an unusual child you are!"

. . . .

Aldó listened to Klára tell about her caution with both relief and resignation. Madame Gretl showed her the house where she lives, Klára explained, and left the choice with her, whether to visit her and have a German or French conversation from time to time. But Klára didn't show her their house—they lived just two blocks away—because she wanted to ask Aldó about this idea first. Aldó praised her for her caution and approved the plan.

"But you should meet her first, too. In my opinion, she's very nice. But I don't know my way around anymore... I don't know what a stool pigeon would look like!"

9. *But we spoke German with my grandparents.*

"Well... and how could I see her?"

"I could go and ask her if you might come with me once, too. Is that a good idea?"

"And who would you say I am?"

"Well... can I say... you are my new Papa?"

• • • •

Madame Gretl awaited them with cookies and coffee. As soon as he entered her apartment, Aldó felt absolutely confident about her trustworthiness. They began with small talk about the weather, the healthcare system, and the food supply situation—phrasing everything in cautiously neutral terms.

Klára's gaze rested, enchanted, on the porcelain coffee set. Yes. Theirs used to be the same; with different paintings, though. Even the coffee pot was the same, with its elegant swanlike neck. But it's not appropriate to talk about things like that today. She waited impatiently for Madame Gretl to pour coffee into her cup, so she could take it into her hands. She began secretly stroking its shell and ear. How fine, how thin it is... Gretl thought she was asking for a second serving—why else would she hold her empty cup?

The conversation soon touched on the most important topic:

"Well, Doctor, you really found a fantastic girl!" Gretl rejoiced.

"She is fantastic, indeed, but it's not I who found her; it's she who found me."

"The same here! She approached me in the store after identifying my first language through my pronunciation of Hungarian!"

"I know. She told me," Aldó smiled. "But that's her! She has a precise instinct for other people and for whom she wants nearby... Last spring, we were looking for somebody who could help keep her French alive, but she didn't like the person we found. Now, she has chosen. She doesn't err often!"

Klára absorbed the praises like a dry sponge. Mama and Papa used to be this enthusiastic about her. At such times, she had thought: that's simply how the world is made.

"Imagine, Aldó, Madame Gretl had worked as a translator for years! She might be willing to teach me translating, too."

"Of course, my dear! I'd be glad to pass on my experience to somebody worth it!"

"I was taught translating by my Mom... but then I was young. I just translated fairy tales and things like that. Now I'm translating serious stuff for Aldó... but still not well enough."

"I always understand what you've translated... And your translations keep getting better every time."

Madame Gretl told some happy stories of her childhood in Austria, her getting married later in Hungary and learning Hungarian; also about her happy, young married years and the trilingual upbringing of her children.

At this point, however, she turned the conversation back to Klára without saying a word about the last decade.

Aldó had the impression that Gretl wasn't Jewish; still, others also had many opportunities for staggering losses. He asked, somewhat embarrassed, whether he could pay an honorarium for Klára's language lessons. Madame Gretl responded with an almost outraged expression, and Aldó said thank you.

"It'll be a present for me to have a child like her around sometimes."

Klára asked Aldó if he would mind their switching over to French now. Aldó couldn't resist the opportunity to hear Klára speaking French—he himself hadn't had this chance since school. After swelling with pride, he got up to take his leave:

"I have to discuss something important with Olgi now... We'll see each other soon, over there," he said.

. . . .

Klára's new worry was how to arrange her many activities into a weekly schedule that wouldn't have Olgi sitting alone at home too much. She kept Tuesdays and Thursdays free, of course, because these were the days with Aldó. Wednesdays were for her English lessons, when she'd get home around four o'clock. Lately, after finishing her homework, she'd often play cards with Olgi, or they'd just listen to the radio. Theater broadcasts were their favorite.

On those days, Olgi began her preparations by mid-afternoon. As if it were a red-letter day. She baked some butter cookies that were cheap and could be squeezed into the weekly budget. She also roasted coffee beans to be prepared later, during the first intermission of the theater broadcast, although usually only guests or visiting doctors were served with such luxury.

Time with Madame Gretl was such a great pleasure that Klára would have preferred spending both Mondays and Fridays at her place, if she wouldn't have to feel guilty about Olgi. But Aldó and the elevator factory helped her through this dilemma. The elevator was finally repaired, giving Olgi back most of her former mobility, while Aldó suggested an idea that had worked so well with Betty Freud.

Grandmothers are also very much needed in the orphanages, he said, and it would be so helpful if she could go—once a week, at least—and teach the girls some needlework. Olgi needed some time to come to a decision, the same way Betty did, but soon she fully enjoyed the time spent there. Before long, she brought the girls all her remnant yarn and spare needles. Tuesday became her day in the orphanage, but she often set off on Thursday as well, if she felt too lonely at home.

• • • •

Klára not only enjoyed speaking French and German with Madame Gretl, but she also used the opportunity to write her German homework with her. Gretl understood Klára's problem with Mrs. Becher completely. She had also had some lowbrow teachers like Mrs. Becher. Klára hadn't known this expression but liked it now very much because Mrs. Becher had, indeed, a strikingly low brow.

Gretl would dictate her such compositions as homework that made Mrs. Becher suddenly regard Klára as a sheep returned to the fold. They laughed about this all the time. Also about constantly mixing up their weekly schedule. As Gretl intended to keep every form of the spoken language fresh in Klára's mind, they decided to use the 'familiar you' with each other on odd-numbered weeks and the 'formal you' on even-numbered weeks, in French on Mondays and German on Fridays. This was really not easy to keep straight!

Gretl taught her shorthand writing as well; first in German, because she had to look up the Hungarian version again, before being ready to convey it. In the first weeks of her new study, Klára only asked Olgi and Aldó to dictate individual words to her. A few months later, however, taking down and re-reading longish German texts—rewarded by the admiration of her people—became her favorite pastime.

• • • •

Klára's seventeenth birthday was fast approaching. Aldó could hardly believe this number. Even though Hedgie not only had been behaving more and more adult-like and had also gained five pounds during the summer: she now looked almost like a young lady.

"Aren't my breasts too big?" she asked with irritation.

Aldó was close to laughing when his new father-daughter reflexes stopped him:

"It's just fine the way it is," he said with a smile.

"But... I won't ever turn into a big wench, will I?"

"Pretty unlikely..."

• • • •

The birthday party was a great success. Klára invited three friends from her class: Ági Feldmann, Juli Szendrei, and Vera Hegedüs. They made a nice group. Aldó pondered Klára's choices. All three guests were still more childlike, although the majority of the class looked like young women already, as he could tell by seeing them on Saturdays as they left the school. Klára always referred to this majority as "the dames" and, not surprisingly, the "smaller ones"—like herself—as friends.

Everybody brought a present: a book, a fountain pen, or chocolate. Only Mama could explain how Klára managed so skillfully as host. Her delicious cakes and her kindness caused Olgi to feel proud when Klára introduced her as Grandma. Klára regarded Aldó's presence as something that goes without saying.

He came over, of course, but tried to keep out of the little circle and kept Olgi company in the kitchen instead. He had to give in soon, however, because the girls invited him to be their game host. Klára introduced her self-made copy of Margit Seilmann's quiz game. She had been busy manufacturing it for weeks.

Aldó also got the task of collecting more questions. He succeeded in persuading Klára to include some less difficult questions as well—otherwise the girls would find it too frustrating and leave the table disappointed. Klára promised Aldó that she wouldn't check the answers to his questions in her books before the game's premiere. And who won the most tokens for her correct answers? Of course, it was Klára. Little presents had been invented for right answers, in proportion to their point value.

While Klára went down to the door to see her guests out, Olgi and Aldó evaluated the day: they've got a wonderful child, haven't they? And Olgi added:

"But I also ask the Eternal daily to bless you, too. Because it's you who made this miracle happen."

. . . .

The next week, László Rajk[10] and his "accomplices" were executed. The verdict of the "people's tribunal" was broadcast in the school, too.

A lot of fighting, crying, and even physical fights—pretty unusual in girls' schools—disturbed the day. During one of the breaks, when the hysterical shouting of teachers and students had become indistinguishable, Mrs. Harsányi, the new Director, asked Mr. Bokor to address the students in the schoolyard.

Nobody had ever seen Mrs. Harsányi tremble, fumble and speak hoarsely before. Except for the young, new Russian teacher—who always seemed to be more frightened than anybody else on the staff—Mr. Bokor was the only man in the school. But this wasn't the only reason for the respect he enjoyed. His unshakable calm had often proved valuable.

The children gathered in the yard. The teachers stood randomly among their students. Nobody blew a whistle to line up, nor was there any other call to order, when Mr. Bokor climbed up on the huge wooden case containing the athletic equipment. Nevertheless, the whole yard fell silent. The four hundred girls and their female teachers awaited his words, as Olgi would await Aldó's turning up when something was wrong. Somebody should finally tell...

10. Communist interior minister in 1946-48, foreign minister 1948-49, main victim of the first infamous Stalinist show trial in Hungary. Executed in 1949, rehabilitated and posthumously reburied in 1956.

And indeed, his voice radiated an inexplicably calming influence, just as Aldó's voice always did. Nobody cared about his words; it was just so good to hear him!

"We all want to live in peace..." he started. "Our duty is to teach and to learn. If we fulfill our duties, and so do others, we can live in peace... We all love our families, our parents, our children, our wives and husbands... We have to make peace with them, first of all... That's our job... When you go home today, children, kiss your mother's hand for everything she does for you..."

He suddenly became embarrassed, because he knew the number: there were seventeen girls in the school who had lost their mothers. So he went on quickly by saying:

"Should, however, someone else take care of you instead of your mother, love her from your heart, too!"

He kept repeating thoughts like these and everybody was glad to hear them. They were ready to believe that those were the issues of importance right now.

"If you go back into your class now, dear children... and my dear colleagues... start a conversation about feasts, about love, about the family..."

Mr. Bokor climbed down strikingly awkwardly from the case. Mrs. Harsányi approached him and thanked him for his speech. The crowd started to disperse slowly. Bokor explained to the director defensively: involving children in politics while the general atmosphere is still so upset, may not be a good idea. Mrs. Harsányi nodded in assent. It might be her Jewish descent that veiled from her ears the fact that the speech she just heard could have been lifted from a section of the Catholic mass.

In the remaining two hours, there was peace—or rather, a mournful silence—in the school.

. . . .

Dear Diary!

Ági Feldmann told me in the break that her father already arranged for her aunt to take her, should he also be arrested. But Ági hates her aunt! Even her father never said a good word about her. Still, Ági just nods in agreement, but she knows for sure how to commit suicide. I tried to reassure her. I told her that I doubt her father could be carried off. If this happened, however, she could move in with us! I am sure Olgi would welcome her, too, and we have two beds in the children's room. Aldó also likes her. How can you figure out who will be carried off? Is it really true that Aldó won't be arrested? He's never been rich the way Ági's father used to be.

. . . .

A week later, Elvira asked Aldó out into the hallway. The telephone technicians 'visited', she said, while pretending to show him blocks of prescription forms. There was, though, nothing wrong with the phone.[11] Now she asked him over to the locker for spare medication. The chief accountant disappeared last week. In the printing house her husband works for, three old social democrats had already been taken away. Only her husband and one more guy are still left from the old guard of the management. Aldó kept nodding. Elvira didn't expect anything more from him. Hedgie would be careful of what she said, wouldn't she?

11. Bugs were installed into telephone sets by hand.

Yes. She is lucky not to have any children, she added, so she doesn't need to be worried about this, at least. Here's a new block of patient registers. Wonderful.

. . . .

The Freuds invited them again for the following Saturday. The depressed mood of the family was no surprise. The children were hard to get rid of: they went to their room for only a few minutes at a time. Finally, Betty succeeded in winning their attention for some activity, so the two men were at last left alone. Mishi was visibly working up the courage to speak while Aldó awaited the bad news.

"Aladár... I want to tell you something... I don't sleep well recently... like probably many others don't. But after falling asleep, I always wake up suddenly—like being shaken—as if being asked to give an account... and what I see then is your face or that of my father."

Silence.

"I... joined... them."

Aldó asked after a while:

"Have the telephone technicians come by recently?"

"No. Why?"

"I'm just asking. They sometimes come without being called."

Mishi apparently didn't understand what Aldó was talking about. Even though he felt uncomfortable about it for a second, his own topic was more demanding than his curiosity:

"I thought it over carefully. And they told me to. My father used to own factories! I have to prove that I'm on their side. My children mustn't be left orphans again! I have to keep my family together!"

Aldó was silent. But, at length, Mishi's begging look made him reply and say, at least:

"I can understand."

Mishi was not convinced yet.

"I won't participate in any witch hunt! I am a teacher! Not a policeman!... Also, they keep promising that there will be no harm done against us Jews anymore."

It occurred to Aldó now that at least two Jews had been executed as "accomplices" of Rajk. Isn't it just the same, whether your father is killed for being a Jew, or is killed and just happens to be a Jew?

"Aren't you worried about Hedgie?"

Aldó was revolted by this question. It seemed like blackmail at best, and at worst, a piece of propaganda. Actually, all Mishi wanted was self-justification. Still, by asking that awkward question he forced some truthfulness out of Aldó that he could've spared otherwise.

"Yes, I am worried, very much. But I don't know of any solution that comes with a full warranty. If I knew one, I might be bought, too, I'm afraid."

"You have it easier!" Mishi went on again. "Neither your past nor your job makes you suspicious. They have no reason to do any harm to the son of a rabbi!"

"Have you been able to detect any logic to their choices?"

That was a sentence Aldó wished he could take back... If Mishi's belief reassures him, let him be reassured as long as he can believe. Mishi shrank back, and even his voice turned quite thin:

"I won't ever abandon God... Tell me that I haven't committed a sin!"

Pity made Aldó suddenly slump as he answered:

"I abandoned Him, myself. Still, He's forgiven me. That's why He sent Hedgie to me. He'll certainly forgive you, too."

. . . .

On one of those beautiful snowy days, Olgi awaited Klára from school with the news that Aldó had called: He has to go to the dentist after his office hours, so Klára should take her keys along. Oh, yes, he had mentioned something about a toothache earlier, on the weekend.

Hedgie had keys to his apartment since last summer but she had never used them, because she didn't want to be alone there. Not even at home, at Olgi's place. Nevertheless, why not? Aldó will come later. Meanwhile she could finish her homework. Or iron his shirts. Entering his flat, she found a long letter and a piece of chocolate on the table. She was scared at first on seeing the letter, but only until she read it.

. . . .

Hedgie, dearest!

It might not be bad news that the dentist only has afternoon appointments and I won't be at home today when you come over—given that I have an old debt to you that I could pay off a bit this way.

I know you'd like me to talk about my family. I can't. But I got the idea that you could see our old photo albums—if this is all right with you. If this isn't too hard for you, if you want. You can find them on the lowest shelves of the left-hand section of my wardrobe. You can have a look at anything you'd like. There are no secrets; it's just me who is unable to look at them. I only beg you not to say or ask anything about it. One day, later, it might be different but I am not ready for it now, for sure. I'm not as strong as you are.

I will ring the doorbell before I come in. Please put the albums back in their place before opening the door. If there isn't a long line at the dentist's, I can be back by around four o'clock. But don't worry, please, even if I don't come until six—sometimes there's an incredible number of patients waiting for him. Also, you should eat when you're hungry, because I won't be allowed to eat with my fresh filling for hours anyway.

Take good care, little one! I'll hurry!

Aldó

. . . .

Klára ran to the wardrobe, opened its left-hand door and squatted down to the lower shelves. And began to cry. Why? She frequently looks at her own albums, always without crying, while talking to all of her people in the pictures. Should Olgi meanwhile enter her room accidentally, she would quickly close her album but she'd never feel depressed about it. Just the contrary, she feels as though she's invited into the real world for a short time again, from this "vale of tears." as it's often called, isn't it... But now, she is squatting and crying in front of the albums. Since whatever scares Aldó must be scary.

Nevertheless, a bit later, she decided to look at the albums. She found eight of them. She got more and more excited while making a pile of them on the big table. First she watched them cautiously and then she chose the one with the most beautiful cover. Her bad feeling was about to disappear, replaced by the excitement she feels whenever expecting a world of fairy tales to come forth.

"Ali, Ilona, and the Sunday circle, 1927." They're laughing, how handsome they are and so very young. Yes, Aldó must have been only twenty, a feminine hand, with nice, clean-cut lines.

"Cool Valley, 1929."[12] Backpacks, several young people in the background. The two of them embracing.

"The silver wedding anniversary!" "Ali and Mommy." "Daddy and the Reithoffer girls"—meaning three old ladies, Mommy among them, standing in a circle around the old, bearded man sticking out his chest in his armchair. Daddy wears black in every picture, and "beanies" which—according to Grandpa—should be called by their proper name, kippos, and not "beanies" as Papa used to call them.

Daddy is quite like Uncle Weiszkopf, Grandpa's friend who was a rabbi. That's a nice story! And what a beautiful son they have! Mommy's face is somewhat sad, but she's smiling faintly in every picture, while Daddy looks rather severe. Well, in some pictures he tries to smile too. But he doesn't overdo it.

12. Name of a neighborhood in the Buda hills, in Budapest.

“Falk Miksa Street. Ali studying on the balcony.” He is neither shaved, nor combed and looks wrapped up in his book. On the next picture, he looks up, somewhat shy and embarrassed, as if he’d just noticed he was being photographed.

“Ilona and the Moppet.” Oh, well, in her belly! Is she expecting a baby already? A beautiful girl... or woman.

“Hosting Mamele and Papele the first time.” Oh, that’s a funny, mischievous man! He must be Ilona’s father! The mother is also fleshy and has an easy smile. She and Ilona are cuddling up to each other. In another picture, Ilona is explaining something agitatedly to her father.

“Daddy congratulating his Monsieur Doctor.” They shake hands with each other, while Daddy—finally! — has a real smile. It’s a long, arcaded hallway with a huge crowd around, most of them wearing black gowns. Aldó is grinning. Aldó is earnest. Aldó is waving to somebody. Aldó is embracing Mommy with one arm and Ilona with the other. Ilona’s got quite a belly by now!

“Celebrating my Ali.” A formal supper, long tables, fancy dresses, twenty-some people.

“Ali chatting with Moppet,” his ear on Ilona’s belly, Ilona smiling at him, Ali concentrating.

On the next page: “Welcome, darling little Gábor!” followed by some Hebrew letters, unintelligible to Klára. Ilona, lying in bed, smiling, with the baby at her side. Ali, hugging her shoulder... and holding the baby... then the grandparents also holding Gábor.

Any pictures from the wedding? Klára began checking the other albums. Here they are! "Hassene! Finally!" well, her Hebrew knowledge is enough for that: "Wedding!" How beautiful Ilona looks! And Aldó, too! Good for them! ...So many old people... but here are some young ones, too... and children... Beanies all around, embroidered tablecloths or whatever they are made for... fancy decanters... and the dresses!

It'll be four o'clock soon, she has to hurry up. Which album contains more pictures of Gábor? Here! Gábor might be about three here, leaning over the crib of the new baby, István! Gábor's eyes are black like Aldó's. Also his lips have the same nice line as his father's. He is just like him! Ilona's eyes are light. Beautiful. Are they blue or green? But her hair is dark, as well. How nice she is... Interesting that "Moppet" had been on his way already, before Aldó graduated. Klára could remember Papa's story about his asking for Mama's hand: first he showed her parents around his newly furnished consulting room to reassure them that their daughter would be abundantly provided for.

Walking tours again... with Aldó holding one child on each of his arms... He plays football with his little boys... Ilona washing her son's scraped knee at a pump. Her dress is so nice: a wide, light skirt with flowers... she is still like a young girl... Aldó carrying Ilona on his back, both laughing... Birthday parties and other celebrations again with grandparents around... Aldó lying on the couch with his leg in a cast, smiling. Gábor standing proudly with a school bag on his back... The two boys and a huge dog... with István gently bending over the back of the dog...

Big family, in front of the synagogue... sadness... black clothes... who died? More and more captions are missing...

The bell! Klára shudders. Oh well, that must be Aldó! Still, she claps the album shut as if she had been caught doing something forbidden and shouts out with a trembling voice: "Just a sec!" She collects the albums hastily and puts them back into the wardrobe.

In the first hour, they watch each other's face from time to time, quickly turning their eyes away again—as if it were just a regular day with tooth treatment, homework, shorthand writing, fried bread for dinner, Olgi's aching knees, and books to be lent to Jutka Freud.

. . . .

The next week, the two of them went shopping. They were looking for a nice winter outfit for Klára. Aldó enjoyed watching her try on the new clothing. After leaving the store, he suddenly said:

"My dear Mother would be so happy with you..."

Klára waited uncertainly and considered whether a response would be appropriate or not. She decided only to look at him.

"She always wanted to have a daughter."

Klára took Aldó's arm.

"But after my birth, she couldn't have any more children."

They walked along on the street, Klára carrying the package with her new, knitted dress. And then they were waiting for the streetcar.

"My dear Father got angry whenever he heard her talking about this. He was, of course, convinced that nothing could be better than a son. Mommy, poor thing, kept apologizing: of course, she is happy with me... she would be even happy with ten sons—it's just one single daughter she wished the Eternal had given her.

The streetcar came and Klára asked her first question after the second stop.

"Your father might have thought that your Mom was blaming him for not having any more children. Don't you think so?"

Aldó looked astonished: how does this child know to draw such connections? It took him several years of gynecological practice to understand how much hostility infertility might generate between couples.

"Do you?" he asked with that smile his face always showed when running into a piece of Hedgie's wisdom. But on this occasion, the real wisdom lay less in her train of thought than in her sensitivity in leading him back into the past so painlessly. For instance, she refrained from asking how it had felt for his mother not to have a granddaughter, either.

Mommy passed away in the very month when the Second Jewish Law[13] came out, and Ilona had been pregnant for some weeks again. They didn't dare bring a third child into life. They mourned Mommy and their unborn daughter at the same time.

"It's possible, isn't it?"

13. The Second Jewish Law—out of three—defined Jewry based on genetics, not on religious faith. Anyone having two Jewish grandparents was regarded as a Jew. Rights to study, work or own properties were even more restrictive than those introduced in the 1920 Numerus Clausus.

"Yes, it happens sometimes. But I don't know the truth. Because my parents wouldn't have talked about things like that."

"I read about this in that article in the *Gynäkologische Rundschau* Madame Gretl and I polished it up together, remember?"

• • • •

One early evening, Mishi Freud rang the bell—Mishi who usually asked for permission before even making a phone call. That's why, in the early days, Aldó had suggested dropping such formalities as soon as Betty's contractions came on.

After entering Aldó's room, Mishi instantly went to the phone, his hands following the wire down to the floor, and unplugged the receiver. They gave each other a silent nod of agreement. And suddenly, he changed to a breezy behavior he'd never ever shown before.

"I just thought I'd drop in for a bit!"

"A great idea..."

"I'm bringing back Hedgie's books that Jutka's finished reading. These children will need different kinds of books in the future..."

His inappropriate, overdone laughter scared Aldó a lot. This demeanor of Mishi's was completely unknown to him.

"What's wrong?" Aldó asked.

Mishi sat down on the couch and started drumming his hand nervously on his leg. Both his face and his body looked thinner than usual. There were new shadows under his black eyes. Grimaces came and went across his face.

"The kids?" Aldó asked.

"They are fine, thank God... my only trouble about them is that I don't know what to train them for... Do you want to be an informer, my girl, or a prison camp inmate? You can choose! Both are fine vocations!"

The wrinkles all drew together on Aldó's face. Mishi's state was as alarming as it had been after the war. The poor thing has never been strong, but his students adored him—the same way he adored beauty: Byron, Schiller, Rimbaud... Mishi has always been Betty's oldest child, and they rarely had a problem with this casting. When their children were born, Betty spent the time between contractions sending reassuring news to Mishi in the corridor: there won't be any problem, just keep calm. And indeed, at that time, there was no problem—yet.

"I only came for a minute," Mishi went on.

"Did something happen, Mishi?"

"Not yet, but I am afraid it will. Aladár... God's truth, but I really don't want to go through this anymore... and then the children..."

"What don't you want to go through?"

"At least we had thirty humane years... They won't have a single one! Nowadays, I keep thinking that our little ones might have left with their aunt at just the best possible moment... while the entire curse is falling upon our two girls' heads now... and upon all the other kids still around."

Aldó could say nothing in reply. Mishi went on:

"We're marching in the same direction we did from '38 on! Just at a higher speed... Everybody will have to report on everybody. What else could the purpose be of collecting data about everybody except to corner us? To get a chance to squeeze anybody's balls, anytime?"

"You have no reason to be afraid, Mishi."

"Do you, you think?"

"...No."

"Because they're informed about you, too. The same way as they are about me."

Aldó managed to set his astonishment aside with impressive speed:

"So what? Let them go hang! The entire leadership is paranoid. That's why they want all that information. They can't possibly intern the whole population!"

"Aladár, let me say what I have to say, and then I'll be out of here instantly. I'm neither a friend nor a Mensch anymore... I have to report on five people each week. But you'll never be among them. They know that we know each other. My job would be to find out more about "your unclear relationship to that minor girl." No, never! They're sick! Can you see? Humankind turned sick! But it's me who will go mad over it!"

During the night, while tossing and turning in his bed, Aldó felt sure that Mishi was right. Mankind is sick. And Mishi will go mad. But what will happen to Aldó? And to the kids... still around?

• • • •

Aldó cooked dinner in the kitchen while Klára ironed his shirts and shouted over to him from time to time whenever something new occurred to her. For instance, today Mrs. Wiesmann discovered that Klára took her notes in shorthand. She dictated quite rapidly and applauded her for reading back precisely what she had dictated. The class admired Klára's accomplishment, as well! Aldó also transmitted signs of admiration from the kitchen.

After finishing the shirts, Klára stepped to the wardrobe, opened the left-hand door cautiously, and peeped in. Her letter was still lying there, apparently untouched since she'd put it there, a week ago. Well, he hasn't noticed it.

She decided now to leave the door open an inch, making it easier for Aldó to notice. But... what if even this much would hurt him? She shut the wardrobe. Then she opened it again and took the letter. Slowly, she approached the desk, opened Papa's briefcase—that belonged to Aldó now—and put her letter in it. After a second, she opened it again and placed the paper into the side pocket—a less eye-catching part—of the folder. Now only the greeting was peeping out. She wasn't fully satisfied yet, so she pulled a folded newspaper and a small book onto the folder. Well, it should be neither too eye-catching nor invisible! When she turned, she noticed Aldó unexpectedly standing in the doorway.

"What are you doing, Hedgie-girl?"

First she was embarrassed, but soon she realized that this could be just the right opportunity to talk about it. Such a letter can't possibly violate Aldó's request! She was just about to speak when Aldó jumped the gun:

"Come on, dinner's ready!"

“Aldó dear... I’ve written a letter for you.”

“Is that what you put there just now?”

“Yeah... Don’t worry... it won’t hurt... the last thing I want is for you to get hurt. But... if it makes you unhappy, just let me know and I won’t write any more letters like this.”

Aldó went to his desk and began following the clues.

“...in the folder...” Klára lent a helping hand.

Aldó was just taking the briefcase when Klára added:

“Or... read it instead when I’m not here. I did it that way last time, too. But you haven’t noticed.”

“I’d rather read it now. Do you mind? You want me not to answer?”

“Not that... just so it won’t hurt you... This is an answer to your letter. Kind of.”

Aldó opened the folder and saw right away where it poked out. He sat down on the couch and so did Klára—the way they always do when they feel orphaned. The chlorines. The letter looked reassuringly short even at first sight.

. . . .

My dear Aldó!

I am not stronger than you. My trick is to think only about things that were beautiful and to tell myself about those. Try it! It works!

I love you very much.

Hedgie

. . . .

As they gently embraced each other, they happened to hold each other's back—symmetrically. Aldó needed several seconds to correct the mistake and to take Hedgie with her arms folded—as usual—against his chest, because Hedgie is a child.

. . . .

At their next encounter, Klára told the story of Papa's proposing to Mama. She talked about his new consulting room and also about how Papa kept boasting to everybody that during the dozen years of his marriage, he'd never ever touched Mama's dowry. Aldó didn't respond but his face was cheerful. It was, incidentally, the first time ever that Klára had talked about her father with any criticism—mixed, however, with forgiving love.

"It's not quite the same sequence we had..." Aldó replied.

Klára grinned back: of course, she knows that! And she waited a bit. Aldó thought a while before coming out with a surprising offer:

"If you want... I can write it down for you. I'll give it a try."

Ten days later, after a Saturday lunch, before going to take a nap, Aldó put a thick envelope on Klára's desk:

"Read it after I've left."

Klára could hardly wait for Aldó to leave and that was unusual, of course. While saying goodbye, she asked:

"And... can I ask questions about it?"

"Well... alright... I don't know... Sleep well, my baby!"

"Are you coming only for lunch, tomorrow?"

"Yes, because I want to continue with my article... But in the afternoon, we'll take Olgi to the movie, as well."

Klára cuddled up on her couch with Aldó's envelope. So many pages! Olgi should just go to bed, she will join her later; she has something more important to do now!

. . . .

Hedgie dear!

I'm done, at last, with my undertaking. This is the final version, after many others. I followed your advice completely: I only wrote about things that were pleasing to remember without explaining anything of the background.

You might find it peculiar that I wrote in the third person about myself. When I first "heard" the story told that way, I thought it's just an escape—as if it wouldn't be my story. It's also true that nothing I'm telling you here was my own experience, but I was told about them either by my dearest Ilona or my father-in-law. Both of them had a great gift for storytelling. Listening to them was just like sitting at a movie and watching the funniest film. Although I'm lacking in this gift, I'll try to reproduce their stories, more or less, for your sake.

I compiled all the connecting sections from their little remarks on this topic over the years. May my dear father forgive me! As you can see, sometimes I was almost gripped by the writer's fantasy. But, actually, every single element mentioned here had once come from their lips. I might enjoy writing this way because it gives me the chance to talk a bit like they used to and to feel their love again.

I'm making up some notes for you, which might help you to find your way more easily.

The Kerns – Ilona's family

Papele, Mamele – her parents' nicknames

Ali – the nickname they gave me

Internship year – the last study year for medical students, to be spent full-time in hospitals

Cottage – Summer-place of the Kerns in Cool Valley, Buda

Aunt and Uncle Wagner – couple from Cool Valley taking care of the garden and the cottage (I spent two months at their place after returning from the concentration camp. God bless them for it!)

Rabbi Körner – my dear father

Audience – questioning, admittance, meant with irony here (My father-in-law used to use that word.)

Aldó

Lastly, I wrote you about another short event I'd experienced myself. It feels good to remember it, as well. You'll find this on the last page.

. . . .

New page:

As usual, Mr. Kern was sitting behind his desk, and also as usual, he was preoccupied, rummaging through a manuscript. He pretended not to notice that Ilona wanted something. He'd heard more than enough for today about her pink-rose dreams and her Ali, he thought. Ilona sat down in an armchair at the end of the desk and kept her eyes on her father in a threatening manner until he finally looked up.

"Papele! If you don't approve our wedding, we are going to make a baby tomorrow!"

Mr. Kern was somewhat astonished by his "little" daughter's loose tongue but, actually, he didn't mind it too much. He mused for a second and then asked:

"Didn't you make one yesterday?"

"No..." Ilona grinned.

"Alright. In that case, I still can swat you now. I would have felt sorry for my grandchild..."

"Papele... we'd like it so much... He finished this year and did really well again, you can see... All he has left is his internship year!"

"That's just it! He still has that year to go. By the way, I haven't heard him proposing to you."

"He wouldn't dare! For that very reason!"

"He's perfectly right! A man should marry only after becoming able to provide for his family."

"But we don't need so much money yet... We could coast along in the cottage!"

"...Meaning that every silly detail has already been figured out... with Ali commuting daily from Cool Valley to town, leaving you alone for the whole day? Terrific idea!"

"Surely the Wagners wouldn't mind staying with us even after the summer. Papele... please..."

Mr. Kern's silence was quite promising.

"Didn't you and Mamele want it so badly, once?"

"Of course we did. But neither of us had a father with such a mellow heart...

Ilona summoned up all her girlish charm, embraced her father's neck, and asked:

"But I do, don't I?"

. . . .

The next day, Mr. Kern called Rabbi Körner and asked him for an audience. They'd never met "officially" before, just exchanged a few words in the synagogue, after Rabbi Körner had finished the Friday night service. The Kerns had visited that synagogue only because Ilona wanted them to see Ali's family. The Kerns hadn't been very taken with the rabbi. In person, he even exceeded his reputation of being the most austere rabbi in Eastern Europe.

They were, however, happy not to find the slightest trace of this in his son—and not only because he was so shy and warm. Mr. Kern had always been ready to incite him to more bravado and was glad to lure him over for a family dinner. Some of his remarks revealed how painful he found it that his sons no longer thought of chatting with him as a special, rare treat, an enjoyable pastime—and now even his daughters were beginning to feel that way, too.

Rabbi Körner could find some time to meet with Mr. Kern in four days... Please don't resent it. Well, he did resent it, but he appeared in the rabbi's office on time. If the issue were not that of his "youngest, dearest offspring" and Ali, he'd find it completely absurd to go and "ask for the boy's hand!" In addition, the rabbi affected not to know anything about the strong bond in the making between their families..

However, Mr. Kern had quite a respectable social rank and an impressive fortune, too. His publishing house connected him with the intellectual elite of Budapest on a daily basis, while his bookstores provided a considerable income for his family. He was, of course, too liberal-minded for the rabbi's taste. All in all, the rabbi seemed to have less of a problem with the family than with the fact that he couldn't help noticing there was something in the lives of others—called intimacy—that he had never allowed himself and his loved ones to experience.

"These children... would very much like to be united."

"Should the Eternal Father have the same intention with them, then the time shall come."

Mr. Körner had no idea at the moment how to best a rabbi in topics like the Eternal. He felt suddenly as helpless and furious as he used to when he as a child, being lectured by his father. And, indeed, he began his reply in that frame of mind, but soon found a more suitable continuation, capable of smoothing the edges a bit:

"Alright, but how shall we parents figure out the intention of the Eternal... if not by seeing them loving each other as strongly and enduringly as they do?"

The rabbi's wisdom seemed somewhat meager in matters of love. Mr. Kern grasped the opportunity provided by the ensuing silence:

"Should the Eternal Father commit the timing of the wedding to our trust, I—for my part—would readily approve it."

"My son is not an adult yet. He has neither a diploma nor an income."

"He will have both within a year. I'm willing to shoulder their expenses until then."

"My family could never accept an offer like this."

Sitting, mute, Mr. Kern's expression grew harder and harder, although his features were not made for that. He was much more prone to outbursts than stony-faced silence. Now it was the rabbi's turn to smooth things out a bit:

"Don't misunderstand me, Mr. Kern! It's not a financial question to me, either. It's about principles. A man should first prove himself."

"He's already proven himself... to me, at least."

"How?"

"By the way he is made. He can certainly enjoy that much acknowledgement from me after four years' acquaintance! However, should he have given you the impression of being a swindler in the previous twenty years, then either I'm mistaken in a terribly stupid way, or he's changed drastically."

The rabbi didn't answer. He might just have been ill at ease or about to mellow. Mr. Kern completed his lesson with one more thought:

"I enter into several dozens of contracts a year, you know... Most of them are built on mere confidence: I trust the talent of the author and believe that he'll keep to our agreement. I gladly pay advance money. I've never been cheated. Should I, however, set as a precondition of the contract that the authors show me their Nobel Prize first, I would never have become the house publisher of those with a great name today."

. . . .

Last page:

On our first wedding anniversary, our first son was born. We had kept the pregnancy secret for months, being afraid, with good reason, that our parents would add this to the list of our irresponsible actions. I had no income in that year yet, and it was quite uncomfortable to imagine that even my child would be provided for by my in-laws. Of course, they were overjoyed to hear the news.

By the first of August, however, I got a job in the maternity ward of the St. Stephan Hospital. This had been only a vague hope for me during that year, with no guarantee of anything. But the chief doctor apparently liked me and when he learned that our baby was due in the last week of August, he disbursed my first payment by the twentieth of the month.

My father-in-law, of course, also visited us in the hospital. I can remember running after him down the corridor to give him my first installment on the previous year's expenses, from my hand directly to his. He instantly upbraided me in his well-known, arch tone: "I'll tell you right away what you should amortize! Spend it on your son! And on your wife!" "I'll spend the rest on them, anyway," I replied. "You will spend the whole sum on them, young man! You got it?"

I never knew a man with a bigger heart than his.

. . . .

On Tuesday, Klára put an even shorter letter than last time into Aldó's briefcase:

My dear Aldó!

Thank you for the storytelling! Please keep telling me, if you can, about Uncle Kern because he is so sweet! What was the name of his publishing house?

I love you,

Hedgie

. . . .

Aldó's reply was already waiting for her in the folder on Thursday. Stories about Albatross Publishers and the tricky ways Uncle Kern had filtered out business partners who'd been about to cheat him. (But the cheats were never the authors!).

The correspondence quickly picked up speed. Hedgie, too, used this channel to tell the stories of her earlier life, although she could have told them without paper. For instance, about how she got her name—after her great-grandmother who'd died just before Klára's birth. Or about her climbing into her newborn brother's crib and telling her parents that she'd rather keep playing the role of the baby herself. She was only twenty months old but spoke fluently.

As Papa often said, she would make up for her missing pounds by learning a new language every other year. Indeed, she spoke three languages by the age of six, without putting on more than ten pounds during each of the two years. Mama disagreed with Papa's chart, stating that Klára weighed twenty-seven pounds at her second birthday. That's true, Papa kept arguing, but in the first nine months she had enjoyed special catering, contributing significantly to her later statistics. Aldó smiled delightedly when he heard the story about the crib and asked:

"So you already had the same habits by that time?"

"What?" Klára asked with the same smile although she didn't yet know what was so amusing.

"You climbed into the beds of men who'd just dropped in, even back then! And here I thought I was the first."

Aldó never wrote about his children, but always found something nice to tell—most of the time about the Kerns. There he enjoyed not only the twenty-plus family members gathered on festive days, but also the noisy gaiety, the laughter, and the outspoken attitude. All these were remedies for the shortages of Aldó's childhood.

The leather briefcase worked as their mailbox, being checked regularly by both of them and making them happy with every new consignment. Hedgie's advice worked quite well for Aldó. Many good memories popped up suddenly as he wrote his letters to Klára. Not every piece was meant for Hedgie, of course. It just felt good to remember.

Besides, many of them were not Aldó's own experiences but tales told by Luca (the nickname Aldó had used for Ilona when they were alone together). Those always had a happy end—that one she told once about Aunt Wagner, for instance.

Their married life wasn't the Wagners' first encounter with the couple—Luca and he had been using the cottage for their secret dates for years. Depending on Ali's study timetable, they chose different days for their "excursions." After their first few times in the cottage, Mrs. Wagner—visibly worried—looked for an opportunity to talk to Ilona in private:

"Missy dear... excuse me for the question... Are you sure the little Doctor is aware of what he is doing..."

"Yes, he is, Aunt Wagner... Besides... he's not doing anything."

"Yes, of course. I just meant, beyond that."

"Aunt Wagner, you won't give us away, will you?"

"We won't, Missy... of course not. You just watch out that even nature won't give you away. You can entrust us with anything else. But I beg you to keep in mind that... if you fail to be cautious... your dear father will just lead you to the rabbi for an early wedding but my husband and I will be kicked out, for sure... And in that case, even our priest can't do anything for us."

. . . .

Aldó's memories didn't always obey Hedgie's instructions. The previous story, for instance, brought back to mind the period when the Wagners had given him shelter: It was in June of '45, just after his return from the concentration camp.

• • • •

Before going to Cool Valley, using the last ounce of his strength, he had hunted down every place in town with even the slightest hope of offering any news about his family. Strangers opened the door to the cottage. He didn't say a word, but just kept going to the Wagners' nearby house. He could only remember Mrs. Wagner embracing him—although he must've been so smelly and filthy—and calling her husband from the house, crying:

"Józsi! The Doctor is back! The Doctor is here! ...The others should return soon, too..."

He was absolutely sure that nobody would ever return (although, he allowed himself one more year to maintain his delusions); that's why he stepped out of the scene at this point. He woke up in a bed, hearing Mrs. Wagner begging him: "Drink! Just a little bit..."

The summer was awfully hot. He was lying on a couch put out on the veranda. All he could remember from the first weeks was Mrs. Wagner coming out from time to time, bringing a full plate or mug, feeding him by the spoonful and talking to him. Early each evening, Mr. Wagner always came to take him to the kitchen where the bathtub stood, and helped him take a bath. Sometimes even in the daytime, because his trembling muscles were relaxed best by lukewarm water. On the hottest days, Mr. Wagner put a wooden tub in the sun and filled it with water. Its temperature felt so pleasant by noon that sitting there felt like finally getting a break after non-stop running. Off and on, Mr. Wagner shaved him, too. Although that was really completely pointless, he let it happen, too.

By the time the plums on the tree bending over the porch were about to darken, he was already feeling well enough to invent clever ideas for suicide. He noticed by now how Mr. Wagner would leave the house in the morning and return for lunch. The couple whispered in the kitchen, close enough for Aldó to overhear: "They haven't been seen there, either." "No list... there isn't any anywhere." "I don't have any more ideas!" Or: "I can't swim after them in the Danube, can I?" And Mrs. Wagner replying: "If I'd stay by his bedside, he would eat it by himself." Or: "He said a few words today."

All this must have happened after Kormos popped up, lying on the porch and trying to catch Aladár's eyes, which kept following the pattern of the blocks up and down, from left to right and back, endlessly. The same scan suddenly revealed Kormos' black eyes and soon his whole curly, black shape. When he made a weak attempt to obtain evidence of having seen a real dog, Kormos stood up, approached him and started to lick the hand hanging down from the couch. Later, he always fell asleep best when holding Kormos' paw. He wasn't aware what a huge sacrifice the Wagners had made: They would never have let their neighbor's dog, so filthy and full of fleas, come into their garden before. They might have thought now that this wasn't much worse than letting in Aladár with his scabies.

It was Kormos with whom he first exchanged thoughts. Most of the time, of course, this was just a mute conversation. Still, it helped him a great deal, because the strange voices recently housed inside him would shut up for the short time he was speaking with Kormos. He had no doubt that Kormos had come from the Beyond and was, like Aldó, just temporarily residing in his present skin. That felt reassuring, like a connecting link. They spent much time considering philosophical questions and agreeing that they could find no answer. It was, again, Kormos who succeeded in taking him for a walk in the garden.

One afternoon when the plums were already about to fall, Mr. Wagner returned home with an old Jew. The man sat down, asked no questions at all, and just started to breathe the prayer Shema Yisroël. He kept watching Aladár's face but soon finished with the silence, and stood up to recite the Shemoneh Esrei. After the nineteen blessings he fell silent again, waited some more, and went on with some psalms. Aladár hadn't opened his mouth. It felt like listening to a goodnight story as a little child. He also closed his eyes, but soon had the feeling as if Daddy wanted to shake him and say: "Behave as is proper for a Jewish man!" Well, he couldn't anymore... but Mommy's goodnight story felt so good.

It was almost dark by the time the old man stood up. "Thank you," Aladár said as a kind of farewell. Mr. Rosenberg asked him if he wanted him to bring tefillin for him next time. Aladár remained silent, but thought his face was clearly showing "No." The old man said just: "I'll bring it along and you'll decide whenever..." Well, Daddy could never say a sentence like that, Aladár mused gratefully, and eventually he decided he owed the old man one more "Thank you."

Mr. Rosenberg kept coming every second day. Nobody would've believed that within a week Aladár could converse almost fluently with the old man, and that, after only one more week, he'd leave with him for town. To be more precise, he just accompanied Mr. Rosenberg, who had started to make arrangements for Aladár's future life. Although Aladár saved the tefillin, he never ever put them on.

Two years passed before Mr. Wagner told Aladár the story about Mr. Rosenberg: at the point when the Wagners had felt that—despite every effort they'd been capable of making—results were still poor. It occurred to them that, in the case of a fellow Christian, they would call the priest. The next day, Mr. Wagner went to the office of the Jewish community office and came forward with his request to the doorman(!). The doorman was distrustful and unpleasant. He asked Mr. Wagner whether he had come merely to get rid of his harbored acquaintance. And why doesn't he take him to a hospital if he is sick... As if there would've been any hospitals functioning in a normal way...

When Mr. Wagner tried to explain that the doctor's father was a rabbi named Körner, but that he didn't know his Christian name, he was lectured by the doorman that no Jew has a Christian name! At this point, Mr. Wagner lost his patience and began to yell at the doorman: He could well understand that Jews now hate Christians without exception, but how could the guy withhold help from a fellow Jew, when Mr. Wagner is only asking for someone to come and pray for his sick one? The doorman deflated instantly, went to the phone, and said a few words to somebody. In a few minutes, Mr. Rosenberg came shuffling down the stairs. He listened to Mr. Wagner repeat his story. He had known Rabbi Körner. Mr. Wagner should wait a minute, he said, and disappeared up the stairs again. After returning, he just said:

"We can go. I only had to bring the prayer book along. May our God bless you for your mitzvah."

Drinking wine in the late-summer garden made Mr. Wagner rather talkative. It was in the year '47 and the first time they'd ever talked about that summer of '45. He mentioned, for instance, that even though Mr. Rosenberg's request for a blessing felt good—especially following his altercation with the doorman—still, considering the poor state and tattooed arm of the doctor, he would have preferred the blessing of another god.

(By the way, Aldó had had the numbers burned off his arm recently, at Hedgie's request. Hardly anything remained of them now. Of course, he still can see them.)

Mrs. Wagner mentioned on that very summer day in the garden, "Nights used to be pretty difficult at the beginning." Aldó had a vague image of somebody else having been there and soothing his nightmares a bit. He asked about it. Yes, the old midwife from the next street... since they couldn't have paid for a doctor's visit—and, anyway, the local doctor not being a best friend of Jews—and Mrs. Wagner wanting to get an ointment for Aldó's wounds.

The midwife came over, indeed, and thought it appropriate to come again every day, for weeks, at the late hour when Aladár's hell was about to break loose. She'd massage and stroke her first-ever male patient, mainly his spine, the back of his neck and his limbs, for well over an hour. And she kept talking to him, explaining what she was going to do next. She always left around midnight, and the Wagners then had a chance for a quiet night. From time to time, she also brought a little bottle of milk for her patient, something that counted as the biggest treasure at that time.

Mrs. Wagner asked her once where the milk came from. First, the midwife hesitated to answer, but then she said: "From a mother." Aldó didn't remember that either.

After learning all this, Aldó wanted to see the midwife. Mrs. Wagner brought him to the house. He would've felt easier if he just could have watched her from a distance. But he couldn't. The only thing he knew about her was that she used to be a nun when she was young. They entered the house. The midwife had a stern face and pretended not to know the reason for Aldó's visit.

Oh, yes, she said, some ointment was needed and I brought it a few times... She politely offered her guests a seat, but kept almost completely silent. Neither Aldó nor Mrs. Wagner felt at ease when choosing topics for conversation. Most of the time, she kept her eyes fixed on the floor, sometimes glancing quickly at Aldó's face. It was impossible to find out what she might be thinking. On their way out, she passed her hand over Aldó's back. Aldó thought he recognized the hand.

• • • •

Now, he visits the Wagners every month. Mr. Wagner died last year—although Aldó kept bringing him medication after medication, to no effect. Since then, after Kormos died, Mrs. Wagner could no longer tell in advance when Aldó would pop in. Kormos used to tell them. He sat down in front of their door in the early morning whenever Aldó was expected. He was always let in immediately, and Mrs. Wagner not only prepared an extra slice of meat for lunch, but also gave Kormos some delicious reward. After lunch, Aldó always took the dog for a walk. When Kormos became visibly sick, Aldó wanted to give money to his master for the vet, but the man was convinced that those who apparently wish to die should be left alone and allowed to die. That was a viewpoint Aldó and Kormos shared, too. They had discussed it extensively for a long time.

Mrs. Wagner longs for Aldó's visits even more since she was left alone. He has never mentioned Hedgie to her—maybe because Mrs. Wagner was the only important witness to his unchanged, prior devotion. She had known Ilona so well, and they will certainly meet again soon. But... no, he will take Hedgie along to her next time! Ilona knows about everything, anyway. Why should he excite unnecessary pity in Mrs. Wagner, who would so much like him to have a family again...

• • • •

January 3, 1950

Aldó and I visited Aunt Wagner in Cool Valley. She is so sweet! It's interesting that she worries about Aldó the same way Olgi does about me. She asked if he eats well, if he has finally bought a scarf, and also if we could come again in two weeks (me, too!) because she'll start butchering her ducks then and we can take one. She said "Grandma will certainly prepare it for you." It turned out that by "Grandma" she meant Olgi, because Aldó had talked to her about us. Last year, it was still Aunt Wagner preparing the duck for Aldó, for him to take home. Yes, I can remember eating it, but I didn't know where it came from.

Aunt Wagner asked if we could join her next time to visit the cemetery, to see Uncle Wagner's grave, because Aldó did that before, too. I saw Aldó whispering something into her ear and knew instantly that he doesn't want me to go. But I told them right away that I am not afraid of the dead. Mama, Papa and my other loved ones don't have a grave here anyway. The same with Ilona and the boys... I could at least bring some flowers to Uncle Wagner's grave.

Chapter 3

Fox Hunt
(January-March 1950)

Now Hedgie was starting to be invited to parties with boys attending, too. Even though her friendship with girls hadn't existed for more than a year; she was now a regular guest at their birthday parties. Even Aldó was surprised to see the high social standing his Hedgie had earned. Klára herself remembered she used to be the opinion leader of her one-time class, which might not have been accomplished by just her sharp mind but also by her dignified attitude, showing a measure of integrity even at the worst times. If she belittled something or somebody, that carried a lot of weight for the other girls, while her standing up for others—for Ági Feldmann and Ica Lakatos, for instance—had made her classmates cautious about doing them any harm.

Aldó now had two new kinds of assignments. On the one hand, he had to help Hedgie buy high-heeled shoes, a feminine handbag and nylon stockings as accessories for her knitted dress. On the other hand, he had to worry about whether Hedgie could take care of herself in every respect at such parties.

Aldó hadn't had the faintest idea how much sexual education Hedgie should have—besides, despite his profession, he didn't feel able to give her even the smallest amount of instruction about these matters, just as his parents hadn't been able to say a single word to him about sexuality, throughout his whole life. As a result, he could remember experiencing embarrassing problems as a boy, and he figured that girls would probably bump into even worse surprises. Without having had Ilona's blessed upbringing in the background, their relationship would've failed, for sure. Ilona's talent for being happy had always been their main resource—not only in love but also in other areas of life. This seemed genetically missing in his family. Only Ilona's make-up training had triggered this ability in him; and Ilona declared him a gifted and diligent student. Without it, they couldn't have come out of the crisis after Gábor's birth, and would have suffered more and more from a mutual feeling of being rejected. They didn't have any trouble of this kind after István's birth anymore.

Aldó's second deep concern regarding Hedgie's parties was about her political caution. In the universities—as rumor had it—one of the students in every study group had been assigned to report. Aldó thought he could handle this particular issue much more easily, but to his surprise, Hedgie reacted defensively:

"You really think that among these kids...? The boys also come from a high school!"

"My thoughts won't change the way things are going, Baby. University students may only be two or three years older than your group, but they still have stool pigeons among them, everywhere! I wish I weren't right about this! But... whatever you have not said, you can never be sorry for, later."

Klára kept silent. Her face revealed that she was somewhere far away.

“Yes... you can...” she answered slowly.

Aldó sensed immediately what she might have meant. It had often occurred to him in recent years how many nice things he had not said to his loved ones or what he had not done for them. He had refused to play football with Gábor in their last year, he hadn’t let István tell a story to the end, and he had failed to laugh about Luca’s jokes, although he was aware that she had invented them just to cheer him up. He also often recalled their last night together before being taken to forced labor service. He wanted to make love with her but—given that no safe place had been found yet for the children—she pushed him away and said: “I’m sorry... my mind is far away...” Although, that would’ve been the only thing capable of distracting him, however briefly, from the fact that they had been lining up already in the slaughterhouse. Had Luca been aware of this being their last chance to love each other, she would’ve made another decision, surely.

Aldó approached Hedgie and caressed her hair, but she withdrew.

“You are angry now...”

“Yes, I am! Because you are spoiling my mood...”

Now it was Aldó’s turn to feel sad. And that of Hedgie to appease him:

“You know that I won’t say anything to cause trouble for us later!”

“That’s what I wanted to ask of you. Nothing else.”

"Will you, then, pick me up at ten? The address is on your desk. But, please, wait for me downstairs so I don't get ridiculed. But I'll be on time as always, you know.

. . . .

By the end of January, Hedgie had already attended a couple of parties with boys. Aldó had to notice by now his having nurtured the seedling of an appealing woman. He was proud, indeed, but more worried, at the same time. In contrast to body hygiene—an area in which he could not only provide her with a healthy attitude but also with many helpful instructions—sexuality remained an inaccessible topic for him. Finally, he decided to loan her a book from the library, written for adolescents. He was just looking for the right words to use while putting the book on Klára's side on the couch. But she was quicker in finding words:

"That's a dumb book! I looked at it briefly in the school library. In my opinion, those things are... not as written there... But Aldó dearest, I don't want to go to bed with anybody... if that's what you're worried about... Boys are just impossible... Nuts!"

Aldó had to laugh:

"Well, I'll certainly be the last one to push you. I only want you to know about the biological aspect of it... And I'd like to add that love is much more than that... but you can't learn it from a book. I'd like you to be clear on the matter of a boy asking you to..."

"Vera has already kissed one of those idiots! And another one tried to rub against me! But I told him: If he even touched me, I wouldn't hesitate to kick him in the right spot! He got offended by that! Funny... What are you laughing about now?... Aldó... but you and Papa weren't... such... nuts, really... were you? These are so...slimy... their hands keep sweating... and their smell is so yucky...Why don't they use deodorant like you... and me? I would never want such a guy!"

She waited for awhile, Aldó was just smiling, so she went on:

"I would order boys to be withdrawn from circulation... as long as they are no... proper men!"

"Circulation is, however, just what makes them into proper men!"

"Really? Alright, but not with me!"

. . . .

February 22, 1950

Damn it! Aldó was right! There is a stool pigeon in the class! Harsányi told us before our Russian class that she'd heard how many kids from our group attend evening parties where "bourgeois" views incompatible with socialism are declared! What's wrong with bourgeois? And also that some were praising American Imperialism and swinging their hips to the crazy American music. That must have been at Kati Veress's party, I'm sure! Fortunately, I didn't say a word about such things, because I never do anymore.

In Juli Szendrei's opinion, that stupid numbskull Novak must be the stool pigeon. And Juli won't go anyplace anymore, either. Ági Feldmann started to cry. I don't know why, but Harsányi said "she must have a bad conscience!" Bullshit!—poor Ági would hardly speak at all. She only gets invited to the parties for my sake. Alright, she might say this or that recently, but never such things! Anyway, we won't go to any places anymore! I don't know if I should tell Aldó about this. He might get even more nervous. Although he really should know that I watch out.

. . . .

A patient of Aldó's complained about their family pediatrician. Their child needed a thorough examination right away. Aldó called Pista Seilmann immediately and referred that family to him. He also asked how they were doing at home. Pista's reply was brief and insipid. Somebody must be around in the room, Aldó thought.

"Are you in a hurry?" he asked, remembering suddenly that he hadn't yet told him about the great copy of Margit's board game that Hedgie had made.

"Any other medical questions?"

"Nothing urgent... I just wanted to discuss with you some matters about puberty."

"I'll call you as soon as I get some time free."

. . . .

Pista called the next day, late in the afternoon. Hedgie was also there. The receiver had an unusual crackling sound. Pista began the conversation by saying only his first name. The background noises revealed that he was talking from a phone booth on the street. He is "ready to bring back that book," he said. Is the time convenient?

Soon, Hedgie ran to answer the door. Pista gave her a huge smile:

"Oh well, this little birdie is also here!"

Aldó didn't believe he had many reasons for being so cheerful. While Pista was looking for a comfortable seat, Aldó unplugged the phone. His hands signaled: let's stay on the safe side. Klára took a seat between them. Pista made some more attempts to keep up his "nice-uncle-face." Hedgie, however, soon realized that this was not the topic of the day. During the long minutes of small talk, she assessed her chances: If Uncle Pista wouldn't tell his story while she was around, neither Aldó nor she would learn anything. If she left the room, at least Aldó would get a chance to listen, and then could tell her later what he'd been told.

"I'm going to make you tea," she said, her first time ever offering to feed somebody.

She tried to move around in the kitchen without making any noise—words might get through, this way. But, there were very few coming through, so she sat in front of the gas stove, waiting for the water to boil. She wasn't aware of being sad, as she had become quite familiar with that feeling again of late.

Aldó was waiting motionless for Pista to start talking.

"This is my last visit, Aladár...because I don't want to cause you any trouble... Nobody has seen me entering your house. Even my daughter has broken our contact."

"What?"

"Her husband is working for the Ministry of the Interior... A list has been compiled of those having a relative living in the West. Margit is on the list, of course, as well. My son-in-law sent a message that we shouldn't see each other anymore, because he doesn't want to get in trouble... We have to consider the consequences for the children..."

"...can't be true..."

"It is! Of course, the lives of my grandchildren are more important than ours. They haven't lived yet..."

"You have to choose?"

"It's still a bit better than in '44. Then, you couldn't even choose."

Aldó's devastated feeling was soon replaced by a healthy doubt:

"Do you think that the Minister would forget your being his father-in-law and Margit being your wife if you don't see each other?"

"I really don't know. But that's what Rudi asked me to do. My Kati still came to see us, secretly... She cried bitterly... I did, too... Things should get better soon, she said... nevertheless, as she left, she tore her collar [14] when leaving... This world keeps expelling us... Even though, as long as our children stay alive, we shouldn't complain."

After remaining quiet for a while, Aldó spoke from the sane half of his brain again:

"No. I don't want to believe that. This Rudi is an asshole—haven't you always said so, too?"

"He is not a genius, for sure. But this is not his idea. I don't want to cause trouble for anybody... Margit's son conveyed a message to us saying that he'll try to smuggle us out of the country... But that might not be any good for

14. In Jewish tradition, tearing a collar is a sign of grieving for a close relative.

my daughter, either, I'm afraid... I don't have anybody I can discuss this issue with."

"Pista, I can imagine by now many terrible things happening—but not that! That's absurd!"

"I wish that you would be right, Aladár dear. But let's wait until..."

"Why couldn't I visit you, for instance?"

"You also have to think of Hedgie, and of yourself, too. Should a miracle happen and this 'numbers war' be called off, I'd come the next day, jubilant to see you! But until then, we'll be in hiding. That's what I wanted to tell you."

Aldó began to mumble, but Pista stopped him:

"The time of moralizing will only come after the numbers war. You won't help us by visiting us... Well, I want to say something else, too."

"Go ahead!"

"You haven't entitled me to. Yet, I just don't know when we'll see each other again. May I...? I want to say...that I might not have survived these years without Margit. Love heals and only love does... Find somebody..."

"I have the child with me... giving me, indeed, a lot of love... and it does heal me."

"One needs a spouse, too. Believe me."

"Ilona is here with me."

"...Yes. And should the Eternal send you somebody one day, remember my words, too... Hedgie! Is tea ready yet?"

Klára brought the tray in, handed out the mugs and put the little bowl with the cakes in the middle of the table.

"Look what I brought for you from Aunt Margit!" said Uncle Pista as he turned toward her suddenly with a forced smile.

And he took a big, flat box out of his suitcase, wrapped into a newspaper. As it became unwrapped, a lovely, colored box was revealed. It seemed familiar to Klára. Of course! The board game! Her expression suddenly turned distrustful—the same way Aldó's did.

"We hardly ever play anymore... but you liked that game so much... didn't you?"

"I did! But I made a copy of it, Aldó and me. And whenever we'd come to your place we would play with this one here."

"A copy? How did you?"

"Aldó and I compiled one hundred and twenty questions which we used to play with my friends at my birthday party... Thank you very much, Uncle Pista, but you should take it home and we'll play with it when we come over. I will also show you my copy!"

"Well... alright, Honey."

Aldó had a strong feeling that they must keep the game. He didn't know why but he said suddenly:

"Would you... after all... leave it with us for a while, we could compare and get some more ideas from it..."

"Of course!" Pista replied, greatly relieved, and placed the box on the table as if he had gotten rid of a huge burden.

He would show up again as soon as possible, he said at the door before leaving. He gave Aldó a quick hug, then he patted him twice on the shoulder in a male-comrade manner and whispered:

"Take good care of this child... and of yourself, too."

While Klára was having her bath, Aldó opened the box. He went attentively through every pile of question cards, lifted the inside bottom drawer and also the felt bed of the sand clock. He checked everything, to no avail. There was nothing unusual in there. Seemingly, he was just dreaming...

. . . .

Next day, a circular arrived at every office of the clinic: all colleagues preparing any paper for publication must submit it in advance for approval by the Party committee. Those concerned are advised to obtain a brochure detailing guidelines from the Party office.

. . . .

Three weeks later, early on a Monday evening, the bell rang. Aldó answered the door with trepidation because he saw through the milk glass window the contours of a much larger shape than that of Klára. It crossed his mind quickly that the secret police wouldn't come at eight, but only after midnight. A Jewish man of about sixty, with sad features, stood in the doorway.

"May I come in?" he whispered.

Aldó nodded by instinct and closed the door behind the man.

"I'm bringing a... letter from Pista Seilmann."

His face didn't promise anything good. He took an envelope out of the inside pocket of his coat. Aldó's address was written on it in Pista's neat, clear and unmistakable handwriting. He handed over the letter and didn't move. He seemed to want to sit down. Aldó invited him in and offered him a seat in the room. And opened the envelope.

. . . .

My dearest, warm-hearted friend!

M. and I have decided to end it all. We do this with easy hearts because it will bring some ease to others. That's the most important thing. Our options were poor. We could either have consented to something we were not willing to shoulder—neither before God, nor before Man—or do something that would be another descent into hell, and that's what we don't feel strong enough for anymore. Besides, the latter wouldn't save any trouble for our loved ones.

We are only sorry for causing pain to you and to some others whom we love. We trust God, and that he will take good care of you and the child. We also trust his forgiveness for our self-justice. Give a kiss in my name on H's sweet, smart head. Thank you for being my friend for seventeen years. God bless you!

P.S.: Please, burn this letter in the presence of our mailman, so it can't ever cause any trouble to either of you.

. . . .

Aldó sat there with the letter in his hand. He read it again. He might have been reading it for the tenth time when his tears began to flow. The strange man was sitting motionless in his winter coat. He often looked up at Aldó whose eyes were only on the letter.

. . . .

The growing light at dawn was something he could still remember. Then he suddenly awakened at quarter to eight. He started getting ready hastily, but soon stopped himself. He would get to the clinic whenever. It was close to nine when he finally arrived there.

He thought that nothing or nobody but Hedgie could set him in motion anymore—nothing inspired, nor scared, nor astonished him. Still, Elvira succeeded in generating a mixture of these feelings in him right now. This was still the same Elvira with whom he hadn't talked about anything other than office matters in their first years. In '47, Elvira had remarked after seeing out a hysterical patient, that she couldn't stand any form of self-pity, whether in an individual or in a group of people.

Upon hearing that, Aldó prolonged his office "quiet rules" by one more year. Actually, it was only Elvira's growing attention to Hedgie that had brought any substantial change in their relationship. Before then, there was only one time when Aldó saw anything human in Elvira. It happened, coincidentally, shortly after her remark about self-pity, when a beautiful young woman had entered the office—with Ilona's dazzling blue eyes, and even her glance! Something like electricity hit Aldó instantly. He began to tremble, of course. Although he had been able to stop his trembling for the past few months by using a special technique, that didn't work this time. To avoid her look, he headed toward the window by a roundabout way, and bumped into Elvira's astonished face.

"I request that you see my colleague in the afternoon shift... I have too many patients... I can't take more."

"But I was waiting for my turn in line!"

"Please, do leave."

"Why are you sending just me away? I'm surprised that your reputation says you are a decent doctor!"

"Please... go."

That was the point when Elvira took command. She sensed that something was wrong. She ushered the woman out, with such difficulty that their dispute was heard from the hallway. Elvira came back upset:

"Doctor, she wants to report you! What shall I do?"

This was the first sentence from Elvira that Aldó would ever recall with gratitude: she wanted to help him without knowing what his problem was.

"Call her back," Aldó replied, still staring at the street.

When the woman returned, he just said:

"You would never report me. That's not why I asked you to come back. I just want to prevent your thinking that the problem was with you... My reasons are... completely private."

"One shouldn't have any private reasons while doing his job," the woman grumbled.

Aldó regarded this pronouncement as fake as her previous threat. He was glad, however, that her aggressive ways as well as her voice sounded strange to him.

"I have to beg your pardon."

He didn't want to say anything else. Since he hadn't heard any noise from that direction, he turned his head toward her and caught sight of her eyes again. How could she talk so much nonsense with the eyes of Ilona! He trusted her eyes, rather than her words. And that's why he confessed, with his back to her.

"Twenty years ago, I met exactly these eyes. She became my reason for being, she and our two children. None of them is alive anymore."

"Excuse me... please don't be angry at me," the strange voice said, in a less strange manner now.

"I'm not angry at anybody. Anger needs strength. And I don't have any."

Silence. Aldó turned back again.

The woman is crying. A woman is allowed to, of course. The magnet is pulling at him again. He approaches her with unsure steps; reaching out for her hand, kissing it, and returning hastily to the window.

"Please, do leave..." Elvira whispers.

Aldó turns away and stares out the window at a carriage in the street. The horses are struggling on the icy asphalt.

. . . .

When Aldó entered his office, Elvira jumped up, ran to him, took his arms as if she wanted to shake him and said in an unidentifiable voice:

"You do have a phone, don't you?"

Elvira thrust her head against Aldó's chest for a second. He waited apathetically for Elvira to detach herself, and asked in a hushed voice:

"Is Peter all right?"

He had never pronounced Elvira's husband's name before. She nodded and jerked up her head impatiently—like horses do—as if asking what's up. Aldó replied just by tightening his lips. He didn't move.

"As soon as you get changed into your jacket, Doctor, we should check the storage cabinet in the hallway for things we've run out of here."

Aldó nodded. But he still had not moved. That surprised him, too. He was standing around in his coat and hat. Elvira was puttering around:

"Doctor... go and get changed..."

"...I don't know."

Elvira's zigzagging eyes revealed that she was now racking her brains, the same way she had done more than a year ago when trying to find out from Hedgie's confused words whether she wanted to register or not. The only difference might be that history, since then, had given her several make-up lessons in compassion.

"If you don't feel all right, Doctor, you could take some sick-leave, once in a while..."

Aldó's head made a long sequence of moves—from refusing, through considering, to accepting the idea, finally.

"I'll come with you to the Internal Medicine office... right?"

"No need to..."

"Yes, it is... much better that way."

Aldó understood that the essence of the idea was not to support him as a sick person. And he nodded.

"I'm going to tell the patients who need urgent attention to come back for the afternoon shift."

. . . .

The two of them set off down the hallway.

"What happened, for God's sake? You look terrible... Hedgie?"

"She's fine, I hope."

"Haven't you seen her recently?"

"She'll come this afternoon. With her... things should be all right."

"You don't want to say what happened?"

"Things we don't know can't be fished out of us."

"Has somebody been taken away again?"

"No. There are people who won't let that happen... but leave voluntarily, with dignity... once and for all."

Why is he saying so much to Elvira? That's not a good idea. Nevertheless, Elvira is just about to cause a second surprise today:

"They can't do any harm to you... Don't worry... Not to you, anymore..."

Aldó stares at her, for a long time. Is that what occurs to her right now? Is she really worried about him? Not just about her husband, about the Social Democrats, and the union secretary who used to work as assistant for the clinic, and disappeared last week? And besides, why does she think he's invulnerable?

"If there weren't Hedgie, they wouldn't find any vulnerable place in me anymore... I'd be glad to leave then, too."

"You can't do such a thing! Because you have Hedgie..."

"I won't do it, Elvira dear, for sure... It's just that it's hard."

"They will pay for it some day, and bitterly... They can't deport half of the country... They can't succeed in that."

Meanwhile, they reached the Internal Medicine wing and sat down slumped and unguarded on an empty bench.

"We know about similar successes during history, though," Aldó commented.

Suddenly, the new head physician of the internal division popped up at the nearby corner of the hallway. They only knew him by sight, but he knew exactly who they were.

"Doctor Körner! Are you waiting for me?"

"...I only want to get a prescription from a colleague for my upset stomach."

"You're really looking bad. Come on in to my office!"

"I'll await you here, Doctor..." Elvira said, and joined Aldó in his improvisation by telling the internist, "He is also dizzy..."

Well, that was exactly the last adventure Aldó wanted that day! In the office, however, nothing special happened. The head physician—being about Aldó's age—tried to be affable, and asked only a few of the compulsory questions regarding the "general atmosphere among colleagues" and so on. Aldó was feeling so miserable, indeed, that no amount of extra effort was needed to show his inability to engage in a discussion, all the while keeping his hand on his stomach. His digestion had been paralyzed for three years in the same hopeless and torturing way as it was this morning. Since having Hedgie, Aldó had been able to forget about such troubles—because life had become digestible, until last night.

The head physician pressed around Aldó's stomach gave him two prescriptions and saw him out while giggling about his own joke:

"First you have to get a clear stomach before you can get your clear mind back!"

. . . .

"He gave me a three-day sick leave, damn!" Aldó complained to Elvira. "So I have to stay at home tomorrow, too."

"You can make up for your lost sleep, at least. And please, excuse me for taking you there. I don't really know where to go anymore."

"That's not a problem... And the idea about the upset stomach could work for the afternoon, too. Hedgie will come over. I have to compose myself."

. . . .

Hours passed while Aldó was lying on his bed, still dressed. From time to time, he fell into a slumber, often awakened by bad dreams. He then checked the clock— how long could he lie here, stupefied? Sleeping in the camp used to be like that. Such a complex mixture of everything— whenever they had been allowed to sleep, at least. Who might have found Pista and Margit? How did the letter get to the "mailman?" How will Pista's daughter survive all this? Should he call her? And then?... He fell asleep again. Pista's funeral. But Pista is standing somewhere behind Aldó, mingled in with the mourners. Pista returns Aldó's surprised look by placing his index finger in front of his mouth: Pssst, he shouldn't disclose that he is there! Aldó's blink reassures him: Of course, he wouldn't!

He stepped out of this dream again, like stepping out of shallow water, and noticed, worriedly, that his limbs were unwilling to move. The time of Hedgie's arrival was alarmingly close. She could always read his face too well. He didn't feel capable of performing even a small part of the show that might be able to deceive her.

"Something has upset my stomach," he started.

Klára was taking stock of him:

"...You didn't mention it last night."

"It started only after we talked. The night was pretty hard... I didn't work today, either."

"I'll make the bed for you... Why did you put away the bed stuff? And why are you dressed for the street, Aldó dear?"

"Because I did leave for the clinic in the morning, but came home right away..."

"How about seeing a doctor... one that knows about stomach problems?"

"Yes, I got a prescription from the internist there... I just forgot to pick up the pills from the pharmacy."

"I'll go and get it for you, but let me make the bed first. Sit down over there while I'm making it... You should have taken your pills already, you know, if you... Or did you feel so bad? Well, never mind... Did you vomit, too?"

Everything is fine; Klára is not suspicious. She is buzzing about like a real mother, like Olgi. After finishing the bed, she looks for the prescription and the money but then stops suddenly:

"Wait a sec, I have to call Olgi first! I want to ask her how to make the soup she always cooks when I am sick... because there might be things that I have to buy from the store... Take your pajamas meanwhile... Oh, my God, Olgi is at the orphanage now! ...I'll call Madame Gretl, then... she must also know how to make caraway seed soup."

Aldó let himself rock gladly into Hedgie's fairy tale—just like the girl's school had done at Mr. Bokor's peace-talk for a short while last October.

Klára made her soup, a lot of tea, and boiled potatoes for dinner. She also watched over him carefully while taking his temperature and giving him his pills. Aldó obeyed her in everything.

Later in the evening, Klára pushed Olgi into accepting her wish: she wouldn't go to school tomorrow, because Aldó needed her now. Besides, it had been so long ago since she'd missed a single day! Pushing Aldó's protest aside was not difficult. Olgi wanted to talk to him, too. She cross-examined him. Aldó ended up at almost believing every bit of the story he had invented for his ladies.

Klára asked for the telephone and boasted to Olgi about her cooking skill: The soup turned out quite well, she reported.

"Oh, it was really delicious!" Aldó intervened, loud enough for Olgi to hear through the receiver.

"He should be feeling much better if he can enjoy food by now," Olgi commented, and Klára conveyed it.

Aldó was annoyed at giving himself away so rashly. If his judgment on the course of history were correct, he should relearn that old Spartan rule of keeping your mouth shut.

At nine o'clock next morning, the bell rang. Oh, no! Fortunately, it was just Olgi with a full shopping bag. She is going to cook a light chicken stew, an apple compote, and bake a sponge cake. She also has found some leftover rice on the kitchen shelf that would "discipline his digestion," for sure. Heaven forbid, Aldó pondered, it's disciplined enough!

"I'd prefer to eat potatoes."

“I didn’t buy any, Aldó dear, but I can go and get some...”

“There are some at home.”

Olgi was busy with her assignments for hours. Hedgie read short stories aloud to Aldó. They also played chess. She let him sleep, too, when he looked tired. Whenever she stood up from his bedside, even with great caution, Aldó opened his eyes instantly.

“You can sleep peacefully, Aldó dearest, I won’t leave you! I’m going to call off my English lesson, too.”

“You shouldn’t!”

“I don’t want you to be left alone... Wait a minute! Olgi dear! Do you have anything to do this afternoon?”

“Nothing, Sweetheart. Why are you asking?”

“Could you take care of Aldó while I go to my English class?”

“Of course, I could!”

The chatting of his ladies in the kitchen sounded like muffled humming to Aldó. He was smiling with half-closed eyes: Luca dearest, are you sending me the angels, one after the other— to lower the level of night-soil in the cesspool I’ve been tossed into once more? I couldn’t imagine this happening again... Are you saying that letting the shit recede to below my chin should be a great relief, since mouth, nose and eyes are all above that line? Alright, I’ll do my best to appreciate it.

He didn’t feel like getting up, even in the afternoon. It was unusual for his body to be so stubborn. Since having gone back to work—in early ’46—he hadn’t spent a single day on sick leave, nor had he been sick, either, at least, not any more so than on other days.

When Klára was back from her English class, she started to organize the next day: Olgi should come over as early as possible because she had to leave for school right after seven.

"I'd like to go to work tomorrow," Aldó said half-heartedly, instantly pushed aside by Hedgie:

"That's nonsense, Aldó dear! You are not feeling well, and you have sick leave for three days anyway! You're not going to go anywhere tomorrow! Your patients will wait until you'll return. Instead, you should go on writing your article... You could do that even when lying in bed. How far along are you with it? I'm ready to type it for you, anytime."

She is a perfect mother, Aldó thought. Not only do Hedgie and Olgi like being told what to do when feeling weak, it seems he does, too. The reason might be that your loved ones give you instructions you won't dare to give yourself. At first, he wasn't willing to admit to himself how much he longed to splash around in... what's called family; family—that's always more than just one molecule of chlorine; where you can hear others chat around you—an experience all three of them had been deprived of for years.

So he bestowed his favors upon Hedgie by following her pushy instructions. He also considered giving Elvira a call. She shouldn't wait for him tomorrow in vain. He had never called her before, but he knew that she had a home phone. He soon found her number in the telephone book. Elvira seemed worried—as if she thought there must be a serious reason for his staying at home a third day. Finally, she accepted Aldó's reasoning about Hedgie's overprotective attitude. She closed the conversation in her usual, soldier-like style: Thank you for your call.

Aldó realized, with a bad conscience, that Pista hadn't come back into his thoughts since noon. At night, he had a dream, however. He and Pista were sitting on a bench, close to the fence of the concentration camp, waiting for their execution. They were not allowed to talk. They were just watching each other's faces, completely calm, and considering, relieved that this mute exchange of thoughts would be their last experience in life. When he woke up after this dream, he saw Hedgie turning around in the bed. He straightened her blanket and watched her for a while. It felt so good that she had stayed with him tonight again.

Next morning, Olgi called before Klára had left: She will be there soon, she only wants to buy some fresh things in the bakery, she said. Aldó hurried his washing up and dressing. Meanwhile, his mind kept recalling Margit's easy smile and fluid movement... What a short time they had known each other! He avoided recalling Pista's face. Since Monday, he had reconsidered over and over again what to say to Hedgie if she asked about Pista—knowing that she constantly kept an eye on her small group of people. Now an idea popped into his mind: they had left for America, to Margit's son! But that's also something Hedgie mustn't tell anybody. That's a good idea! The Almighty hasn't offered anything better... Aldó's disproportionate relief revealed that he was willing to believe this version of his own story the same way he believed about the upset stomach.

Olgi arrived again with heavy bags. Aldó sat by her in the kitchen and helped her peel potatoes. They chatted about

Hedgie. Later, Olgi dictated some recipes for dishes that Aldó wanted to make for Hedgie sometime.

The bell rang around noon. It scared Aldó less this time than it did yesterday. Elvira stood in the doorway.

"I only wanted to see," she started, "if it's not just goofing off."

"Of course, it is! I am sure I could have worked today... It was just that Hedgie-girl was still worried so much. Yesterday, she even skipped school. And now, dear Olgi is here."

"Well... so you have two nannies, Doctor! That being the case, I would also prefer to spend my days at home!"

Aldó has never seen Elvira's face as kind as now. She went on:

"Results are striking, however! I can see how much better you must feel now. I really don't understand Hedgie's reasons for still being so worried. If I were you, I would tell her to stop now..."

"Denying somebody the right to care for another would be as cruel as denying somebody the right to being cared for!"

. . . .

On Saturday, the two of them were playing chess while Olgi was sewing in her own room. She had found quite a nice piece of fabric in her closet—without remembering anymore where it had come from—that would be perfect for a young girl like Klára. They have been designing a two-piece dress together for weeks now.

Aldó and Hedgie hadn't spoken for a long time when he realized that he didn't know the reason for Hedgie's being so quiet.

"Are you in a bad mood, my baby?"

"No... just... Novák's party is right now. Juli, and Ági, and I were also invited, but we won't go anymore. It's absolutely certain that Novák is the stool pigeon in the class... She is so self-important around Harsányi, all the time."

"Well... if you are cautious about what you say, you could still attend... There must be other kids there that you like."

"We are not going to attend, because she must have told a lie recently. Harsányi threatened us by saying that the eyes of the Party could see every one of us, and that she knew Mari Szentpéteri had been putting down socialism like an attack dog. Only Novák would say something like that to her!"

Olgi entered the room:

"Klára-baby, your skirt is ready for a trying-on. Could you pull away from your game for a few minutes?"

"No point... Olgi dear... I'm not going anywhere anymore."

"How can you say such silly things? Having a few kids around who are not suitable for making friends is no reason for sitting home all the time! There are many places where you could go and have a nice dress on!"

"I don't miss that. I'm fine here, at home. Only you mustn't be carried off by the communists! The three of us are just fine together, aren't we?"

This was really not that sort of attachment Hedgie's old people would have wished to see.

. . . .

The newspapers were loaded with triumphant news: "The working class keeps gaining ground" and "Workplaces are continually being weeded out to the public's benefit." Aldó stopped pushing Hedgie into any entertainment with her classmates. He chose to take over the job of providing a facade of normalcy. The two of them went to concerts, for instance—with Hedgie in her beautiful new outfit. Attending a concert at the Academy of Music wasn't easy for Aldó, since he had never been there without Ilona. But he used a magic word now, for situations like this, by saying to himself: Life is about Hedgie now; that's why Luca and the Eternal have sent her to him. Remembering that, the concert evening was fine for Aldó. Klára didn't share with him her own first memories about the Academy, either.

Next day, Elvira told him—once again in the hallway—that two doctors, one from surgery, one from dermatology, had disappeared. The surgeon seemed, right at first sight, to be a thoroughly decent man of peasant background who—according to Elvira's information—had held a high position in the Smallholders' party. What the disappearance of the other doctor was about, Elvira had no explanation whatsoever.

That same week, a same-floor neighbor of Aldó, Mrs. Bauer, whispered to him while both were waiting in the staircase to pay their monthly rent to the house manager. Had he heard the news that Mr. Ferenczi from the fifth floor had been carried off last night? And that she is deeply worried, because her own husband also owns two stores in town.

Wednesday afternoon, Klára knocked at the door of Aldó's office. "What's wrong?" Elvira asked worriedly, but didn't get a proper answer. Okay, she would ask the doctor to step out as soon as he was finished with his patient. Aldó appeared soon, took Hedgie by the arm and began pacing about with her.

"Ági was rushed to Lipót Hospital by ambulance! Mrs. Mestrovich told me. Ági's aunt called her to say that Ági had taken a whole bunch of pills! She didn't show up at school yesterday... I called her, but nobody answered the phone. Mrs. Wiesmann said Ági is just sick... Her father must have been carried off, for sure. Ági had told me that she couldn't live with her aunt even for one day! Aldó, let's go and see her in the hospital! I don't dare go alone."

Aldó sat down on a bench and pulled Hedgie to his side. He kept nodding. "One day, sooner or later, we'll be all gone," he recalled Hedgie's words from one of their first encounters. The plan works, even quicker than intended! Hedgie was surprised to see that Aldó wasn't able to react in a more reassuring way. She couldn't recall when she had ever seen his face having such disciplined dread, but it seemed familiar to her.

"She will survive, won't she? Mrs. Mestrovich also wants to visit her... but couldn't find out yet which department Ági might be in... because the operator was not willing to give any information... She also warned us to be cautious... Why? What's wrong with me visiting my school friend? You will come with me, won't you?

"Yes. I will, if it's possible. But you shouldn't go anyplace right now," he said, standing up from the bench, and gesturing for Hedgie to move on. They were walking again. "I'll try to get news about her. Meanwhile, don't call anybody about this! If someone calls you about it, divert the conversation immediately. Got it, Hedgie? This is not the time for heroism... One can die here from just following his own moral decency... But we will trick them! I promise to look into it... today—if possible. Now you go, Dearest, and be smart! Don't do anything silly!

. . . .

Aldó ran several blocks from the streetcar stop to Olgi's house so he could get in before the manager had closed the house door. It was quarter to ten.

"Who is there?" Olgi's terrified voice answered his ringing.

"Aldó."

Both Hedgie and Olgi gave a huge sigh when opening the door.

"I have good news!" Aldó said, out of breath, and gesturing for them to follow him into the bathroom. He turned on all the taps to full flow.

"We've been at Ági's place... A colleague and I... he's a psychiatrist who also works for the orphanage and has good contacts with the Lipót. On our way there, he already invented an idea how to... Ági's attempt to commit suicide had been due to lovesickness... No politics! ...Her father might have been carried off, indeed, but the doctor on duty hadn't mentioned anything about that. They only know that Ági was taken to the hospital by her aunt... who really made an unfriendly impression. Ági is out of danger now. What they know from her for sure, is that she won't ever go live with her aunt. János... my colleague made a deal with the guy about taking Ági to the orphanage as soon as she comes out of her... sedated state... Fortunately, she won't be eighteen until next year. No better plan could have been made, for sure. Aren't you happy about this, Hedgie?"

"And... have you talked with her?"

"No. She was sleeping. But I saw her."

"Was she snoring?"

"Of course, she was."

"For sure?"

"She even turned!"

"Can I go and see her tomorrow?"

"I haven't asked... But that's less important now, my baby, than having the chance to help her in a safe way, and to be able to get her out soon... One shouldn't stay in a place like that a single hour longer than absolutely necessary. Tomorrow you should go to Mrs. Mestrovich and ask for the phone number of Ági's aunt... if she has a phone. I forgot to ask for it while there. She must be consulted."

"Was she really snoring?"

Aldó briefly caressed Hedgie's hair and nodded. Then he looked at his watch.

"Now I have to run so the manager won't see me."

He gave both of them a kiss on the face, a rare treat. And added:

"Cheer up, my little one! Compared with what we were expecting, this is great, indeed! All the rest... will come step by step... I wish we could find solutions to other things as quickly as this. Also, Hedgie, we won't talk about this on the phone!"

He checked his watch once more, started to run down the stairs, waving back good night. And he disappeared.

"Aldó!" Hedgie shouted.

Aldó ran back while Hedgie went toward him.

"Thank you... so much... You are the best... Papa on Earth."

. . . .

Ági's stay at the Lipót took its toll on Klára. Before their visit, when sensing Klára's dread, Aldó made some attempt to divert her from the plan, realizing that she was certainly not even aware of how depressing both the place and poor Ági herself were.

"Later... it's not urgent" he argued, but Klára's reply put an end to the discussion:

"One has to be there when it's needed."

Aldó might have accepted her point even if he had known what was going on in Klára's mind: She was recalling her little sister's last days; the way she had sat by her side in an overcrowded room in the Ghetto, not even attempting to clean little Juti out of the poo anymore... and then there wasn't even any poo anymore, just the smell of it... and Juti's weak whining... and Gyuri hiding behind others for several days.

During those days of hesitancy, Aldó twice visited Ági and talked to her, rather than with her. His colleague, János Csillag, also went to see her again. The doctor in charge called Ági's state "pre-psychotic, to say the least." In János's opinion, however, psychotic reactions easily pop up in any deep crisis. Should they have sent all children in '45 with such reactions to a psychiatric ward, the orphanage houses would've been empty. He is ready to take full responsibility for Ági as soon as she's released. She can get out, the answer came, provided she signs a declaration stating that she has given up the idea of a suicide. The doctor in charge heard from Ági's aunt that Mr. Feldmann had, indeed, been displaced into a "work camp." Since the doctor seemed just as depressed as his surrounding environment, Aldó saw no reason for making up any fake story for the guy.

He talked to Ági about her school friends; how much they are expecting her to return, especially Klára; and that there would be a good solution if Ági wants it, too. She sat apathetically by Aldó's side, on a bench in the hallway of the hospital, strongly sedated. After some twenty minutes of silence, she spoke at an almost normal speed:

"You should take care of Klára instead... for her, it makes sense."

On Saturday, Aldó and Klára went to the hospital together. Aldó walked along the long hallway so the girls could have a private talk. On his return back up the hallway, he saw Klára's agitated gestures while Ági listened to her in the same indifferent way she had listened to him. This might simply be a consequence of the sedatives.

After leaving the building, Klára wanted to sit down in the garden right away, but all the benches had been ruined by dry rot. There might be some intact ones on the street, Aldó suggested, but Klára slowed down even more, like someone who couldn't walk any longer. Aldó leaned back against a big oak tree and pulled his child close. Hedgie began to talk:

"I used to say before, too, that I don't want to live any more... but that wasn't true. I just missed having somebody worth living for... But Ági really doesn't want to live! What should I do?"

"We'll find her somebody who's worth living for. She only has to endure until we can find that person."

Ever since his decisive success on Wednesday night, it hadn't occurred to him what to do for Klára if he, too, were carried off, although, in his evening prayer, he continued begging the Eternal not to separate those who loved each other.

Aldó's seemingly simple solution reassured Hedgie a bit. Nevertheless, she burst out crying in the night, for the first time since they had started spending nights together. Aldó knew from experience what was helpful in moments like that: switching on the light immediately, getting up, eating or drinking, or doing anything linked to the present. Hedgie wasn't surprised, just grateful that Aldó didn't ask about her dream. That's why she was soon able to tell him: A soldier in the Ghetto had tied Ági to a tree, just to make her starve to death, and the others nearby didn't allow Klára to set her free.

Aldó tried to quiet her ("Shall I make a tea?") but she didn't hear him anymore.

"...We stood on the side corridor and Mama asked me to take good care of the little ones... until she returned. She said Papa would return, too. She lied to me! ...I watched her from the railing as she went down the stairs with all other women... and saw the Arrow Cross guys yelling at them in the yard... I kept telling myself that some more friendly soldiers will lead them to work, and they won't suffer any harm... And then... Uncle Schwarz came and asked me: 'How old are you?' 'Twelve,' I said. 'No,' he said, 'you are nine, you understand?'" ...I kept arguing, 'I am short but twelve already'. He kept hissing: 'You are nine—or don't you want to stay alive?... Every child older than ten has been taken away'... It wasn't true either that it was a protected house[15]... It wasn't protected... That's why we had to sneak through the town with the Schwarzes to the Ghetto. Mama said I should take care of Gyuri 'because he is stubborn,' and Juti ''cause she is small and scared'... I couldn't take care of them!"

Hedgie was crying just like when Aldó first tried to get her to go to the orphanage. Aldó put her on his lap. He didn't care anymore whether Hedgie felt his trembling.

"But how could you have been able to?"

"I was supposed to! Any way I could!... When Juti's diarrhea didn't stop, Aunt Schwarz told me not to touch Juti anymore and just leave her. They were afraid of getting infected. But I didn't leave her. Aunt Schwarz didn't mind so much... but Uncle Schwarz got fed up by the evening and dragged me away from Juti. By then, Juti had been put on

15. The Swiss and Swedish embassies acquired the right to offer diplomatic protection for certain houses where Jews had been huddled together. After coming to power, the Arrow Cross gangs invaded these houses as well.

the floor so she wouldn't take up the whole bench... Many people were just standing around... I was screaming that he should let me go back, I can't leave Juti alone, Mama trusted me with her!... Next day, she was unconscious and I started telling myself that she was just sleeping; that's why she had stopped crying... I knew, though, that it wasn't true. By then, they let me sit by her side on the floor... I didn't care about Uncle Schwarz's threat that I couldn't touch her anymore... And Gyuri hadn't been around for days. I saw him sometimes peeping out from a corner, then returning to his hiding place... I didn't try to talk to him anymore... When little Juti died and was carried out, Aunt Schwarz put me on her lap, anyway, maybe to make me shut up... and I peed on her lap... Even if I looked nine... even a nine years old is not supposed to pee like that. But she was less mad about that than for knocking a full plate of food out of her hand... Others ate the spilled food up from the floor."

. . . .

Hedgie was working on the equations had Aldó put together for her. She seemed to be less enthusiastic about her success than usual.

"Did you get stuck?" Aldó asked surprised.

"No... I just want to... ask you something."

"Do so!"

"I don't dare, but I'd like to, very much."

"Go ahead!"

After another minute of hesitation, she came out:

"If I weren't... around, would you get married again?"

“No.”

“But others are! Uncle Pista did, and Faragó’s father, and Bíró and Kôvári’s mothers did, too. Only Ági’s father hasn’t... I wouldn’t want you to be married, although I know it would be better for you.”

“It wouldn’t be better. Don’t worry.”

“Why, then?”

No answer, for a long time.

“Because it’s good the way it is.”

. . . .

Next week, she just said:

“ Aldó dear, are you finished with your new article? It’s been a long time since you told me there were only a few hours’ work to be done on it.”

“I got stuck, somehow...”

“Alright, then, give me the pages already done, for typing... You will get a clearer overview if it’s typed... Meanwhile, you could sit down and do the rest.”

After finishing ironing his shirts, she asked:

“I’m going to iron the sheets also, right?”

“No way! You’ve been ironing now for an hour! Sit down and read your new book... or we can take a walk. Which one would you like?”

“...If you had a wife...”

“Hedgie dear, forget about that topic!”

"But you don't have anybody to do the ironing for you."

"I can do it myself."

"You said you are glad about my ironing your shirts."

"...Because that's... coming from love..." he murmured, and added, even more quietly: "Ironing sheets was never my wife's job, either."

Klára cuddled up next to Aldó on the couch:

"I'd like to give you everything that's love... Because you don't have anybody else, either... But I don't really know how to... because I'm not your wife."

The return to the topic and its more direct formulation scared Aldó a lot. That would disturb any caring gestures between the two of them—which had been so safe until now. His scare blinded him from noticing that Hedgie was pondering this question just as seriously as she had Ági's wish to die, or the deportations. He stood up.

"Aren't you, little dear, reading too many love stories these days?"

Without a word whatsoever, Klára left for the kitchen. She had never resembled an adult woman as much as right now. Aldó gave himself a few minutes before following her. While sitting at the kitchen table, Klára pretended to read the newspaper.

"Hedgie, dear..."

She didn't want to sell peace too cheaply—so she didn't look up yet.

"Hedgie... Now, now... come on... speak to me!"

A grimace showed on her face.

"I didn't want to offend you."

Still silence. Aldó waited while Hedgie raised the price some more.

"There is nothing on earth more important to me than your love, you know that, little one... But our relationship is not..." he tried to cheer up the conversation by recalling their kind, old expression: "I am your adopted Papa, after all... right?"

Hedgie laughed briefly, though still somewhat sulking. Then she blurted out:

"Okay... but why are you laughing me off, while I only..."

"I never laugh you off!"

"Yes, that was laughing off! While I only want to care about you...because you won't have a wife and I won't have a husband..."

"Hedgie, dearest... first of all: you *will* have a husband..."

"I won't! First of all, because I can't stand them, second, 'cause we are not allowed to make friends with anybody."

At bedtime, Aldó was reassured that Hedgie crawled into her blanket the same innocent way she always had before. He felt ashamed: he must have misunderstood that gesture and statement she'd made in the afternoon, and the scare must have come from his own fantasy. Hedgie wouldn't show any bodily desire—her idea must be simply a product of her well-known "strategic thinking." Poor little thing...

• • • •

Ági allowed herself to be persuaded to go to the orphanage; still, nobody around her was feeling calm yet. Doctor Csillag took the view that "it's just a mask at this point, in order to escape from the psychiatric ward. She will be meticulously guarded in the orphanage, and is not allowed to go to school yet." Klára had a bad conscience, remembering what she had promised Ági after Rajk's execution: that if her father were carried off, she could move into Olgi's. Although she hadn't reaffirmed this promise during the hospital days, she was sure that Ági remembered it well. She saw herself as inexcusably gutless...

Doctor Csillag—following Aldó's request—explained to Klára in detail how irresponsible it would be to allow Ági to loaf around at this point. As soon as she was well enough to make reasonable decisions herself, the idea of her moving there could be discussed. Provided everybody concerned could agree on the plan. Even though on the sidelines in this matter, Olgi made no effort to hide her fear of this responsibility.

Doctor Csillag ordered a tiny, but heavy-handed and deeply religious woman to be at Ági's side. Aunt Wallenstein—though not yet fifty, was still called "aunt" by everybody—had pulled several kids out of such pits in recent years. She would spend, in the beginning, twenty-four hours a day with the child. If asked during the several weeks of such "child care" how she could manage it, she'd answer that the Almighty would always provide you with just as much strength as needed for the task. Although many of her fellow Jews disagreed with this thesis, they did envy her strength. Aunt Wallenstein didn't care about any of this. Doctor Csillag understood the other, more pragmatic reason behind Aunt Wallenstein's heroism:

"No Jewish child must die meaninglessly anymore!" Klára entered the orphanage, for the first time in her life.

Within a few weeks, everybody around Ági was able to sleep undisturbed. She was studying again—even if not too much—with Aunt Wallenstein; she waited eagerly for Klára's visit every second day and for the homework she brought along; she had only a minimum amount of medication to take now. Since receiving a postcard from her father, sent from the camp, she had stopped yelling at Aunt Wallenstein whenever she'd remind her of the duty she had to her father to somehow hold herself together and not let him down in any way. By the way, yelling and other emotional outbursts counted as new behaviors of Ági's. Doctor Csillag welcomed them as signs of healthy energies. Aunt Wallenstein also took the view that it was not only an option, but more of an obligation of the troubled child to measure his or her strength against her own and to regain their vitality this way.

. . . .

One night, a shouting male roused Aldó from his sleep. He approached the window with fluttering heart and saw three men wrestling in front of a car across the street. The shouting one was flanked by the other two ("They'll regret it...!"), while looking toward the upper floors, where a woman was sobbing on the balcony. Aldó stood paralyzed behind the window. It was two o'clock.

Next day, Hedgie asked him why he'd fastened the window open with a matchbox while it was already too cold anyway. His answer was that he wanted a bit of fresh air coming in. And he laid out an extra blanket for her.

. . . .

Hedgie arrived in a high mood: she and her friends had founded a 'Secret Society for the Reliable.' There are three of them included, at the moment—Juli, Vera, and Klára—but Ági will also be accepted as soon as she can come to school. They intend to keep increasing the number of members one by one so they will have the opportunity to catch any stool pigeon as soon as she sneaked in. Isn't that a splendid idea? They are going to have their first encounter next Sunday, at Juli's place. Juli's brother and two of his friends from the university will attend, too—who are also reliable as clockwork! Hedgie read Aldó's face as much less happy than she was.

"What's wrong now, Aldó dear?" she asked in the somewhat impatient, condescending voice of an adult.

"How can you tell that they are "reliable as clockwork?"

"They know that about each other... because they also come from such families!"

"What kind of families?"

"Well..."

"That's it, my baby! There is no clear-cut proof whatsoever. Next year will be your final year in high school... If anybody were declared a class enemy on his cadre-sheet, or just noted as being hostile, he'd lose all chance to study anywhere.

Hedgie hid behind her physics book, in a bad mood, while Aldó felt guilty about his discouraging warnings.

"Well, alright..." he started his compensating moves, "if you avoid politics, you'll be on the safe side. There are so many other things to be talked about."

“I thought...” Klára grinned, “that you were going to warn me once again about boys.”

“Well, that’s something I don’t even dare mention anymore.”

. . . .

Aldó knew Juli’s address by heart already. At ten, again, he was waiting for Klára in front of the house.

“Everybody else was still there! It’s only me who had to leave so early.” Klára complained. Although meeting him at ten had been her idea.

“A couple of months ago, I would’ve said you should call me if that’s the case, and I’d start out later. But now... the secret police are on the streets at night. It’s better not to hang around in town... Anyway... let’s talk about something else. Was it fun there, my baby?”

“Would the secret police drag people away from the street, too?”

“Maybe not. At least, I haven’t heard of such a case... But it’s better to bypass any I.D. control, as well. Anyway... We’ll take care of ourselves. Now, let me hear...”

“Everybody was very nice! These boys are so intelligent! They are not pantywaists like the boys from the high school.”

Oh dear, Aldó thought. He realized yesterday that Luca had been just one year older than Hedgie is now, when she had first allowed him to get really close to her. And he had not even been two years older than Hedgie. His only hope now was that Hedgie would stick to her strategy of “kicking the right spot” for a while, and when the time came—by the help of a miracle, somehow— Hedgie would know how to take care of herself. These boys today, he pondered, certainly wouldn't be as protective of a young girl as he used to be.

. . . .

Aldó was waiting for Hedgie to fall asleep. Then he offered his evening prayer, asking for the Almighty's protective care for Hedgie, Olgi and himself. After that, he still recalled the little package he'd put together, in case the worst happened: Hedgie's picture, a few pieces of paper, a pencil, some marked post cards, money, and toilet paper. He watched while Hedgie slept until he soon fell asleep, too.

The same noise woke him up as last week: the noise of a car engine being just switched off.

"Hedgie!"

Hedgie is instantly awakened by his terrified voice. She sees him running to the window. She follows him. Now she grasps the meaning of the matchbox in the window. Aldó looks down to the street from both corners of the window, without seeing any car. Then it has to be in front of the gate, he figures, hidden by the big second floor balcony. And now he recognizes the quiet beep of the bell downstairs.

Their breathing is synchronized. They look at each other. Aldó pulls her toward the couch where they can watch the entry door. They sit there, embracing, staring at the milk glass window. Now they see the light going on in the staircase. At this point, Hedgie refuses to watch anymore. She sits on Aldó's lap, grasps him with all her strength, and buries her head in his neck. Aldó keeps staring at the door.

Tetam, tetam, tetam, Aldó's neck artery says, as he hears Hedgie's heart beating the same vehement way.

"I have written down everything for you, little dear... Olgi has the letter," he whispers.

"No!" sounds Hedgie's sobbing reply.

Aldó puts his hand in front of her mouth... as if that would make any difference in how far away her voice could be heard. As if there would be a place to hide. Shadows appear in front of the door! Tetam, tetam, tetam... But they disappear again... They go further... And the bell of the shopkeeper neighbor, Mr. Bauer, is ringing.

Hedgie isn't aware of Aldó's crying—his choking voice sounds so natural:

"Adonai! How can you teach me to feel relief when a man is being hunted down!"

Hedgie doesn't understand him. She looks at his face.

"The Bauers... today," he explains.

They sit paralyzed and silent.

The last night before Papa had left, he came to the children's room to say good night and farewell. Klára and Gyuri soon pretended to sleep and sneaked out to the dining room. Only Juti was sleeping. The light in the master bedroom was on. They opened the door a few inches. Mama and Papa were lying awkwardly in a diagonal position across the bed, still dressed, as if somehow being tipped over... while Mama was caressing Papa's head, hidden down in the duvet. In a few seconds Gyuri and she closed the door. That was the last time she'd seen Papa. If Aldó were carried off, she would go with him! At least they should die together! But...what if Aldó is alone in the night? He must move over to Olgi's!

Mr. Bauer did not fight like the neighbor across the street. Neither a word nor any other noise could be heard when the shadows passed by Aldó's door again.

They have survived this day, Aldó realized. But tomorrow, another night will come, and many more nights. Will the numbers war ever come to an end? Whose number will be read and called out tomorrow? Still, a numbers war is, actually, much more fair, with both teams having some chances. These people, however, keep coming like hunters surrounding a fox—driving it into its foxhole where it can't escape anymore. How many more foxes are going to be hunted down?

What if this has been their last night together? He knows last nights of life well enough. And those nights following the last ones—those when incurable absences won't let you fall asleep anymore; absences that seemed so innocent before... Has he done everything Hedgie has needed? Was he good enough to her? Has he provided her with enough strength this past year and a half to help her stand safely now on her own two feet? But he is not like Pista; he will endure and return to her, if there is a way back. That's what he also promised in his letter to her. Olgi will hand it over whenever appropriate...

Is there anything he's failed to give her? He should have told her about the boys... to make sure she would only accept the snoring of a man who really loves her deeply, because she can't fall asleep without hearing the snoring of somebody at her side. How will she recognize what real love is? He wished he could entrust Hedgie to the care of somebody.

Suddenly, Aldó begins offering a prayer. He doesn't notice her watching. After he has finished, Hedgie grasps his arms furiously:

"You haven't asked Him to forgive you, have you? Why not the other way around? Don't believe Him... it... them... I could kill them!"

She jumps up crying, Aldó follows her, tries to get hold of her. They are struggling... ("No! How can you be so obedient?") Aldó catches her and holds her tight. She suddenly gives up fighting and embraces him. He starts to kiss her face, her shoulders, her neck...and keeps bending lower, opening her nightgown, giving kisses all over her body and pushing his face tight against her belly... Then, paralyzed, he squats down to the floor.

It takes her only a few seconds to realize what... What? No name is needed here, anyway... And she begins caressing his motionless head...

"It's all right... Aldó dear..."

No answer from the lame bundle of flesh. This scene... has been, somehow, part of their lives before...

"Aldó... dearest... come on... let's go to sleep."

With some delay, Aldó asks quietly:

"Why don't you... sleep... over there... on the couch? You are... not anymore..."

"It's all right the way we always sleep. Come on..."

. . . .

A few hours later, light was coming in, as Aldó lay awake on the bed. He looked at Hedgie, fearfully, from time to time. She was still sleeping. Then he turned his head and started watching the ceiling. He has had many difficult mornings before, but never this sort of difficult morning. How could he commit such a sin? Hedgie had been entrusted to him as a child. Entrusted by God, by Luca, by Olgi and by Hedgie's parents! He betrayed them! He hasn't deserved their trust. He has spoiled her tonight!

Or... is that sheer bullshit? Luca might say so.

("Oh, Ali dear, keep spoiling me, please... it's marvelous! Come on, let me spoil you, too!" she said, though not being even twenty.) But that was something different. Back then, he still had a right to life. Now he only has the right to talk to his love in heaven:

"I've always loved only you, Luca dearest... It was just... like being with you... the last time."

"I know."

" I'll always be yours. That's why I don't want the joy anymore. And my body is learning to accept this"

. . . .

After returning to Budapest from the camp—he didn't call it "coming home" anymore—the misery of his body and soul has kept this trouble away for a long time. After more than a year, though, he awoke one morning, noticing with dread that his body had been—without his permission—wandering on the forbidden path. ("What did you want, you fool? Having joy? Making children? You idiot!") He went to have a bath in the ice-cold tap water, even though he had promised himself in the camp to never be cold anymore—if he survived at all.

After his bath, he got dressed for the street, maybe as another punishment, since it was too early to start the day. Then he soon fell asleep after lying on the couch, and had a dream, seeing Mommy sitting on an armchair next to the couch. How could his dream put her into this unfamiliar, unfriendly setting that he had just moved into a few weeks before...And Mommy said with a worried face: "Stop causing yourself more pain, my little son..."—Mommy, whom her adult son still regards as the only authentic incarnation of the most ridiculous Christian idea about Immaculate Conception.

Since then, he is really less angry when—luckily, not very often—the nighttime surprises him. He only has a bad day afterwards when he remembers a dream about Luca. But it's an absolute No! when he's awake... because that was... truly hell. He has never felt his solitude to be as unbearable as that time.

Luca and he had laughed their heads off when reading about the monks of Tibet with their desire-free life. "There is nothing unusual in that!" he commented, "I also undertake this... well, every second day!" Whenever he switched off the light before Luca came in to their bedroom, she announced her arrival by whispering in his ear: "Is this a day in the monastery?" And he always answered: "Well, I'm ready to change it... but, of course, only for your sake, madam!" and quickly pulled his Luca to him... Also, this nickname... sounded so playfully frivolous to his ears that he hadn't even dared pronounce it in front of the children.

Luckily, we never see the next part of our lives. He hadn't known that he'd have a monk's life for the next ten years. Without believing in Nirvana. But he received this child as compensation. And that's what he has abused right now... What will be the punishment, Eternal Father? Having to lose her? Will he be carried off tomorrow?

Hedgie began to toss and turn in bed... as always before really waking up. And Aldó would always stroke her hair then. Is he not allowed to touch her as innocently as before? That means not touching her at all? He looked at her, almost in grief. Hedgie reached out for him as she always does while beginning to awaken.

"Aldó dear..." she murmured in a sleepy voice.

"Hmm?"

"I made a pledge last night never to mention the Bauers ever again... We just have to say always: You won't be taken away! And then you won't be taken away."

Aldó didn't understand the connection, but Hedgie's voice made him feel much better. He was pondering why to not mention the Bauers? Did she really mean the Bauers, or something else? But he only asked:

"Is that so?"

Hedgie sat up, already in a combative spirit, and shared her instructions:

"Yes! I will say it to myself, and you will say it to yourself, several times a day—and so it will become true... Isn't it time to get up yet?"

Chapter 4

Almost a Life Worth Living (1955-1956)

Joli, just recently hired for the maternity ward, was compiling the quarterly departmental statistics with Elvira. Since instructions for completing this paperwork continually changed, they kept asking Aldó. He was often not sure about the right answer, either, yet he felt it was important to stay nearby. As today's night shift has been uneventful, they felt they might as well use the time to deal with these silly statistics.

Elvira meant that Joli had interfered in too many matters. But Aldó liked her, right from the beginning. She reminded him of a younger version of Aunt Wagner.

The telephone rang; Joli got it.

"A young woman's voice, Doctor."

Aldó has been expecting Klára's call for hours. Today she took her written and oral exams in French simultaneous interpretation. He knew she wouldn't be done until late afternoon. Up to now, she had received an "A" in all but one of her exams.

"I know, my baby, good for me... How was it?... Three cheers! Can we celebrate tomorrow?... What did the Chair say?... Well, it's a flattering offer, but you shouldn't work all summer! This is your last real school vacation!... Well, you'll decide, of course, my baby, but I don't think money should be your first priority now... Will Pepe work over the summer also?... That's not why I'm asking, Hedgie dear... Of course I won't criticize him!"

The women got stuck with their rows and columns once again, so they waited for Aldó to finish his conversation. Aldó hung up, and Elvira congratulated him without asking anything. Joli—confident in her right to speak boldly—asked Aldó:

"How old is this 'baby'?"

Aldó noticed Elvira's kick under the table.

"Elvira dear, stop kicking poor Joli! Why can't she ask questions?"

Elvira looked surprised. Although she has been a mute witness to their relationship in the last seven years, she has not had the courage to make any remarks whatsoever about Hedgie's pampering, because to her, there was no need for any explanation.

"She'll be twenty-three soon. But I like calling her 'my baby.'"

"Is she your only child?"

Oh, my God, Elvira thought, but wasn't allowed to kick anymore.

"Yes."

"How lucky it's a girl! A boy her age would certainly not let his father call him 'baby.'"

"Maybe so."

"I have sons..."

"Doctor, now we really have to finish that awful chart," Elvira fumed, instead of kicking.

Aldó stepped behind her, put his hands on her shoulders, and bent down to her ear:

"You don't need to be so worried about me anymore... but... thank you."

Without really understanding what was going on, Joli felt like an outsider now and that's simply how it was. Elvira turned around slowly and asked Aldó:

"Can I, then, also ask a question? ...Why do you always say, when Hedgie calls you, 'I know, my baby, good for me'?"

"Because she always begins the conversation with the same sentence also," Aldó replied, smiling.

"What sentence?"

Aldó made an attempt to tune his voice to a soprano register. He was in a good mood. He had often been in a good mood, recently.

"It's-me-Aldó-dear!"

"What?"

A second attempt in soprano, with the same spluttering. The third, clearly articulated, version was clear for Joli, as well—the words at least.

"And then I say: I know, it's her, and that's good for me," he went on explaining and added for Joli:

"She calls me Aldó."

Elvira made another quick detour in the conversation:

"Doesn't she even greet you first?"

To add more emphasis, she repeatedly shook her head disapprovingly.

His conversation last year with Elvira suddenly occurred to Aldó.

. . . .

He had told her he was about to be reassigned to the maternity ward of the St. Stephan Hospital. Elvira had burst into tears. This was as shocking as if a man had done so. (Hedgie held the opinion that Elvira must have attended a military school at one point.)

And, still crying, she started to talk about how it had felt to work by Aldó's side in the early years. She had been brought up in a family of craftsmen, in a tiny town where Jews had always been around. True, they had sometimes murmured about the Jewish shopkeepers, envied a Jewish schoolmate for her little treasure, or had found Jews funny for this or that—these had just been innocent little frictions, mostly even reciprocal, just the way it might happen anywhere between two different groups of people.

But there certainly were no murderous emotions! She could not imagine anyone wishing another's death: neither within her family nor among her whole neighborhood! Her father hadn't even been able to decapitate a chicken! In '45, she had thought nothing could be true of the rumor about the murder of the Jews. It had simply been wartime, when many can die—but with equal chances. That's what she kept telling others, as well as herself.

And then, suddenly, a Jewish colleague was assigned to work at her side. A Jew who wouldn't say a single word of truth about the place he had returned from. How could she, then, argue with him? Only the tattooed number on his arm spoke about why he had never been in a hurry to leave for home, even though rumor had it that he used to have a family. Furthermore, hardly anybody ever called him. And in the evening when he thought he was alone in his office, his assistant peeped in and could see him sitting there with his arms trembling. If he were caught, he would hastily recover, with a strange folding gesture of the hands. Only Hedgie's sudden appearance eased the unbearable, unconfronted burden of Elvira's conscience. She told herself: he is not alone anymore, life has returned to normal... why talk about old things?

Elvira had a hard time stopping her tears: as if this were just what had been missing for a long time. Aldó just sat there, embarrassed and quiet. He didn't feel entitled to offer her comfort the way he would anybody else—even though he had become highly proficient in comforting crying women in the maternity ward. (The same maternity ward where he was now invited again; the place he had previously worked, and where he had earned their full respect for ten years.) The place where he hadn't felt the situation unbearable even in '43, although his presence was, by then, only tolerated. Still, no harm had been done against him.

Soon, however, the day came when the young nursing aide refused to change the bed sheets for a young mother who suffered incontinence after her difficult delivery. When Aladár asked the aide to change the sheets, the answer came in front of the whole team as well as the patients in the ward: "I won't take orders from a Jew." The head physician apologized only late in the afternoon, and in private. This became Ali's last day at work because Papele held the view that "Enough is enough!" This same maternity ward, where nobody called or came to see him after he failed to show up.

He was staring at Elvira and the only thing he could think now was that he'd be letting her down by leaving the Clinic. The next day, he called the hospital's head physician to report on the status of their matter—yes, the Clinic wouldn't interfere with his change—and asked whether, by the way, there was still a shortage of assistants. Elvira was hired by the hospital two weeks after Aldó. Neither of them was aware at first that this change would also significantly ease Elvira's life financially. Since her husband's return from the work camp after three years, he hadn't been able to work a single full week. He didn't have a diagnosis. He was just constantly short of breath and short of money. Whether he wanted to or not, he would soon be forced to take disability leave.

. . . .

The chart was almost completely done when the phone rang again.

"Another lady, Doctor," Joli commented.

Aldó seemed to be happy to hear that voice, too:

"Are you at home already, Sweetheart?"

. . . .

The mysterious illumination of the pub must be what appealed to Pepe; certainly, nothing else about it. No comfortable chairs, no appetizing cakes, no good service... still, Klára soon grew to like the boring, sentimental music played by the pianist there. It goes well with kissing, for instance. How exciting to live such a libertine life! The only thing wrong with kissing in a pub is the fact that you can't go anywhere to be alone afterward. If Pepe's apartment could be Mom-proofed, they would never come to listen to the bar pianist, but, unfortunately, this was not such a day.

Olgi likes Pepe, too, by the way. Because he can make her laugh and he offers her a courtly "I kiss your hand" greeting. In Olgi's opinion, such things are always sure proof of a good upbringing. She's almost used to his beard, as well. Nevertheless, Klára wouldn't dare announce to her that Pepe would spend the night there with her. Such a step would instantly ruin all the illusions Olgi had built upon Pepe's hand-kisses.

Pepe also keeps inviting his friends to the pub. Friends from college—no less crazy than he himself—also coming as couples. Right now, he is focusing on keeping Hedgie's sexual interest alive, looking forward to better days to come. They are sitting in the most hidden corner of the room, yet Klára is still afraid of being noticed by some acquaintance. This fear makes her look around from time to time and keep an eye on the entrance door. Soon, Pepe changes his activity in favor of talking:

"Before Iván and Zsuzsi pop in, I want to tell you that I've come to a hard decision," he began, in a faltering tone.

"Quit hesitating!"

Pepe's voice now turned dramatic:

“Well... Regretfully, I am aware of the fact that getting married has become inevitable.”

The chestnut purée gets stuck in Klára’s throat. Pepe begins tapping her back and pouring some pink soda water into her mouth.

“If you suffocated, I’d have to start my search all over again from scratch!”

Giggling doesn’t help Hedgie’s cough at all. Soon she could talk, though:

“Because your plan at the moment would be to ask me to be the victim?”

“Well, if you know a better candidate, I’d certainly consider it.”

“I’ll think it over.”

“Look: as we all know, I’m twenty-five already. I only want to mention parenthetically that you being twenty-three makes you not a baby chick anymore, either.”

“Yes, I have to admit that. Still you could take a look around, too, for me.”

“No problem! Here’s Iván, for instance... with his reassuringly soft belly and his mezzo-soprano voice... He will, however, become a damn good sculptor soon... meaning that he could provide for you quite well whenever you get fed up with interpreting. By the way, I am informed that you’re drawn to painters much more.”

At that moment, they saw Iván and Zsuzsi standing right in front of their little table. Fortunately, it was Zsuzsi who stood closer. She’s thick-brained enough not to put things together too quickly. Their showing up had been on the verge of slipping Klára's mind a moment ago. It was eleven o'clock. Pepe overcame his embarrassment about what he had said, and being eventually heard by Iván, with impressive speed:

"Let me introduce my bride!"

"Jesus, Pepe! You've thrown in the towel! I need a strong drink right away!"

"Right now, he only has candidates for a bride," Klára added, for accuracy's sake, "We are in the midst of the elimination rounds, with me the front-runner at the moment, but there's still a chance I might bolt before the finish."

Iván and Zsuzsi sat down at the table. She began to say how much she would like to be the front-runner in Iván's contest. Iván didn't appear convinced. That being the case, Zsuzsi had no other choice than to talk about her new design for a carpet. She is majoring in textile design and has one more year to go, the same as the two guys. It's tiring to listen to her, because she speaks very slowly, and then stops altogether before every concept needing any degree of abstraction. Everybody knows that she won't find the words she's looking for. Then she starts illustrating her concept in the air, drawing angles and arcs under everyone else's noses, and hoping that it's clear that she meant, for instance, "collision of opinions" or "artistic competence."

Even if her mother's investment in providing Zsuzsi with a mouth soon proved useless, her eyes and hands lavishly compensate the public for the other shortage. She is regarded as the most gifted student in her major at the College of Art. Iván agrees with public opinion: he is proud of her, and hangs on each of her ideas as it develops. A longish encounter, however, bores him to death. He tries his best to be alone with her only when it would otherwise be an offence against public morals. If the snail's pace of Zsuzsi's verbal revelations is distributed among more people, it's easier to manage! A simple gesture you could expect from your friends, after all...

In the past, Klára tried to put the missing words into Zsuzsi's mouth ("Well, whatsitsname...you know what I mean, Hedgie... you're the... intellectual among us!") but she soon gave that up because Zsuzsi always returned to her air-design technique.

She told them once that her reason for speaking so slowly was that her parents had always encouraged her to, hoping her stuttering would improve this way. She doesn't stutter anymore, but Klára believes that even stuttering might help them reach the end of a sentence more quickly than Zsuzsi's present-day strategy.

On the other hand, Zsuzsi was lavishly blessed with female curves and—as Iván put it—she is a great lover. Klára got scared when Pepe reported that news.

"Do you tell him, too, what it feels like with me?"

"Nooooo...." Pepe replied, but Klára was sure he was lying.

Actually, she didn't mind it—too much—because there was something exciting about that. But she didn't say so to Pepe. In the same way, she never told him about her fantasies while making love, imagining Iván watching and approaching them, and Pepe making weak attempts to push him away... and as her movie would come to the point of having two male co-stars, she flies off to heaven. Pepe, for his part, was always sure that he had sole copyright in this department.

Pepe is Klára's first serious boyfriend. Before his time, there was only one boy she chose to go to bed with, for she was impatient to learn at last about male anatomy. And she never regretted that. The boy was nice, skillful, and he had a pleasant odor(!). Nevertheless, the next time he phoned, she asked Olgi to tell him she wasn't at home.

College life hadn't changed Klára's physique too much. Her figure still looks somewhat like a miniature, like Mama's used to. She had noticed for many years how many guys are nuts for girls like that. She was confident of her nicely proportioned figure and was able to say "No" if she wanted. She's been dating Pepe for a year and a half already, without betraying him so far. This might be true for Pepe as well, although only heaven knows that for sure.

Iván was telling dirty jokes when Klára noticed two policemen at the entrance. She saw them ordering the waiter to lock the door. She caught her breath sharply and was close to jumping up.

"What's up?" Pepe asked and turned. "No problem, Hedgie! Do you have your I.D. with you?"

Good God, where had this Pepe been in '44 and ever since? How can he treat it so lightly?

"Good evening, Comrades!"

"Fuck you..." Iván murmured.

"We doing an I.D. check. If you don't want us to use force, please do stay where you are."

Hedgie was trembling while Pepe held her hand. The policemen stood with their legs spread as if they wanted to urinate, just five yards from Pepe's table, and looked around. Zsuzsi was about to draw her first sentence in the air; nobody cared. Hedgie was breathing heavily; Pepe was at a loss altogether.

"What are you afraid of? Hedgie dear, you must be kidding!" he whispered. "It's just a simple raid!"

"I won't... come here... anymore!"

Suddenly, one of the policemen's eyes fastened on them.

"Let's take a look at those hairy comrades over here..."

"Son of a bitch..." Iván kept murmuring.

"Shut up!" Pepe hissed, and launched into a performance Hedgie would never forget.

He stands up, takes his I.D. out of his rear pocket and—without even extending his arm—he offers the cops his little red booklet. He doesn't even step forward and says:

"My colleagues and I are students of the College for Visual Arts of the Hungarian People's Republic. The recent congress of the Communist Party of the Soviet Union called for special respect for artists. Our master at the College who—in a commission by the Party—is working right now on a life-size statue of Lenin for a mineworkers' town, has a similar beard... maybe with more gray hair in it...

The policemen stare in stupefaction until the one with quicker wits replies:

"We do respect artists! It's just our duty to make a routine raid."

"Alright, comrades, then go ahead and fulfill your duty..." replies Pepe in a generous mood, and sits back down and continues the pleasant chat with his friends. "How are you doing, Hedgie?" he asks in a whisper.

"Much better... I just have to... pee... right now!"

• • • •

That was when Hedgie really fell in love with Pepe. She suddenly remembered a story that her motherly friend Emmi had once told, about a certain Laci Kaufmann—a Jew, of course—who in '44 had managed to acquire a military uniform with the Arrow Cross armband. He was raiding his neighborhood with such arrogance, telling any soldier, policeman or other functionary where to get off, that he was soon dreaded by everyone... and he kept pulling Jews out from their useless hiding places, forcing them march under his loud abuse, and dropping them off at safe shelters that had been prepared in advance. He was the Robin Hood of the Jews, as Emmi called him.

Hedgie told Aldó about that evening. She said that the policemen didn't even dare come to their table! The story certainly impressed Aldó, but he kept shaking his head with a smile: "What an impostor..." Hedgie resented his remark, and to make the historic significance of the event clear to him, she also told him the story about Laci Kaufmann. Aldó seemed convinced then.

• • • •

June 20, 1955

I'm done with all my exams! Finally! Aldó dear is proud as hell of my being first in my class. He took us out yesterday to celebrate. I know he wanted to celebrate with me in private, but Pepe can't be left out of such an event. He is jealous enough anyway, even without... The same way Aldó is: What else would make him struggle to control his face so much whenever I start talking about Pepe? Pepe only disciplines himself about this because I threatened to split up with him if he didn't stop badgering Aldó. Of course, I didn't mean it seriously, but I won't let anyone offend Aldó, that's for sure. And my threat seems to work, for the time being.

I came up with the idea of inviting Pepe by suggesting that Aldó bring Erzsi along for the dinner. We ended up inviting Olgi, too, but I know that's not the same for Aldó. Never mind, the two of us will go out next Thursday on our own (for shopping, maybe).

Erzsi was much more relaxed than usual. I disagree with Pepe when he says that we don't need anything from Erzsi except her availability for Aldó. That's male bullshit! I don't want Aldó to be locked up in a straightjacket. But I can't help it, anyhow—whatever happens—because they've moved in together. It would be just terrible if Aldó had to be constantly on his guard to comfort Erzsi for what the hell might be the matter! He didn't even have to pamper me that much when I was fifteen! Well, all right, sixteen...

The dinner was at The Little Cuckoo, so Olgi wouldn't have to get on the streetcar or walk very far. Pepe picked her up at home and Erzsi was also very kind to her for the whole evening. By the way! It's fantastic how happy Olgi has been since Pepe moved in: "There is a man, finally, in the house!" All she had wanted was the magic word of his pledge.

Everything turned out quite well. Pepe's humor suited everyone, as usual. He kept the company entertained the whole night. He told them about his exhibition plans, and also about how many great names would give him letters of recommendation. Also, his pictures will illustrate two wall calendars next year, which means a lot of money. He can't grasp that his first priority now should be continuing his studies in good studios, instead of looking for money. I earn enough by doing a lot of SimulTran. Since the Chair (Prof. Bordás) keeps recommending me to more and more places as an interpreter, my absence from classes is automatically excused.

Despite the high spirits last night, Aldó mentioned in his call today that he had hardly heard anything about me. He wanted to know, for instance, "exactly what words of appreciation my professors had used about my German simultaneous interpretation—because we always ended up talking about Pepe's issues." I tried to explain that giving more appreciation to Pepe would certainly lessen his "bragging." He must keep in mind that Pepe doesn't have a father. Aldó replied that he can't help being his daughter's father and his daughter mustn't be pushed aside by anybody, for any reason! Poor, dear Aldó! Still, I cornered him a bit, by suggesting that he would be better off following the good example of his father-in-law, Uncle Kern!

I'd like it so much if Aldó understood how many of Pepe's ways and things are just adorable! He's always in a good mood (as Olgi puts it: even his eyes laugh); funny ideas constantly bubble out of him; I'm never bored with him; and he likes my being around so much. (Beyond all these, I go crazy making love with him, as well, but that's something I could never talk about to Aldó.)

Well, let's go to sleep. Pepe's been sleeping for quite a while, not to mention Olgi, whose snoring I can hear even here in the kitchen!

. . . .

Since Aldó started working for the hospital, he no longer volunteered for any tasks at the orphanage, but just brought his monthly contribution. (Compared with the first years, the number of children living there had dropped reassuringly—though less from adoptions than from the fact that pupils simply grew up.) Whenever he dropped in, Aldó quickly looked for his acquaintances, Gyula Barta, János Csillag or Aunt Wallenstein. He stopped in front of János's door. Why not see him for a few minutes? Then, he started calculating his chances: János was supposed to be here only on Tuesdays. It actually was Tuesday, but almost seven o'clock. Still, he finally chose to knock on the door.

"Come on in!" the quick answer came.

Entering the room, he saw János and Gyula sitting there. Both seemed depressed—a state often visible on Gyula's face these days. Even the weak light of a forty-watt bulb was sufficient for the diagnosis. He'd better not work so much anymore...

"Hi, Aladár! We haven't seen you for a long time!" János said, while Gyula stood up, asked Aldó quickly how he was doing, and started to say farewell.

"Am I disturbing you?"

"No, no, on the contrary! It's only that I got fed up and wanted to shut my mouth for the day."

"Anything wrong?"

Gyula waved apathetically, so János took over:

"To make a long story short: it turned out today that two of our one-time pupils are working for the ÁVO.[16] That's what provoked quite a fight today in our House."

Aldó mused a while and then asked:

"What sort of Houses are the other ÁVO-guys coming from? With that small a number, we certainly haven't stepped over the limit of the Numerus Clausus[17] yet..."

"Listen, Aladár...first of all, there are, indeed, too many members of the tribe involved in the ÁVO, well beyond the Numerus Clausus. And secondly, our ethics provisions will become questionable if that's the case.

Aldó pondered again:

"Strangely enough, you kept preaching to me for years that my way of life was pathological, for not filling up the space offered by life. Well, those guys certainly do! The space they're given! They're alive, here and today! Or is that still not what you would call health?"

Gyula's tired eyes were almost shut by now. He patted Aldó's upper arm, wished him good night with an inane smile, and left.

16. State Security Authority.

17. "Closed Number," Hungarian law from 1920 that limited the number of Jews (and also of women) accepted as students at Hungarian universities.

"How are your daughters doing?" asked János, meaning Hedgie and Ági.

"Very well! They've both just finished college and are both brides!"

"You must be kidding! Graduated ladies lining up for marriage?"

"Incredible, isn't it?"

Aldó also asked some questions about János's family and then wanted to leave immediately, had János not reminded him of having eventually another reason for dropping by.

"Oh yes... but it's not so important... It's late."

"Sit down, if that's the case," the psychiatrist in János took over, and he lit a cigarette.

Aldó could hardly believe that he might be about to talk about himself. In the last ten years, he only dropped little crumbs about his inner life. For weeks, however, he had been considering talking to somebody about Erzsi. There was just one person suitable for the job: János. Listening in an unbiased way was his profession, after all. What's even more important, he wouldn't tell anybody. Aldó had been trying ways to phrase his thoughts, even though he hadn't made a final decision yet whether to talk at all. "You know... since I got this child, she has fulfilled my life. Since then... I didn't ask the Eternal for anything else."

János turned his armchair away, so all he could see was the filthy wallpaper, and turned his right ear toward Aldó. He did that with a strange effort, as though he were eavesdropping. He also set his glasses—otherwise worn on the tip of his nose—on the table.

"...During our first two encounters, I just felt that she was another monster like me. When I first saw her at the clinic... an ugly, furious, anorexic chicken... I felt like fleeing. I didn't want to be faced with another example of misery... after all, I could hardly bear my own company. But she returned to me. She must have heard me telling her aunt a few months earlier that we mustn't expect any working hormones from such a stature. She wanted to prove I was wrong, and miraculously she produced her first period very soon. She can't bear to be declared unsuitable for anything!

For the next meeting, she prepared German translations for me. A strange, healthy ambition overcame me somehow—God knows where it came from—and I accepted her offer to accomplish things for my sake. I started to push her into standing up on her feet again, into enjoying life, into working, fighting... And she did. It has been no less a healing experience for me, too...

Still, I've been aware throughout the whole time that she'll grow up terribly soon and I'll have to release her... in a nice, healthy way... not only for her own good, but also for mine... so I don't get fired as an elderly father and will get to stay in her life—even if my role becomes more modest—and to have the chance to enjoy grandchildren someday... I've never thought of that period as unbearably difficult. I'd already learned to live alone, without a spouse, without love. So I wasn't surprised at all one Saturday afternoon when I heard her say that she would have been on a date right then, if the two of us hadn't made arrangements to be together. I chased her away to be with her date, just the way I had trained myself for the eventuality of such a scene. I was even proud of myself—even if I was not quite happy.

(János wiped the ashtray with the cigarette butt while still holding his ear toward Aldó's lips.)

"She returned in an hour with the story that she'd found the guy totally boring, and the two of us should go and see a movie, instead. She was twenty-one. I knew instantly that I'd have to find somebody who could fill this gap, because otherwise she would never leave me. I know her. And, indeed, I soon found somebody for myself. We've known each other for years. You also know her because she worked for the House, too. But that doesn't matter. We'd talked with each other from time to time, when the occasion arose. Her story resembles mine a lot... why not do something together sometimes... maybe go to the theater or to the mountains? That would help me ease the growing spaces between my meetings with Hedgie.

(János took another cigarette while Aldó's eyes wandered between the framed pictures of Sigmund Freud and Rabbi Horowitz.)

"Things were going just fine, and both Erzsi and I looked forward to our next encounters with increasing excitement. After six months, we agreed to move in together. It feels so good, after all, to go home and be waited for, or to have the chance to wait for somebody to come home. Still, we promised each other a strictly sibling-like relationship—since love won't work for us anymore. Erzsi also had spent ten years by herself. Well, she had a short relationship with one man during these years. But it didn't work out... for sexual reasons. Erzsi had adored her husband the same way I had adored my wife. Our agreement seemed perfect. We both felt relieved and were proud of our common sense."

"Soon everything changed, however. First we just used the pretext that falling asleep in somebody's arms would simply be reassuring. However, our bodies soon became demanding. As if we were healthy people... For a long time, this had brought us nothing but suffering: severe physical pain, torturing memories, and a feeling of failure. We stopped. Then we went back again. Several times. We kept apologizing back and forth to each other. Still, at least we've been able to talk about it, right from the start. That has helped somewhat. Erzsi often encouraged us to just do things that feel good—since it wouldn't be fair, even for the Eternal, to call us to account anymore. At other times, though, she'd cry and warn us both not to risk resenting and losing each other on account of "that silly issue."

(János fashioned a pine tree out of matchsticks. Aldó was worried to see the sticks getting used up but János took out a new box from his pocket, so the tree kept growing.)

"I don't know why I'm telling you this... after all, there's some progress... and we can't expect any miracle... It simply feels good to talk about it... Now we've reached the point... it's hard to say it...when we both are able to stay in... throughout... but only... in turns... while the other one has to participate kind of invisibly as if he... she weren't there at all... That's humiliating. True, both of us are more willing to give than to receive. Erzsi would reassure me that it's all right; we only have to follow the essence of our agreement: being happy about anything we can get from each other, and not expecting completion... because that's what we've both lost forever.

(János hasn't turned back yet. He even seems to like asking with his ears. He has dropped the sticks, however.)

"Are you with your old partner while you...?"

"...Of course."

"Can you talk to your partner?"

"To Erzsi, you mean?"

"No."

"To... Ilona?"

"Yes."

"...I can. Although, since I've been with Erzsi, I don't often have the courage to speak to her."

"Ask her to let you go... She will. It might be exactly she who has sent Erzsi to you. And Erzsi has to be released by her husband, the same way. Then you'll need nothing more than to say out loud: 'Now you are my partner'."

. . . .

Olgi opens the door and a few seconds later, Pepe and Klára appear, too. Usually, Hedgie would run to answer the door when she expected Aldó. The same way she had done as a young girl. Why was she trudging now? Even Pepe arrived in the hallway first. He struck the first note in a remarkably resolute manner, especially considering his usual uproarious style.

"Aldó, may we really address you as a fiancé?"

"Yes, it seems so... Hedgie dear, how about..."

Pepe was not to be budged:

"Congratulations!"

"Thank you... and how about you, girls?"

"Alright," Pepe went on, "you're not interested in boys, I know. That's a healthy sign!"

Olgi and Hedgie were smiling, somewhat in a daze. It seemed as if they didn't mind not having a chance to talk.

"Hedgie, Sweetheart, you look so wilted."

"Just tired..." Klára replied.

Olgi disappeared into her room. Aldó kept watching Klára, distrustfully:

"I didn't like how you looked on Sunday either..."

Pepe tried to take the baton again:

"She's working too much these days."

Meanwhile, they went into their room. Aldó instantly noticed the blanket—having just been pushed aside—along with the pillow on the bed.

"What's wrong, baby?"

"Pepe, would you please make Aldó some coffee?"

Pepe gave in. If Hedgie decided, after all, to tell Aldó the story, she should do it herself.

After Pepe left, Aldó again looked at the couch from which Hedgie might have just gotten up when he arrived. He noticed the folded, old blanket covering the center section of the couch—just like hospital beds are made for young mothers after their delivery. Hedgie laid back, stayed quiet and avoided Aldó's eyes. Even though she had been pondering for days how to tell him. ("Aldó dear, please don't be mad at me, but this child would've come way too early for us. We only kept it a secret so it wouldn't make you sad. But you don't need to worry; you'll have a grandchild later. Besides, you're not old enough to be a grandpa yet!")

She was sure that she couldn't keep it secret forever, despite Pepe's opposition to it coming out. Still, she couldn't make herself start talking. Aldó was quiet, too. Then he asked:

"You were already bleeding on Sunday, weren't you?"

A nod.

"There is a reason for missing your regular period, isn't there?"

Another nod. Aldó looked down at the floor, and continued so.

"Who decided not to keep it?"

"Both of us."

Aldó put both his hands in front of his face. Klára wanted to say something but couldn't.

"Who was the doctor?"

"A young man from the Péterfy hospital. He was recommended... There are women, he says, who keep bleeding this long... Pepe brought me back to him for a check-up yesterday... I got some vasoconstrictors... But this is the sixth day, and still there's no improvement.

Aldó stood up and went to the phone with an empty expression on his face. He was looking for a Doctor Steiner... What a relief that he's still there!... Acute... uteritis... incomplete... abortion... anemia...hypothesis... I don't want to understand, Klára thought, and I don't have to. Aldó should help! And he is. He's still speaking: they'll be there in thirty minutes.

Aldó hung up and called to Pepe:

"Put some things together for Hedgie... things she'll need in the hospital. Hurry up!"

He had never given instructions to Pepe before, at least, not in such a tone. Klára just watched, without moving or speaking. She didn't feel strong enough to intervene although she saw how angry Aldó was. She hid her head in the pillow. Aldó turned to her, with the same anger:

"What's the name of that guy?... I've never heard his name. How could you allow such a... vagrant... to touch you... in your most sacred part?... Even if you didn't want... it... by no means... why didn't you ask me... to find you the best... baby-killer colleague of mine? ...Also...how many more days would you have waited to tell me? Until you bled out?

Hedgie started to cry. Aldó couldn't help her. He needed help, too. His powerless anger, bordering on tears, made his voice sound strange:

"How could you do that...? Children mustn't be killed! A child wants to live!"

A long silence.

"...And... if anything irreversible has happened to you... I would...make Pepe... I don't know what..."

Klára's crying face was begging: she needs absolution and reassurance now, not that! Aldó couldn't even reach out to touch her face or hand... He was holding his own head with both hands.

Pepe suddenly appeared in the doorway and looked at Aldó with disdain:

"You can stab me, if you want. But Hedgie needs something else now. Reassurance."

Aldó only gave him a nod and thought: "Go screw yourself!" Of course, it was easier to be mad at Pepe. He was ashamed to be rebuked by this scamp, because Pepe was right.

Pepe started to grab nightgowns and underwear from the closet and put them in a bag. He turned to check out the silence behind his back, and began to feel a little pity for Aldó, too. Even though he didn't like him, because Aldó kept... holding Hedgie in his hands. Aldó had always been Hedgie's first priority. Pepe just felt like a welcome playmate, while Aldó was God! See, he is even allowed to yell! True, up until today, he had always shown the face of a benevolent God. Today's performance contained, at least, more realism...

What will happen to Hedgie in the hospital? Will she be all right after that? Damn, now this whole matter has to be entrusted to Aldó, whatever their earlier plans had been. There seems to be no other recourse than to bring her to another doctor. She is getting worse and worse every day.

"Can I call the taxi?" Aldó asked.

He ordered a cab while Pepe asked Hedgie about what other stuff she needed for the hospital. Olgi was standing in the doorway with dread on her face. Aldó stepped close to her and said:

"Everything will be all right... It's better if a real doctor examines her, as well. We'll call you."

"Why does the Almighty keep punishing us?"

"He won't, Olgi dear... Refoenu Adonai..."

Olgi nodded to show she understood her homework and trusted her teacher. Pepe made a condescending face, and then walked over to Hedgie, gave her a handkerchief, and helped her get up.

"Should I come, too?" he asked.

"What would you like, Hedgie?"

What Klára said was not quite what she was thinking:

"Alright, come along..."

Aldó felt relieved by her answer—at least Hedgie wasn't angry with Pepe. He didn't want any discord between the two of them, after all. He might even be wrong in his anger toward Pepe. Yet, still... his scholarship that is going to start in the fall must have prevented them from keeping this kid. He's so selfish... They would've managed with the baby, even without any help from him. Yes, now Hedgie will certainly say: "Look at Papele's example!" Of course, he realizes that Hedgie can't compensate him for everything. It's her life, her partnership, and her aborted baby! ...If only he could at least be sure that it wasn't Pepe who took that baby from Hedgie! That Hedgie had felt the same way about it.

Klára chose to sit by Aldó in the cab, while Pepe took the front seat, feeling offended. There was silence. Hedgie's tears continued running. By now, Aldó was able to embrace her. Neither of them took note of Pepe's presence. Many minutes passed before Hedgie asked her first question in a quavering voice:

“Aren’t you going to love me anymore?”

“I can’t help doing so... I’m just very angry right now.”

“Can you feel love while you are angry?”

“There’s no other way to survive.”

Aldó was once again ashamed of demanding her contrition instead of providing her with comfort. He tried to mend his ways:

“Things will blow over soon...”

• • • •

August 17, 1955

I’m home at last! The inflammation is almost completely gone. Aldó has calmed down, too. And he apologized for “not being able to react better” before taking me to the hospital. I told him I understood this completely—that’s why we didn’t want to tell him. But he kept saying how bad he felt about his behavior. I asked him, however, to make amends with Pepe, personally. This time, I’m sure that Pepe was right. He is not a criminal for having a condom tear! It’s not true either that we’ve “killed a child!” It was nothing more than a one-inch group of cells. But I couldn’t convince Aldó about my truth, in this case. I didn’t have the faintest idea about his having such sentimental feelings about the uterus.

I had to cancel four days of interpreting because of this. Pepe needed the money badly, to begin his big painting.

I still have to see Doctor Steiner every other day for a while, to reassure Aldó. Incidentally, it was great to see Aldó moving around doing things at his new job. He makes a much more confident impression than he used to at the outpatient clinic. This is his proper place! Elvira also kept coming to see me. She also looks much more animated than in the old days.

. . . .

Aldó ordered Klára not to look for a job before mid-September. Those who'd hire her, he argued, would insist on her starting right away, for sure, and she has to keep resting for a few more weeks. Of course, she'll find a job—considering her outstanding abilities and already excellent reputation!

At the end of August, Klára got a call she just couldn't resist pursuing. She took a taxi—to avoid Aldó's censure for "hanging around town irresponsibly"—and went to see the Chair of the French Department. This promised to be something important.

László Bordás was a decent man. He couldn't keep it secret, though, about being a member of the Party, while still hinting to the students what they needed to be cautious about: what kind of invitations not to accept; what kind of issues not to interfere with; what kind of relationships to avoid. Any Western language department would have many such traps. He phrased his secret instructions in an amusingly allusive and flowery idiom, perfectly understood by the students. They forwarded Bordás' messages to each other: "This might not be the best time to raise the issue..." "This is of secondary importance at the moment" or "It's not necessary to deliver individual points of view in that case"—all meaning: Shut up! Nobody knew how he was so sure about whom to warn and whom not to... Nor had the students been mistaken about where to stop the chains of information.

Klára knocked at the door labeled "Department Chair." Bordás came out to meet her with an old-fashioned gentleman's charm and suggested without delay that they look for a seat in the cafeteria. That reminded Klára of Aldó's inviting her for a walk whenever he wanted to discuss something. Bordás might, however, only mean it as a gesture to show his respect for her having already graduated, she thought.

"We might disturb the colleagues working over there," he explained, since "The walls are thin."

"Of course," Klára replied, in the manner of a well-tamed student. She was disappointed, though.

. . . .

Hedgie asked the whole family to come and listen to her story. Since her "disease," Aldó hardly ever came alone. Erzsi was worried, too. Being the sort she was, fretting wasn't a difficult task for her, but this was the first time she had ever been anxious because of Hedgie. And Pepe-Mama often dropped in to bring cakes or fruit for her. Pepe was spending more time at home, as well. Not to mention Olgi. Klára was pampered from all sides, and that felt good. Now, everybody was interested in her story.

"Well, he offered me a position. I could teach simultaneous interpretation... since they "haven't had such a fantastic student for many years" in that field, he said. I reminded him of what he already knows: that my technique can't be taught; it's not a conscious effort; I don't know how I'm doing it when I switch off my own voice and hear only the speaker's. Well, he tried to make light of that problem because he had an even bigger problem to deal with: they can only offer positions to Party members!

Surprisingly, he said he is aware that this is not my preference... still, I should consider the offer... after all, this is where we have to live. Of course I will consider it, I said. Oh, damn, what a mess! Can any of you think of a workable solution that doesn't mean dealing with all that horrible Party stuff?

Addressing the question to all of them was mere politeness, since nobody except Aldó would state an opinion on such an issue.

"Unfortunately, that's not the biggest problem here," Aldó began. "I'd be very worried about you, if you..."

Now Pepe's face showed its first disapproving grimace. But he didn't turn his eyes away from Aldó, who felt strikingly reassured by this exchange of glances.

"What's up, Pepe?" he asked.

"Tell me, Aldó, is there any situation on Earth where you aren't worried about Hedgie?"

"You win! There is none."

Klára was laughing, too, when she interrupted:

"Let him finish, Pepe!"

She was extremely happy about her men getting along so well. They had cleared the air during her hospital days, and that seemed to have made their relationship better than it ever was. Also, she didn't at all mind Aldó's worrying about her.

"Well, whoever teaches simultaneous interpretation can't avoid being used for political discussions at the highest level. You told us that those interpreters were always selected from the college staff. But interpreters are inevitably witnesses, and witnesses can often be silenced by radical means."

"Aldó, you are constantly seeing ghosts!" Pepe jumped in, without hiding his outrage any longer.

"I wish I were wrong!"

"You think that reply compensates for your being such a wet blanket?"

"Pepe, leave Aldó alone! He just wants the best for me!"

Olgi and Erzsi quickly took refuge in the kitchen ("Just to bring some sweets.") Surprisingly, Aldó didn't seem at all offended. After some thought, he locked eyes with Pepe again:

"I also used to feel irritated whenever my father told me things like that."

"Then why are you saying the same stuff?"

"Because—even if I'm aware of young people's overwhelming need to believe—at my age, we know how much a belief can lead to a fatal crash."

Although Pepe never liked to let such talk go unanswered, this time, he swallowed his reply in the making ("Why don't you let us crash a bit?"), because that would have indeed been baloney. There was silence in the room, interpreted by Aldó as permission to go on:

"It's never a good idea to be chosen by the top guys... Once in the camp, we had to line up, and were asked if there was a doctor among us. By that time, I had witnessed many similar selections there. We never saw those volunteers again. We couldn't tell, of course, whether they'd had good luck or bad. Silently, I summoned my father: what should I do? The answer came right away: "No!" So I kept silent and a guy, about thirty, came forward. He was found the same evening, not very far from our barracks, dead. For years to come, I was angry at my father for giving me the wrong advice."

Pepe didn't show as much aversion to the story as expected. He just nodded. Then he stood up and—seeing their anxiously inquiring gazes—he reassured them:

"I'm just going to take a leak."

After the two of them were alone, Aldó came with a proposition: how about asking Mama or Papa about the job? Hedgie immediately heard a clear "No!" from inside herself. Aldó blew his nose in relief, as strongly as a steam locomotive. Hedgie smiled:

"What else could they have said, after hearing such a story!"

. . . .

September 20, 1955

I got a job! Through Aldó! It's perfect! It's a tenured position as translator at The Medical Weekly. *The monthly workload is minimal (so is the money...), but I have to spend hardly any time in the office, and I can take extra translation or interpretation assignments elsewhere, as much as I want! It's just that my employee's booklet will be registered at the* Weekly *and they expect me to complete a few articles each week. There are no politics involved in that job, for sure. I'm totally familiar with the language of medicine, of course. Both Pepe and Olgi are very happy about the job, too.*

Professor Bordás wasn't mad at me at all. He had known my answer, he said, in advance, and he is just sorry about it. At the bottom of the staircase, he added: he feels even more respect for me after that decision. And he disappeared before I could respond. I feel sorry for him, because he must've sold out like Mishi Freud. Of course, he has a family to think of, too. My position is easier.

Also! Ági's wedding will be next Wednesday! A huge wedding in the synagogue! Ági has really turned super-Jewish since she's been dating Andris. Others of our sort would do anything to forget where they had come from, but not Ági and Andris! Of course, it was Aunt Wallenstein who gave her the first push ("Blessed be her name!" Aldó would add now. Or does one only say this about the dead?). And he is right, of course. Ági and Andris even won her father over to the religion, as I heard. They're doing a lot of silly Orthodox things even Aldó smiles about. The whole process seems so relentless that I finally made a threat: I told Ági that if Andris went so far as to have peyes[18] *by the wedding, I'd convert! True, I have no idea yet which faith to leave and which to join, but I'll find out before Wednesday!*

. . . .

Klára was in the editorial office every Tuesday—for a full day, in principle, but it really only meant arriving around ten and leaving soon after lunch. This was not due to it being an easygoing workplace, but because of the absurd scarcity of desks. All her colleagues mainly worked at home, including Klára. Only the Editor in Chief and

18. Sideburns worn long by men and boys in the Orthodox Jewish community, based on an interpretation of the Biblical injunction against shaving the "sides" of one's head.

his two slaves—the secretary and the young typist—were office-bound. The section editors had to share the two available desks whenever the galleys arrived for a quick proofreading. On Tuesdays, one of these desks belonged to Klára.

The Editor in Chief always did his best to appear to know everything. Granted, his German was quite tolerable. His English, however, left much room for improvement. Luckily, French was completely unknown territory, and Klára instantly realized—like everyone else there—when the old guy was talking bullshit. She was skilled by now at waiting patiently to be proven right, using the big dictionary here as her main resource. The boss had invented the habit of calling Klára simply "Young lady," just to reinforce his more and more shaky authority... while everybody else had a first name! (By the way, he graciously let himself be addressed as "Doctor-in-Chief.") "Actually, this form of address is quite all right with me," Klára explained to Pepe. "After all, I'm much more a young lady than he is a doctor-in-chief!"

Klára had been working for more than two months for the *Weekly* when she happened to see the boss running nervously up and down the corridor. It was the day for submitting all the week's manuscripts to the printer. The idea of offering some help suddenly popped into her mind. By revising two or three articles, she could speed up the work a lot. Somogyváry—that was his name—looked at her the way parents would look when their small child offers financial advice—a benevolent, condescending smile. Then he started to fumble among his papers, and finally took out the bottom copy of an article and handed it to Klára. The letters on the carbon copy were barely legible.

Now Klára had a chance to display her great intellectual talent. Being nourished by the works of the best Hungarian writers, she had more work to do on this manuscript than just arranging words in the right order. First she wrote her modest remarks in pencil on the margin, but soon she got fed up: hardly a single sentence stood solidly on both feet. After discovering the second serious medical mistake in the text, she jumped up with indignation and ran toward one of the shabbier typewriters (which was out of use, anyway). The task required rewriting six pages, plus putting a new ribbon into the typewriter. She was a bit annoyed at not having a shorthand book available. Rewriting the text completely, based on the original, would be much quicker than correcting every sentence.

When Somogyváry—an hour or so later—bustled out of his office again, Klára was already working on the third page.

"What are you doing, young lady? Already discouraged by proofreading?"

"That article's unusable, but I'll be done with it around three."

"Well, well... And what's wrong with it?"

"The translator not having a working knowledge of Hungarian might be forgivable, but somebody who thinks that hyperemia is an increased deficiency of blood, because he had only heard about anemia before and can't even read the letters... and who makes 'melanchoma' out of 'melanoma'... 'the dejected tumor!' ...he should just change professions," Klára explained, more and more amused.

Somogyváry smiled appreciatively for a moment (that was exactly what Klára had aimed for), then he looked for one last chance to question Klára's competence:

"How do you know, by the way, what was in the original?"

At this point, Klára was clear that their roles were about to switch: Somogyváry would dance to her tune in the future, and not the other way around.

"Well... even this jerk remembered to reference the original for his translation... and the *Rundschau's* are right here on that shelf."

She closed the journal she was working from, to show him the cover. The Editor in Chief raised his eyebrows and peered at Klára's typing:

"Congratulations!" he said, and he really meant it this time. Even if he regularly found a lot of joy in putting people down, as Editor in Chief he had to appreciate the advantages of competence, after all.

"Considering that you're a beginner..."

"I've been translating medical literature for my father for seven years."

Somogyváry began to turn the pages of his memory:

"Well, yes, Feri Szepes told me when recommending you that you are the daughter of Doctor Körner, right?"

"Yes."

"Is, then, Wiener, your married name?"

For you: sure, Klára thought.

"Hmm... well, Doctor in Chief, must we use that guy for translating? I could take some more articles... Translating would be easier than correcting those."

That was the first time she could see signs of common sense emerging from Somogyváry's mind. The arrival of the thought was forecast by a violent scratching of his head:

"Doing ten to twelve translations a week would be impossible for one person... Should it, however, turn out that you can proofread at a high level of competence, I'd prefer you to contribute to that task. I'll check what you've done so far."

In January, Klára only did translations for the *Weekly* when an unexpected situation required her to. Proofreading took much more time than translating the amount negotiated at the beginning. Still, she was proud enough of her quick promotion to generously ignore the change in her workload. Aldó began to strut around as if his child had been nominated for the Nobel Prize. Although Olgi didn't know anything about the Nobel Prizes, she, too, had a daydreaming smile on her face whenever she heard her Klára-baby's successes mentioned.

Thus, Somogyváry was thoroughly won over, and soon took the brave step of calling Hedgie "Klára-dear." It sounded really much better than "Young Lady." He started boasting to the section editors about what a wonderful language expert he had acquired. Most of them had already noticed the sudden improvement in the translations.

Klára had more and more business to do with the section editors. She seldom sat at her desk alone. Recently, she had to run from one to the other, manuscript in hand, to discuss details of her corrections. She was more and more fond of the bustle in the office—and of her own role in it. When she had no interpretation assignments elsewhere, she'd go three or four times a week to the office, so that the papers with her corrections could be retyped uninterruptedly.

She never told anybody in the office that she'd always ask Aldó's opinion first, when a correction had to do more with the content than the language. Well, by that time, Klára had enchanted not only Aldó, but also the whole editorial board. Who could ask for more?

. . . .

February 10, 1956

Today I heard something terrible in the office. It started when that Doctor Szemerkényi was, once again, engaging somebody about politics—in the same unguarded way he always does. Up until now, I thought that only provocateurs did that, and I'd never responded to his chat. Today, though, I had to change my mind and now think that he simply can't grasp where he is living! The ophthalmologist whom Szemerkényi chose as the target of today's tirade against the regime tried to put him in his place and suggested more cautious phrasing, whereupon Szemerkényi replied that they can kiss his ass! Aldó says this is certainly not the key to a long life (at least, not a life spent outside of custody.)

Anyway, Szemerkényi suddenly said: victims are not just found on the gallows, in the camps or farmyards for displaced persons, but also are those who committed suicide back then. One colleague, a pediatrician called Seilmann, one of the best souls ever to walk the earth, committed suicide with his wife to avoid serving as informers! I couldn't breathe for minutes. As soon as I could move, I went to the toilet and threw up.

Then I wanted to call Aldó, but realized that it's not something you can discuss on the phone. Later I thought I'd rather not tell him at all. It's better that he think they went to America. Half an hour later, something else occurred to me: what if he also knows about it, but just didn't want to tell me? How can I find out the truth? Only by talking with him.

But still... if Uncle Pista said they were leaving for America, it's still better if Aldó thinks about them that way. Does he, however, know the truth?... Then, his reason for telling me that story was to make me imagine them in America! Which one of us owns the truth, and which one the benevolent fairy tale? I think I won't say a word, after all: talking about it would either destroy the fairy tale Uncle Pista invented for Aldó, or destroy Aldó's fairy tale invented for me. It's a good idea to write a diary to help think things over.

Poor Uncle Pista, poor Aunt Margit, God rest your souls! Now I understand why you gave me the board game. Thank you for always being so nice to me! If you meet my family, little Juti will play with you, for sure. Good for you all up there, all together! I still have to stay, I have things to do: taking care of Aldó and Olgi because they took care of me when I needed it. Also, Pepe is counting on me. I'm so sad that you can't be our pediatrician whenever we have a baby!

. . . .

Olgi was surprised by Aldó's call: Erzsi and he wanted to invite her for lunch next Saturday.

"You've never come to our place by yourself... and the kids have something to do this weekend, anyway," Aldó explained, and even offered to pick her up. "You will come, won't you?"

That's the nicest birthday present she could get, Olgi thought; being together with Aldó is always a treat. And Erzsi is a very kind person, too. It's strange that the kids forgot her birthday this time. Last year, they made such a nice celebration and this one is her seventieth. They must be very busy now. That's all right. The only important thing is that their lives be good. At her age, it's all the same anyway when you were born—it's such a long time ago...

Aldó rang the bell after eleven. Hedgie had been busy for hours, getting Olgi ready for the trip: checking if she looked good enough, giving her a beautiful hairdo with her curling iron. Olgi didn't quite see the point. She would be proper for the Aldós anyway, as always, and would never walk around looking untidy—what does it matter which scarf and brooch she wears as accessories? She was completely gussied up as she puttered around the kitchen to see if there were some leftovers the kids could throw together for lunch, because today, they wouldn't even let her cook. Well, they shouldn't leave without an ordinary meal!

"Aldó, please, take care of Olgi's stomach! Don't overfeed her...you know, at her age it's..."

"Klára-baby, I'm not a child anymore! I never pack my belly full! Look at her... she thinks I'm...."

"It's all right now, it's all right... stop fighting.... Can we leave, Olgi dear? You look beautiful!"

Aldó and Olgi were finally out. Hedgie and Pepe watched them go. Olgi was about to swing her left leg, the one with more climbing strength, onto the first stair step. ("Shall I go and get the elevator for you?" Aldó asked. "No, dearest, I must manage.")

Hedgie and Pepe closed the door and gave a huge laugh, relieved:

"Well, let's start the job!"

And they braced themselves to move the furniture, so the big table and the many chairs they were going to borrow from the neighbors would all fit in. Pepe discovered that the armchairs were quite heavy, but that was no news to Hedgie, since she and Olgi had to lift them whenever they cleaned the apartment.

"Why isn't Andris here yet? This is no job for 'weak women'! Your honored father will throttle me if you overstrain your little belly!"

Since he was squatting anyway—to roll up the carpet—he gave a quick kiss on Hedgie's belly.

"Pepeee, you really can see now that he should worry about you, too!"

"About my belly?"

"Not quite. But the time might come for that, too... By the way, we asked Andris not to come over until after twelve."

"Damn..."

But they didn't need his help to put up the decoration, so they started to stick the huge pictures on the walls and doors. They planned to cover every vertical surface with life-size pictures of former actors.

"Give me Kabos, first... he'll make her laugh right away... Now, a prima donna... the dramatic Karády... alright... How about Gombaszögi next, she liked her a lot, too..."

"No, now a guy... the handsome Pál Jávor, she was in love with him!... How about Nijinsky, don't you want him yet?"

"No, that should be in a central spot, in Olgi's room."

There were at least two dozens pictures, all put at Olgi's eye level. Some finally found their place in the kitchen.

Hedgie hadn't known before that Olgi had been a fan of the theater in her younger years; nor about her having been trained in ballet as a little girl. Her devotion to theater must be a leftover from her love for dancing. Hedgie had only been aware of Olgi's listening to theater broadcasts with great affection, but she never heard any more on that topic. As Pepe began to come over to Olgi's place more and more frequently, and Olgi regarded him more and more as a family member, it was Pepe to whom she started to talk about theater. At the beginning, these were only little things, but the cheerful reception encouraged her to say more. An artist has entered the family! An artist who must understand this dream, she thought.

She recalled a lot of stories about her favorite actors and actresses, about the rumors surrounding them, and performances of special note that she had attended, with tickets her husband always bought as a surprise for her.

A few months ago, Hedgie had discovered in a second-hand book shop a bound copy of *Theater World* covering all of 1937. The idea of organizing Olgi's birthday party around that theme came instantly. She meticulously collected the names mentioned by Olgi (some of them even sounded familiar) while Pepe acquired pictures from the *Theater World* archive. Enlargements were made by Pepe's photographer friend. Another present, beyond *Theater World,* would be a pair of tickets to four performances at the nearby Comic Theater, a place close enough for Olgi to walk to. She hadn't been to a theater since the war. Olgi could choose which family member she'd like to accompany her to each performance. She might not even have heard that the Comic Theater had been renamed Theater of the People's Army. Well, her eyes might not notice the new sign when she entered the theater.

The huge paper flowers—made by Pepe—could also be stuck on before Andris came. ("They shouldn't turn out too modern, Pepe, because Olgi won't understand that!") The wooden finish of the closets could hardly be seen after they were covered with flowers. Paper coils were hanging down everywhere from the ceiling, the lamps, and the windows. Balloons, which took quite an effort to blow up, also became part of the decoration. Hedgie and Pepe argued for days about aesthetics, since Pepe found paper coils and balloons kitschy and childish, an assault on his artistic concept. Hedgie, however, countered that Olgi would be happy to see balloons and paper coils. Their intention should, after all, be to make her happy—not themselves.

When Andris and his father-in-law, Mr. Feldmann, arrived to help move the bigger pieces of furniture, the apartment already resembled a ballroom just before closing hour. Except for the chairs, all the furnishings of the apartment had disappeared.

"Uncle Feldmann, why is Ági going to come alone?"

"She isn't, Honey. The girls from the House will meet at our place and come over together. Because we explained to her that with her nice big belly, she'd only get in our way at this point; better for her to rest a bit until then."

Pepe-Mama arrived with two full baskets. First, she put the meat in aspic—made by Hedgie at Pepe-Mama's place, based on her instructions, and kept secret—in the icebox, along with the huge birthday cake. Pepe-Mama volunteered to be head chef. She cleared off the counters for all the food they were expecting, and took out tableware, napkins, glasses, and plates. The boys went to get the big table and chairs from the Patakis' on the second floor while Hedgie ironed the tablecloth. She still had to find a second cloth for the gift table...

It was clear by now that all twenty chairs wouldn't fit into Olgi's room, so the "children's room" also had to be rearranged. Pepe gave permission to Uncle Feldmann to arrange the leftover paper flowers any way he wanted. Now the signs with "God bless you" "and keep you" "Olgi dear" "to 120!" were pinned up. Meanwhile, Pepe-Mama kept feeding the staff since there was still a lot of time until four o'clock.

Madame Gretl also came earlier than appointed. "Helping hands might be needed," she commented. They were, indeed. Gretl seemed to be a real expert in preparing punch. It had been her idea to plan the party as a potluck. At first, Hedgie was afraid of asking the older people to bring something along. But as it soon turned out, everybody was happy with the idea. Piroska, Olgi's sister-in-law with a lot of common sense, insisted on being told what to bring—after all, everybody would bring something anyway. "It would be pretty embarrassing to see my flodni[19] become the eighth one of its kind!" It was easy to see her point. Finally, everybody was told what sort of contribution she was expected to make— sweet or salty, solid or liquid— and anything else was entrusted to "her very special creativity."

The men were busy arranging the heap of furniture while the women set the table. Hedgie prepared the bathroom for the huge crowd while Pepe was arranging the presents already there, with artistic care. Andris ran down to the flower shop to get the bouquet ordered the previous day and some decorative leaves to be spread on the tables.

At half-past two, Emmi rang the bell. She needed some extra time, she said, because her layered cake could only be put together on site. She also brought along the records, as promised, of the popular cabaret-duettists of the pre-war times, Hacsek and Sajó, borrowed from a friend of hers. (Olgi couldn't understand last week why her gramophone suddenly had to be repaired. Still, she proudly put out her reserved set of needles and kept listening to her old records made by the Tonalit factory, one after the other.)

Soon after Emmi, Aunt Piroska and her husband arrived with several pans of meat pie that still needed twenty more minutes in a preheated stove. The Patakis from the second floor didn't see any reason to stay home any longer, after loaning their big table and all of their chairs. They brought the wine Pepe had been storing with them for days, plus their own homemade raspberry soda. Pepe and Hedgie were hurriedly changing into their Sunday clothes in the

19. A popular, very rich Hungarian-Jewish dessert with layers of walnut, apple, and poppy seeds between the layers of the dough and with apricot jam on the top.

bathroom when six girlfriends from the orphanage arrived, all swarming around Ági's swollen belly. They brought enough food to feed an army. This part had been organized by Ági. She invited those who had been most devoted to Olgi and still visited her. There are so many of them, an amazed Hedgie marveled.

"It's such a long time ago when I last saw you on a Saturday! Once you had meant Saturday to me... you, Olgi and Aldó" said a touched Ági.

(During the years when Uncle Feldmann was deported, Aldó had always arrived from school with "his two daughters" for the Saturday lunch. Ági had spent the whole time with them until Monday morning. On weekdays, however, she'd preferred to stay in the orphanage. She made several friends there and became—for the first time in her life—a support for others.)

Everybody kept the three o'clock appointment. That was needed to leave spare time for a final arrangement of the buffet table and the presents before the guest of honor arrived. Hedgie "ordered" her to come—via Aldó—at half-past three. Uncle Feldmann was already on the balcony looking for their arrival, so the candles on the cake could be lit in time.

"Why seven?" Ági asked.

"No, that's seventy," Pepe laughed. "You can't expect a 'zero' candle to be visible!"

They could hear the elevator start up. Then the squeaking as it stopped. Snap, its door closed again, and the key turning in the lock. The cake stood on a small table, fully illuminated, in front of the entry door.

Twenty people squeezed together, hardly breathing, behind the closed doors of the rooms. Not a single sound came from the hallway. What's up? Aldó's voice, soon: "Well, there are some interesting rearrangements made here...it seems." More silence. Then, Erzsi's voice: "Olgi, dearest, don't you have birthday today, just by chance? Because it looks pretty much like a..."

At that, Hedgie gave the starting note for the chorus:

"God bless you and keep you, Olgi dear, to a hundred and twenty!"

And they burst out of the rooms. Olgi had been, seemingly, busy with her tears for quite a while and was holding onto Aldó's arm. After being attacked by the crowd, she grasped Erzsi with her other hand. For safety's sake, Aldó put his free arm behind Olgi's back. She was overwhelmed. She was surrounded.

"Olgi dear! Look around!"

Olgi nodded and cried.

"Come on, let's guide you through the exhibition!"

Olgi was smiling and crying.

"Hey, let her come and look around! Olgi dear, whom do you choose as your guide?"

Olgi was crying.

"Aren't you happy?"

Olgi kept nodding. Hedgie helped her out by lending her voice:

"That's just her way of being happy..."

• • • •

The radio was on continuously. The Free Hungarian Radio. The voice of Imre Nagy.[20] That's good news. Maybe. But what will happen next? Will the Russians really march out? And who will march in? Is it true what was said about a massacre in front of Parliament? Rumor says that tanks are roaming around, but not shooting—so far. The Patakis from the second floor said that one can hear abuse of Jews on the streets. Both Russians and antisemitism... isn't that too much in the name of "freedom?" "Why are we always in the wrong place?" Klára wondered.

In the first days of the uprising, Pepe was coming and going, bringing fresh news each time. Iván and two other friends came to pick him up and—despite Hedgie's protest—they left to have a look around town. They invited Hedgie, too, but she was even more afraid of that alternative. From the fourth day on, however, Pepe only hung around the phone. He spoke to everybody, without caution. From time to time, he reported on the news he heard: yes, terrible, there were many dead around Parliament. Iván and Zsuzsi had been there, too. Since then, Zsuzsi started stuttering again. But at least both of them were alive. Pepe summarized his news at the end of the day:

"Everything will remain as it was. The ÁVO and the Russians unchanged. They might be cornered now, for a short while, but their turn to corner others will come. They simply have superior firepower. The Carpathian Basin had

20. *Imre Nagy (1898-1958) was leader of the "reform-communists" and prime minister during the 1956 revolution. In November—after the revolution was crushed—he was arrested, executed two years later, and rehabilitated only 1989.*

never been and will never be the Valley of Liberty. One has to leave this region!"

. . . .

They didn't even bother talking in a low voice, even though it was well after midnight. They had been quarrelling for hours. Klára was crying. Even Olgi could hear Pepe's voice, and that made her cry in her room.

"Now's the time! You can't tell how long this opportunity will last. Borders can be closed again, any time..."

"I won't leave them! Don't you get it? They didn't leave me! They tolerated me when I was intolerable... while I was doing nothing but abusing them... Even though I was nobody to them; and hardly anybody even to Olgi. Still, their only desire was to make me happy with life! They shoveled joy into me, with all their strength... and they still do."

Pepe's voice weakened.

"My mother would let me go, for sure, if she knew I wanted to leave!"

"Maybe so. But that wouldn't be enough for me to leave her. It's never an accident where you happen to be."

"God's orders?"

"No. My orders. I won't leave them!"

"Meaning, you're going to remain their possession forever."

"You can put it that way. It sounds good! Still, if you want to belong to me, you owe me something, just as I owe you."

Pepe kept silent.

"Besides, it's not just about Olgi and Aldó... Aldó once said I had to stay behind when Gyuri left in order to keep watch at my post. I don't know how he put these things together so exactly... but that was the truth, indeed. And that's the case today."

"Because Aldó is a genius, as we all know... Alright, Hedgie, I didn't mean it... it's not an insult... stop crying..."

Olgi thought about this. If Klára could be happier somewhere else, she'd certainly let her go. Aldó would do the same, without question. Life would immediately lose its purpose, of course. But that would be her last loss. Because the time she has left will likely be short. She should ask Klára. She should offer her the choice. She should offer her life.

"But my post... is not the same anymore." Klara replies to Pepe. "I gave up waiting for them to come home a long time ago. I only want to keep their place reserved here. Every one of us was killed or chased away..."

"Like my father and his family..."

"...but they'll never chase me away! I'll stay here forever... to leave some trace of their having been here... my parents, my grandparents, my siblings, and my cousins... There were thirty of us around the table on big holidays... Aldó's family had been twenty, without guests... I'll live here, even when I become nothing more than a monument!"

"For a monument, you can't be called oversized..."

• • • •

The next morning, Hedgie spied on him and worried because neither version A (guffawing) nor version B (fuming) was apparent in Pepe's behavior. How to find out what was going on in his head? Is he going to leave? If that were the case, it would be best to get over that hump as soon as possible. Gyuri had left once, too. That was also hard. But she'd gotten over it. She'd get over Pepe's leaving one day, too, if that's what was coming.

After a few short phone calls in the morning, Pepe announced he'd go and get his mother. She shouldn't be left alone at home. There's more and more fighting reported all over town. Hedgie got scared: what if he was planning something else... In a moment, though, she settled herself down. No, Pepe has never been sneaky; he won't just run away. If he decided to leave, he'd say farewell. Just the way Gyuri did. And Mama. And Papa. That last thought brought some relief, and she felt ashamed of the previous ones. Pepe had asked her to see what Olgi thought of his plan. Also, whether his mother could sleep along with Olgi in her double bed.

Pepe took off. Hedgie kept recalling Gyuri's face. Does he have any idea what's going on in Hungary? What do they know in France about the situation here? Did he care at all? Whom could he talk to about it? There are two Hungarians among his friends, but they lived outside of Montpellier. Sometimes he visited Charlotte, too, he wrote, and talked to her on the phone. Hedgie tuned the radio from the Hungarian stations to look for a French one. She found one, but didn't hear a word about Hungary. Calling Gyuri would be an idea...It's been more than an hour since Pepe left.

. . . .

October 27,1956

Pepe-Mama lives just a few blocks away. What if Pepe decided to leave, after all? But there was nothing farewell-like in his departure. Should they also bring a blanket, he asked. No, Pepe won't deceive me. Not about something like this, in trifles, maybe, for convenience sake. How would life be like having only Olgi around again? Aldó's life is also further away than it used to be, and that won't change. He has his Erzsi. He never abandons anybody, but what about Pepe? Do I know him at all? Is he interested in anything other than playing? Am I doomed to be deserted by everybody?

. . . .

The key was jingling. That's Pepe! Finally! Hedgie threw herself on Pepe's neck. Olgi immediately invited Pepe-Mama in warmly.

"What's up, Hedgie? I'm not returning from the North Pole!"

"Yes, you are."

"Alright... if you think so. The temperature would almost fit."

Olgi helped take the baskets into the kitchen. The very same baskets that Pepe-Mama had brought on Olgi's birthday, with ugly crystal glasses on top. Now there was canned milk on top, along with cooking oil, sugar, rice, flour, and a few jars of homemade jam below. A small tin box labeled Neocarbolax stuck out from one of the baskets. There was, however, no medical carbon in it, but two thin necklaces, a bracelet, a couple of brooches of dubious beauty, and the Schaffhausen wristwatch that had belonged to Pepe's father, having last shown the correct time in the prehistoric era. Pepe pulled his mother's wrinkled clothes out of the backpack. Hedgie joined them in furnishing Pepe-Mama's camping place.

The phone rang. It was Aldó calling. Hedgie listened with a worried expression. And then she reported:

"He's going to leave for the hospital! A terrible idea... there is shooting everywhere...! He just wanted to let us know. Everything will be all right, he said. How can he tell? He must go, he said, because his colleagues have been working without a break for four days... Erzsi is crying bitterly, of course. He asked us to call her from time to time, and to stay at home. Why's he leaving, then?"

Hedgie expected Pepe to start teasing about Erzsi's crying. But Pepe surprised her once again:

"I'm bringing Erzsi here, too," he declared with a resolute expression.

"Don't leave again! Isn't it enough that Aldó is about to head outside?"

"No woman should be left alone at times like this... You can't tell how far things will deteriorate..."

"Erzsi's in a safe place, Sonny," Pepe-Mama intervened, "I would've stayed at home, too, if you hadn't been so pushy!"

"The situation is getting worse every day, as you can hear. Anything might happen! I really don't understand why Aldó couldn't just stay put where he was!

There was no way to talk Pepe out of his plan. He ate a big slice of buttered bread, donned woolen underwear, plus an extra pullover under his coat. He turned back for a last remark before leaving:

"I'll call you when I arrive there. If you don't hear from me within a couple of hours, the only reason will be that it was better not to keep going but to hide somewhere... And not because I was shot!"

"What's the guarantee?" Pepe-Mama asked, terrified.

"...The fact, Mom, that when I was eight, the old gypsy woman predicted that I'm going to have a long life, remember? Well, stop yammering, that won't help anything!"

. . . .

All three women sat in numb silence in Hedgie's room. Olgi kept asking from time to time if they wanted anything to eat. They didn't. For a while, Klára tried to distract herself by imagining a bulletproof bubble around Aldó and Pepe. She also put a magic compass in their hands showing them at every corner the safe way to proceed.

Aunt Schwarz had commanded them like that in '44, while they were sneaking through town from the falsely called "protected house" to the Ghetto. Aunt Schwarz held Klára's and Juti's hands; Uncle Schwarz held Gyuri's. The gander with the unerring nose was clearly the aunt. Klára was fully aware of the dread felt by her grown-ups, but she took it for granted that they would reach the Ghetto. She hadn't suspected, however, that she would leave the Ghetto one day without Juti being around anymore.

Almost two hours had passed since Pepe left when the phone rang again. Hedgie picked it up:

"Oh, thank God!" she said and explained right away to Olgi and Pepe-Mama: "It's Aldó! He made it to the hospital safely!"

It was hard not to notice Pepe-Mama's disappointment at not hearing from her son instead. And that feeling was understandable, after all.

"The doctor's bag worked great," Aldó began his report. "I took it along as a visible ID. The insurgents stopped me at the Pest bridgehead, peered into my bag, and started to call me Doctor. I told them I was on my way to a childbirth. Two of them accompanied me for a while and explained which routes to avoid. The grand boulevard and Üllői Street are beleaguered... They also helped me find a detour around Boráros Square... Narrow streets are safe. Before parting, they promised that the children being born right now would live in freedom... I have no idea how they can be so sure. Still, that was touching. I would never have thought to say farewell to an armed stranger with words like 'Take care!' But that's what happened... Also, imagine... Erzsi wanted to sew a red cross on my coat before I left but I was against it. There could be many problems with such an insignia. I—for my part—have had pretty unfavorable experiences with the yellow star, while nowadays it seems it's those with a red star who have difficulties surviving."

Hedgie was astonished to hear Aldó speak in that manner, especially on the phone. But she was glad to join his laughter. Pepe-Mama kept pacing nervously:

"Pepe can't call us if the line is busy..." she murmured.

Her remark immediately reminded Hedgie of her other worry, Pepe, and she hurriedly invented a pretext for hanging up. The three ladies had agreed not to mention Pepe's adventurous errand, in case Aldó called prematurely. He should only learn about it after the two have arrived safely.

The bell rang. Gyuszi Pataki from the second floor stood at the door.

"Rumor says," he began, "that the son of the district physician was shot dead yesterday in front of Parliament. In addition, there are more and more fights with live ammo all over the city. For God's sake, Pepe should stay out of that crazy game. Our sort has already taken its share from history. Oh, is he only half Jewish?...Well, that's enough, too... Where did he go? To Bartók Béla Street? What a crazy idea! Well, I better stop babbling. But please let us know when he's back. Just for us to know he's alive."

Half an hour later, the phone rang again.

"I can't understand your hanging around the kitchen stove instead of taking a nice stroll in this beautiful weather!"

"Where are you, Pepe?" Hedgie asked, almost crying from relief.

"Where should I be? At my new girl friend's, of course... But I'll walk home with her soon."

He suddenly reduced his volume to a murmur. Erzsi must have come nearby.

"She is about to get ready, but first she resisted the idea. An empty apartment could be plundered, she argued. I asked her if she wanted to defend the tableware in person! After all, whoever came to plunder the apartment would first knock her on the head! So, finally, she agreed to leave the teaspoons to their fate... There was nothing unusual in the street... I haven't heard a single shot... from nearby... Yes, that's true, the quay is an open space, but that's its advantage! You can see the whole area around. If you walk close to the wall, you can't be shot from any direction... there is no opposite side close enough!"

Hedgie was glowing. Pepe is victory himself. He is survival!

"Let me hand it over to Mama...she's almost crying to hear your voice. And if she begins to cry, there will hardly be any usable woman left for you!"

An hour later, Aldó called again, terrified, and said he couldn't reach Erzsi by phone. "She might be over at the neighbor's." Hedgie offered as her first sop to Aldó's fantasy. But Aldó had tried there, too, of course: they hadn't seen her, they tried ringing the bell at Erzsi's, but she didn't open the door...

"Well... alright then... she is on her way here with Pepe."

"Good God... this Pepe!... Are you sure it's a good idea?... It's very nice of him, but no one should be out wandering around town now!"

"You arrived all right, too, didn't you?

"It was a close shave..."

"An hour ago, you told a somewhat different story... Anyway, we'll call you as soon as they arrive."

And indeed, they could call him in twenty minutes.

. . . .

Aldó and the other three members of the medical team couldn't leave the hospital for more than a week. Their relief didn't show up. Judging by the nearby detonations and the radio news, neither Haller Street nor Üllői Street were passable. The hospital, however, proved to be safe. There were plenty of potatoes and dried peas in storage. Sometimes, even fresh bread and apples were distributed. Washing water was heated on the department stoves. The central laundry closed up, because all available coal was needed for heating. Both patients and staff washed their laundry by hand, individually. The new mothers took turns boiling and hanging diapers all day long.

The team's biggest concern was to avoid any raging contamination among the newborns. The medication stock on hand was not enough to cope with such a threat. Nursing bottles were sterilized according to the strictest regimen.

Still, every team member was able to sleep a few hours every day. No new deliveries took place anymore, because no families would risk the trip to the hospital. Any mother due to deliver, and having both courage and some help, seemed to have decided on a home birth over the past few days. Nevertheless, the department was full to capacity during the whole time, because no mother there would risk leaving the hospital.

The four members of the team shared night shifts with the babies and shared all other tasks, like serving food or transporting the babies back and forth every third hour. The flow of mother's milk started to ebb; extra food portions had to be begged for in the kitchen. Whining became non-stop. Newborns were crying all day, too, most likely the result of milk loaded with hormones of anxiety. Aldó and Pali Steiner spent the daytime using techniques to reassure the mothers. Magdi, the senior nurse, proved to be a good psychologist by inventing a joke-telling contest. Others were playing Bar-Kochba,[21] initiated by a young mother with unusual common sense—that spread quickly in most of the wards. The panicky whining ceased then for a few hours. Also, it was touching to see some mothers breastfeeding others' needy babies.

There was an exceptional woman among them. Her baby, born with a severe birth defect, had died the day before Aldó arrived. She had already been prescribed the injection intended to dry her milk supply. After calling Aldó to her bed, the woman said with tear-stained eyes:

"I don't want to have my milk cut off... There are many babies here without enough food... I'm ready to feed them."

"You'd be cheating your own body this way," Aldó argued. "What will you do later on at home?"

And suddenly he thought of himself having been healed by Hedgie... But what nonsense to think of any similarity here... They are two different stories!

However, this woman asked less for his permission than for his support:

"I have two healthy children at home. I'll overcome my grief sooner or later... But let me say farewell to my own baby by offering others a mutual gift from both of us," she begged.

She belonged to the sect of the Sabbatarians.

21. A game similar to Twenty Questions. The name of any person, any object or concept should be guessed based on questions that can be answered only by Yes or No.

. . . .

Since there were hardly any doctors in Pediatrics, Aldó and Pali had other tasks in regard to the babies besides just looking after them. Aldó learned soon not to be afraid of holding babies in his hands anymore—he had had no time or opportunity for this luxury. He hadn't held a newborn after its bath for thirteen years. By the time it's dressed, it's already a child.

All the babies spent a few hours with their mothers every evening. That also gave the team a chance to rest a bit. Still, none of them had any idea how to spend their free time. They didn't feel like talking about the events outdoors. A short nap didn't work for them, either. Pali acquired a set of cards from somewhere and they spent the time playing "Twenty-one." Pali legitimized this simple-minded game by the argument that during the siege of Budapest twelve years ago, "Twenty-one" had been the favorite pastime for those squeezed together in the cellars. However, he hadn't taken part in those entertainments personally, because, at the time, he had had an important engagement in Auschwitz.

Jancsi Lőrincz called the day after Aldó had replaced him and inquired if he was needed. Actually, he was not... he should stay at home instead. The head physician hadn't answered his home phone now for days; only one other colleague, Géza Weszely, called to announce that he didn't feel like setting out. It's all right, Aldó replied, they can manage without him. Likewise, both Aldó's and Pali's families were relieved that their men didn't move.

The nursing personnel had shown even less interest in the Department. Only one neonatal nurse dropped in, and decided to leave after twenty-four hours. Nobody ever saw her in Hungary again. And as far as Elvira was concerned, she didn't dare to leave her husband alone, because "he would then run into town right away, until he found the site of the most bitter fighting; and then be done in quickly by an asthma attack."

. . . .

November 1, 1956

Gretl has left! It's terrible! She came to say farewell. It's awful. I wish I could go with her, but only if all of my loved ones would come. How will I manage without her? Of course, I understand. Her grandchildren are waiting for her in Austria. I know it will be good for her. She was crying, too. She won't miss anybody as much as me, she said. Why is she leaving, then? Let her just arrive safely! She said she'd send a message. Also, that she doesn't have too many more years to live and wants to spend those with her grandchildren, despite being four years younger than Olgi. She left a set of her keys with us. I should go to her place and take whatever I like. She meant the books first of all—but anything I like. And she told Olgi how grateful she is for having me ("this little ray of sunshine" as she put it) as "part-time granddaughter." shared with Olgi. And "now—with broken heart—she is returning her share." I was crying so much that I don't even know when she finally left our place.

She will be picked up at seven, she said. She must be across the border by now. It's almost midnight. She may even be sleeping already at her grandchildren's. We won't see each other anymore, I know. Gott sei mit Dir, Gretl!

. . . .

The young mothers, well over a week after their deliveries, became less and less vulnerable. Daily news about events in the country soon became not just a question of survival, but one of politics. Violent emotions surfaced. The cozy atmosphere of recent days seemed to allow that, too. The staff did its best to turn the mothers' attention back to the "sanctity of motherhood," meaning: toward taking care of the navel stump or getting useful information from the diapers. Most of the time, this maneuver was successful. One morning, however, while on their usual rounds, Aldó and Pali couldn't distract them from their arguments. One particular mother—around twenty—whom they were trying to coax back to silence, was outraged when she got no response:

"Is it really all the same to you what'll come next?"

"No," Pali replied and left the ward.

Aldó used his argument that Hedgie was very familiar with by now:

"Whatever we think or say can hardly influence the course of events."

The senior nurse, fortyish Magdi Schlesinger, also made her point:

"They should just stop shooting! The main goal of my life is to live without hearing shooting!"

"Exactly!" Éva Orsós, the younger nurse, added.

Several young mothers agreed.

The next time they were playing cards, Pali Steiner ran his eyes over the team:

"Éva dear, how about joining us as an honorary Jew? We are just about to found the Society of Faint-Hearted Jews."

"Why not... if you're willing to take a Gypsy..."

Éva laughed while Aldó was pondering about how easily taboos could be lifted. Pali Steiner went on:

"Of course we are. We've made it a habit to walk hand-in-hand into the gas chambers, as well!"

"Oh, Doctor, stop making such jokes!"

"Do you think, Éva dear, that it was me who invented this joke?"

. . . .

November 2, 1956

I managed to forward a message to Gyuri today: we will stay even though the poor thing tries to organize everything for us in Montpellier. The same way he kept begging me to leave with him in 1947. He should understand by now why I'm staying.

He has begun to write wonderful things since he started his therapy... for instance, that he has already forgiven himself for not being strong enough to stay by my side in the Ghetto when Juti died or after the war. If I could forgive him, too, that would become the most beautiful day of his life. I feel sorry for him. It must be damn tough to be weak. Will we ever see each other again?

. . . .

On the third of November, Aldó called and wanted to talk to Erzsi right away.The news was that he'd be home—meaning, at Olgi's flat—in a few hours! He explained that Jancsi Lőricz had dropped in, and that Géza was also on his way to the hospital. Erzsi started to cry: are you sure you'll get home safely? Aldó promised to. The three other Graces under Pepe's protection also received the news excitedly, but fearfully. They stood in front of the window for hours, started checking the street from the balcony at completely unrealistic times, kept looking at their watches, and were fastened to the news on the radio. Those not standing at the window were busy cooking the festive meal. Olgi kneaded "meatballs" from dry bread and old vegetables, using up the first egg. Pepe-Mama cooked the rice she had brought along from home, Erzsi shredded potatoes for fried balls—needing the second egg—and prepared the dough for pancakes (the last egg). For the filling, there was plenty of apricot jam on hand.

When Klára finally screamed, "He's coming! It's him! At the corner!" they all ran to the balcony and started to yell his name and wave violently, like children. Only Erzsi was crying, paralyzed, and let Olgi embrace her. By the time Aldó came close enough to hear their voices, Hedgie had also taken fright. As usual, Pepe-Mama remained the only efficient one onstage, which everyone else explained by the fact that she was the only Aryan among them. She shoved Erzsi in her back as energetically as a man would do, and urged:

"Go meet him! Now!"

Erzsi indeed set off, soon followed by the others. But everybody else stopped at the first landing. Erzsi and Aldó were standing in an utterly silent embrace. His doctor's bag lay tipped over on the floor. Pepe-Mama gestured for her team to withdraw. Hedgie's eyes glistened as she realized that Aldó wasn't coming home to her anymore, but to Erzsi.

After a few longish minutes, Aldó appeared on the stairs leading to their floor. He held out his arms as if he wanted to hug all of them at the same time. Erzsi followed him, carrying his bag. Hedgie could no longer help jumping out of the row—like a puppy not yet trained. Aldó snatched her up and whirled her around: "My baby!"

Both Olgi and Pepe-Mama got their share of embracing while Pepe yelled from the background:

"Hurrah! The chieftain has arrived!"

Aldó approached him, laid his hand on Pepe's shoulder and said with undeniable festivity:

"You're a hero, Pepe!"

"Well, of course! Bossing so many women around is really something!"

"I wasn't aware of your ever having had a Bar-Mitzvah... there was no visible sign of it until now..."

"Is that something like a bar-becue?"

"Close... but with less smoke!...Thank you, Pepe! Even Laci Kaufmann would be proud of you."

Pepe allowed Aldó to hug him and asked only:

"Laci Who?"

• • • •

Everybody surrounded Aldó as they entered the apartment.

"Which route did you take?"

"Any shooting?"

"Are people walking on the streets? Tell us, please!"

"But first, the meal is ready, with a lot of delicious things!"

"Aren't you hungry? What would you like to do instead?"

"Not 'instead', just 'before'. Take a bath. A full bath! What else could be your point of buying a water heater?"

After lunch, he told everybody his story. Pepe was mostly interested in learning about the forecasts Aldó had heard. Pepe's friends took the view that nothing but a huge bloodbath could follow. The Russians don't seem to be leaving. Why should they, anyhow? The Yanks won't stop them!

Aldó's prudence could always be measured by a clock. His answer arrived slowly, as always:

"Should the Yanks not move a finger for our sake, that might actually reassure the Russkies. They'd have less reason to toughen their rules. We might even have some chance for a better option. They'll probably try to insist that life is only worthwhile here... They are doing the same back at home."

"Will it become more worthwhile just because they insist on it?"

"No idea, my dear boy. My instincts tell me that the situation won't be worse than it used to be."

"Is that good enough?"

"Can you recommend another planet?"

Pepe didn't reply. He didn't say that he'd be satisfied with merely another country. Klára had the impression for the last couple of days that Pepe had—for the first time in his life—grasped the meaning of something new: the point was not merely happiness. He had somehow accepted the truth of his "undersized monument." This was a big departure from his family's pattern. His parents used to hoot down each other's truths. His father even used to tear Pepe's little child-truths to bits, while his mother had not only allowed, but encouraged Pepe to rebel against his father.

By the time the ladies reached the topic of frost-free potato storage, Pepe was sure he wasn't the only one being bored here. He stood up and announced he had something to discuss with the neighbor. A few minutes after his return, Gyuszi Pataki stood in the doorway. It had been such a long time, as Gyuszi explained his goal of dropping in, since they last had a nice chat... How about the ladies coming down for a coffee later this afternoon? Let's give a little rest to this poor man, who's just returned from battle! He meant Aldó, of course.

"Hedgie and I have to drop in at my friends' house next door, anyway... You could discuss current events in the meantime," Pepe chimed in, supporting Gyuszi's ruse.

"Which friends?" Hedgie asked surprised.

"At Tomi's, you know! We should have gone there yesterday!"

Hedgie didn't know, of course. But she could sniff the smell of conspiracy and so she gave in. Pepe-Mama tried to offer excuses while Gyuszi pretended to be offended if she wouldn't come. Erzsi was merely surprised not to be included in the guest list.

Pepe dragged Hedgie into the kitchen:

"The youngsters need to be left alone for a while..." he explained.

"What?"

"...for Aldó and Erzsi to have some time for each other!"

"What for?"

"Hedgie, dearest! One day, I will explain to you what uncles and aunts like to do with each other!"

Hedgie just stood there with her eyes opened wide as Pepe roared.

"You really think they live by each other's side without touching?"

Hedgie didn't have the courage to say yes. Because... Aldó...hadn't wanted... to be a man... for a long time. Once he had said he was old in both body and soul. Or... had things changed since then?

"Listen, Birdie, even the Lord has a cock! And Mrs. Lord has a pussy. Like you do, little silly! Besides, Aldó still stands half a degree lower in rank than the Lord, doesn't he?"

Hedgie followed Pepe to Tomi's without complaint. Before leaving, Pepe pointed out to Aldó several times the keys hanging in the lock, and explained that their coffee break would last about two hours. However, when he started to boast to Tomi that they'd come over there to leave the apartment free for Aldó's lovers' tryst, Hedgie hissed back between her teeth like a spinster:

"Pepe, that's none of their business! Neither is it ours!"

Pepe fell silent but on their way to Tomi's room, he whispered:

"I had no idea that this delayed news would cause you such trauma!"

. . . .

The mattress borrowed from the Patakis was awaiting them on the floor.

May I make the bed? Can I come to you?

Will you come to me? You came home, András.

I'm back at home with you, Luca. I'm here.

You returned safe. All of us are safe.

I'm here again, for you, for you all.

I missed you so much.

You've been waiting till I returned.

Here you are. Here am I. I love you.

It's you whom I love now.

It's you for whom I returned.

We are together again.

I love you. Take me.

Hold me. Accept me.

Take me in.

It's me.

. . . .

Love had never been so easy for them before. As they slowly separated, Aldó's breathing already came from peaceful dreams.

"Don't fall asleep, Bunny... they'll come back soon."

"...Just a little bit," Aldó answered. At three o'clock. And he kept sleeping. He had come home. And he was waited for.

. . . .

Waking up was beautiful, too.

"Aldó dear! Get up! Dinner is served! You won't be able to sleep tonight!"

Since he couldn't sleep the night through, indeed, Aldó would watch from the balcony as the Russian tanks rolled in along the boulevard in endless rows, in the early dawn.

But his loved ones are alive. All of them.

Epilogue

Farewell to the First Generation (1957-1967)

Zoltán dear!

The closer I get to the present day, the harder it feels to tell my story. Less so about Pepe, since I no longer think that our marriage was a complete mistake. But talking about my old ones passing away is really hard. Last week, I ran through my shorthand diaries from fifty-six on and found some quite telling episodes to share with you. From the sixties on, however, I find that many of my statements are so unfair that I'd rather just give you a new summary of the important events.

You were sent to me by Aldó—I saw that in your eyes, right away. You are so much like him and you know exactly what he knew about love. What really makes a big (huge!) difference is that you let me love you as an adult woman. As we know, Aldó overdid his effort to send me a younger version of himself. Still, I can now see that it's no accident that you are the younger one of us. The reason can only be that I have to pass on all the love that I've received, while you have to receive whatever life still owes you.

I love you, Klára

. . . .

November 18, 1956

I thought I could never set foot in Gretl's empty apartment. But Pepe and Aldó kept nagging me not to wait until the authorities closed it up and made everything disappear. They both offered to come with me. But to me, it feels like grave robbing. They invented the idea, however, of putting Gretl's favorite objects in boxes to take and store in our cellar, in the hope that one day we could send them to her. Also, that we should make another group of items I'd cherish as memories of Gretl. And—if I don't want to take anything "as a grave robber"—we should simply leave everything else behind. They are both so sweet for understanding my point! Yesterday, we finally went over. They put me in my place only when my whining "delayed the job." Aldó came over beside me sometimes and whispered: "She is in a good place, you know! And she's alive!" We always say about our loved ones who have left that "They are in a good place."

But I'm unable to look up at Gretl's window.

. . . .

March 21, 1957

Aldó will be promoted to Head of the department! (Ever since his boss defected, it's been Aldó leading the department, anyway.) Hip, hip, hurrah, I yelled, but his face revealed that he was unable to feel any joy. He looked rather sad for days, and just kept smiling politely. Nevertheless, Erzsi and I decided right away to make a huge celebration on the day of the promotion. My dear Aldó protested at first. So yesterday, I took him to Café Savoy, our usual haunt for such conversations. I knew for sure that it was about Ilona and the others who had left.

Erzsi is not the right person to hear things like that, I'm sure, because she would start crying and then she becomes the one who needs comforting and not the other way around. That must be hard for him.

Well, he kept talking about trifles in the café, and I was waiting for the chance to talk, at last, about the real issue. But he suddenly said: "Let's go, it's late!" So I had no choice but to jump right into the middle of it while we were at the door: I know they—up there—are also happy, I said. He hugged me right away (we also walked home this way) as he kept talking. About how proud Ilona had been when István was born, telling others that, "her husband is not only the best father, but also the best doctor in the hospital—she had been told. However, that wasn't, strictly speaking, true..." Aldó explained to me.

He told about his father's shy pride at Aldó's graduation from medical school. Also, about how Mamele would tease Papele whenever things were in a jumble at his publishing house: how could their daughter, Ilona marry a successful man with a decent profession if she herself could not! That was only a joke, of course, Mamele being so proud of her husband in reality... And Aldó told about how little eight-year-old Gábor recruited patients for his father: Gábor's school friend had mentioned he was getting a new brother or sister soon, and said his mother wasn't satisfied with her doctor. Gábor quickly recommended his father to the boy, whose mother soon turned up in Aldó's office.

Dear Aldó asked me when we reached the house door again: "Are you sure they're glad?" Of course, I said, "They are glad about any joy you have!" He listened as if only I could speak the truth. And he added, quietly, like a child:

"Yes... and it was my sweet Ilona who allowed me to have Erzsi, too."

. . . .

June 30, 1957

Olgi dear, get well again! You can't do that to us! We'd rather carry you in our arms; all you have to do is make your kidney okay again. I can spend a lot of time at home and so can Pepe—you won't be alone too much. It doesn't matter if your legs are not so great anymore! Please!

Aldó says there is no better nephrologist in town. If there were, he'd already have taken Olgi there. "Let's be patient!" I'm scared because I know he's right. If there were a better option available, he would've taken it by now.

And, I go crazy when Olgi starts explaining where to find what, back at home. I can't listen to that! I keep telling her not to bother me now—she tells us what is where whenever we need to find something. The same way she's always done. But, hearing my protests, she just keeps silent and caresses my hand. Although, last week when I was telling her about buying the washing machine, and promised to show her how it operates, she just kept nodding! Olgi dear!

. . . .

July 7, 1957

We celebrated Aldó's 50th birthday. But we couldn't take Olgi home. Even though her doctor had promised last week...

We all have been pretty depressed, despite our efforts to focus on the birthday. Aldó has stopped talking about better options. We went to see Olgi. I took special care to buy a present for him in Olgi's name. But Olgi said it's not important, the main thing is to see Aldó... once more... and she said... goodbye to him.

I simply couldn't listen, and left the ward. Aldó didn't say a word on our way home, either. We just stayed in each other's embrace.

. . . .

August 9, 1957

Aldó keeps trying to reconcile us. We shouldn't fight so much. Alright, but Pepe really doesn't understand that I'm absolutely not interested in his silly ideas right now! Not even when he's just trying to cheer me up. He has never lost anyone except his father, whom he never liked. He has no idea how terrible it feels not having dear Olgi anymore. Even though he liked her, too. A lot. He says that crying every time I stumble across any reminder of Olgi won't help. But I can't help crying. I didn't cry when Mama and Papa left, because I couldn't tell they were leaving forever. They had just flown away. There had been no closure.

I'd like so much to sleep over at Aldó's! I don't care if Pepe likes the idea or not. But Erzsi is there, too. Well, I'll ask Aldó tomorrow if he'd be willing to leave town with me for two or three days. I'll cancel next week's interpretation. I'm unable to focus now on anything! I don't even care if those guys won't give me any more assignments, because I've cancelled."

. . . .

February 7, 1958

Today I found an incredible item among Olgi's papers! Aldó's letter to me from March 12th, 1950. When he was thinking he might be arrested, too. I cried all morning after reading his letter (Pepe wasn't at home, fortunately.) I've always known that Aldó loved me. But I had no idea how much! I love him, too, like crazy.

He wrote: "Any joy I have been able to experience since the war has come from you and through you. I even take breath through you." And "You are the only meaning in my life, but you are reason enough for me to do my best to survive and return to you." "I hope I've been a good Papa to you in the recent year and a half, and I hope the time will come when I'll be your father again. Your Papa and Mama might also be content with me, I suppose. What's your opinion, little one, as a versatile critic? Whenever I think of the wonderful young lady you've become since I've known you, I can't resist asking your parents for a bit of appreciation for my part in this. You must know, of course, that I'm aware of Olgi's and your parents' huge part in your turning out to be so wonderful."

He also wrote down for me whom to turn to when I need this or that, and whom to be cautious of; what to do and what not to do in different critical situations; things like that.

I called Aldó at the hospital and sobbed into the receiver that I love him very much. But then I couldn't keep talking, and hung up. He returned the call, terrified, and asked what was wrong! By the time he called back, I was able to tell him what it was all about. He asked me if he could read the letter again.

. . . .

January 4, 1959

Why didn't my little baby want to stay with me? We wanted it so much! Why don't I deserve a baby? Ági already has two. And they are so sweet! Pepe is also very sad. Why don't I deserve to become a mother? I have cried so much that by now, I've stopped feeling anything.

Aldó keeps comforting me by saying that, next time, I'll carry it to full term, for sure. But I could see on his face, too, how sad he was. Doctor Steiner took the view that my uterus might be somewhat immature; that's why I couldn't carry it any longer than half of the full term; also, that these few months of pregnancy might have helped for the next time.

Yesterday I asked Aldó whether or not that's bullshit. Of course, he said, "No, no," but it didn't sound very convincing. I also asked him whether my having been a "late bloomer" might have played a role here. That's nonsense, he argued, since my hormones have functioned perfectly for ten years. Mama, Papa! Olgi dear! And all the others up there, hearing and loving us! Please, send us a baby again, and I'll take very good care of it!

. . . .

March 20, 1960

Aldó and I will be together at the Gynecological Conference! Aldó will read his paper—that was already very much appreciated last year at the conference in Szeged—and is now completed with new data, while I'll be interpreting for the Germans.

The whole thing turned out quite funny. First I mentioned to Aldó how much I'd like to attend. But he said I must understand his not being in a position to propose interpreters for such a forum. As it turned out later, he mentioned something about me, after all, making the secretary scream out: "Are you serious about her being your daughter? She's the best interpreter we have! But how can she be your daughter with a different name?" Aldó solved the puzzle for her, and told me that the woman began begging him to try to get me for the job. Well, he might have exaggerated... although Aldó has never been inclined to touch up a story. Anyway, the only important thing is that the two of us will work together! Aldó dear and me.

. . . .

May 4, 1960

Pepe won a new prize! —for that piece that he struggled with the most since I've watched him paint. This is great! Pepe is so happy! I just felt sorry for him when I heard him ask Aldó a second and third time to say still more about what he especially liked in his painting. He's still starving for Aldó's appreciation, although Aldó has done his best in the last few years to give him as much praise as possible.

Also, it's definite that two or three of his pieces will be included in the Hungarian exhibition in Rome. I'm so proud of him! I know he is damn gifted. He is also hoping to get the chance to go to Rome for the opening. I warned him not to take it for granted, since nobody ever got to do this without being a Party member. He was angry and blamed me for discouraging him. I'm just being realistic, I said. That's just the problem, he replied.

Nevertheless, we've been getting along quite well again recently. As soon as he feels appreciated, his cheerful, benevolent and generous ways return. I wish he got more of this! And I wish I were finally pregnant! Having a little daughter to cuddle, Pepe would have his daily dose of heaven. 'Cause I should have a daughter, of course, for Aldó's sake as well. Pepe also awaits the good news every month. The two of them agree completely that I have to be "put out of order" for nine months when I get pregnant. Alright, I just hope not to become completely demented during that time. What would my baby say to a demented mother?

. . . .

Zoltán dear,

I'm going to tell the events after sixty-one only in little nutshells because it feels so very painful, even now.

In sixty-one, I got pregnant again, but was able to keep the baby for only a few weeks longer than the first time. The family—including Erzsi—was in grief for a long time. First one, then another of us would break down, with Aldó doing it in the most private but still visible way. Whenever that happened, everyone else composed himself or herself quickly. Still, I remember this period of time when the four of us clung together as closely as never before.

We had some wonderful summer vacations together, with even Pepe-Mama joining us once or twice... Our first journey abroad was to Prague and, a year later, to the East German Baltic Sea. Sometimes we traveled with our friends—to Poland, for instance. Pepe had a few really successful periods—that of his Munkácsy-award, his two exhibitions in France, and his short-lived students' workshop—bringing out his good side again every time. Whenever he felt short of appreciation, however, he'd become less and less tolerable. Once he threw punches at the director of a museum and got arrested. I never told him the secret behind his release after a week: Aldó asked Mishi Freud to find a contact who could intervene in Pepe's favor. And it worked.

I was able to travel to the West as an interpreter at conferences from '61 on—more frequently than almost any other profession made possible. Before leaving Hungary the first time for a Western country, I sent a message to Gyuri that I'd be in Holland soon. Two days later, the bell rang, with somebody bringing Gyuri's letter (of course, we never risked using the regular mail for such exchanges). I should let him know exactly when and where he could find me, because he was going to meet me there.

Although we cried throughout our first encounter (two evenings), we parted as happily as if we had retrieved every beauty of our previous life. Unfortunately, this lasted only for a very short time because, after our second encounter, full of laughter that time, the stool pigeon in our delegation came up to me on the train while we were traveling home and said: if I want to avoid having my service passport withdrawn, I must stop seeing my brother; he's warning me out of sheer good will (he was a bit tipsy), and he won't report on me yet because he likes me, but he won't risk it another time—he's being monitored, as well.

That meant Gyuri and I couldn't see each other for another ten years, because he couldn't convince himself to come to Hungary. As if there were no fascists in France! Yes, he said, but he hadn't heard the shouting! —For him, the Holocaust is only connected to male Hungarian voices; it might sound silly but his reactions keep coming from his gut, not from his head.

Pepe grew terribly jealous of my trips, reaching a peak in '63, when Aldó also got a service passport for a conference, and the two of us could travel together to Salzburg. (Of course, being a couple, Pepe and I could never get a Western passport at the same time. He was outraged about being the hostage of the authorities for making sure I got back to Hungary—exactly as they meant him to be.)

I was surprised to see Aldó's easy-going ways while in Austria: he agreed with me that we shouldn't care about whether we were being watched or not. Actually, we weren't watched, but couldn't find a reason for it. So we decided to visit Gretl in Graz on our way back home. I had a last chance to tell her how much I owed her, how grateful I was... She listened to our stories as fondly as if we were her son and granddaughter. She died a few months after our visit.

That was the happiest week of my adult life until that point, because I was with Aldó. I was pondering about going to heaven with him one day and getting a duplex as our well-deserved and appropriate home, should the authorities be a bit more fair up there than down here. While Pepe would only be a friend in the city... Aldó might have meant something similar when he told me, a few years earlier: "Erzsi's been aware, right from the beginning, that the one single issue she could never contradict me about was you. Because she would lose, right away."

Another great experience in Salzburg was to feel like a fully qualified citizen, for the first time in my life. We really had *not* been watched there. We could live our lives—meaning nothing more than leaving a letter for each other every afternoon at the information desk of the conference about where to meet after work (Aldó addressed my letters to "Miss Hedgie Wiener"); or walking down to the hotel's swimming pool in robes laid out in our rooms; or walking around town till midnight without any fear or obligation to report to anybody.

I can't remember any other happiness after the Salzburg trip until I met you in the summer of '70.

Erzsi had her first heart attack in the spring of '64. Her second one, the next fall, killed her. They had ten years to give each other. Beautiful years. At that time I hadn't yet realized that they really had lived by each other's side like an old couple that had aged together over many decades. Their similar history might have brought this about, even though neither of them had really turned old.

My motherly friend, Emmi, told me once—with her unconditional admiration for Aldó—that he must really have had the ambition to "bring me up" and then release me without making me feel guilty; by taking Erzsi, he found the right tool for this goal. Emmi's comment made me feel bad because it sounded pretty realistic. Later, though, I was relieved to see how much joy Aldó had found in his new relationship.

I've never been as mad at Aldó's God as when He robbed him of his second wife. That's really something inexcusable for a "good" God! Whatever He's done to me can be explained somehow: I'm not an angel, perhaps... But Aldó was an angel!

After Erzsi's death, my only concern was to make Aldó live. That didn't help my marriage, of course. Still, this way I could offer him nicer days, weeks, and months. One month after Erzsi's death, I got pregnant again. It seemed as if I wanted to make one more effort to give Aldó a grandchild. Later I thought for many years that I'd killed Aldó by this very step; that I shouldn't have pushed so hard to make it happen, since all of us had guessed that the outcome would be the same. (He had never blamed me for that abortion when I was twenty-three. Once I told him, sobbing, that in a friend's view, that abortion might be the cause of my failure ever since. But Aldó dear said only: "That's something you can't tell... That baby might not have survived, either.")

When this third baby also had left me, and I was lying in a life-threatening state of toxic shock for two days, it wasn't only Pepe who reached his lowest ebb ever, but also Aldó, who might have given up life on the spot. My dangerous state—following Erzsi's death just by a few months—must have been the last threat he could face. His backaches started within weeks, and we soon got the diagnosis of leukemia.

Pepe reacted as though it were my private delusion that Aldó was ill, and that we'd lost another baby and Erzsi as well. He was unable to cope with these facts—to such an extent that during some disputes, I was already thinking that he couldn't be sane. He was talking crazy bullshit as if facts don't count! ("I told you not to try again; why are you so upset now?" he said just a few hours after my miscarriage. He got fed up with the lamentation of lost babies... "These are simply fantasies... Why not care about your job, instead?" That's what he said after more than ten years together... I never had an orgasm with him again. He knew that this was my ultimate turning away.)

First, I tried to push Aldó into every possible treatment. He sabotaged them in a discreet but clear-cut way. Then I started to blackmail him: how could he do that to me! He gave in to my reign of terror for a short while, tolerating the painful, dead-end treatments. After his first really painful attack, he pulled me close and whispered: "Please release me!" After crying for a few days, I assented. I thought to myself: I'll release him, but I'll also follow him right away. I'm not willing to stay behind all alone at the railway station ever again.

That made everything more bearable again. Thanks to his enormous strength of will, Aldó dearest was able to work solidly for another year. Later on, he chose his better days to drop in on his department. If he called in the morning with the news that his day looked promising, I immediately left everything behind and we made our plan for the day—including a visit to his hospital. My only happiness in that period was to see how many people loved him, and how deeply!

By the end of the summer—1966—I moved into his place. I refused any interpreter assignments, and did translating whenever he was sleeping or well enough to entertain himself. Around that time, I told him, without any preamble: "I'm getting a divorce."

And he answered right away: "I know. But don't worry, my baby, you're going to have somebody who will love you a lot, and whom you'll be able to love a lot, too. I'll send him to you. After all, I won't have anything else important to do up there. Luca and I will pick out the best one for you!"

He could still laugh. And I could also laugh because I had my secret, safe solution. (Or, did I have an earthly alternative in my head? Otherwise, why did I care about whether to get a divorce or not?) We had our agreement where to meet "up there" when "the time comes." Unfortunately, he caught a remark of mine revealing that I planned to meet him much sooner than he had thought. First, he started to beg me. Then, he accused me of blackmailing him: I had promised to release him, he argued, and that's no release! Finally, he reminded me of his story: what he had gone through before, and how long he had waited for me, and later for Erzsi, to turn up—and yet he had made it! "You won't have to wait as long, and you'll make it because you're my daughter!"

Concerning Pepe, he only said: "Don't hurt him! He is offering as much as he can. You are the only one he'd do this much for." My waiting period turned out, by the way, to be only a few months shorter than his had been.

The time came when Aldó couldn't get up anymore. Elvira and I had organized a complete nursing service around him. The two of us agreed that he shouldn't spend a single day in the hospital. We needed help twenty-four hours a day—the days when we were left alone after midnight became rare—because he refused to let me take care of him physically. ("You should remember me the way I was for eighteen years"). In addition to the paid nurses, somebody from his staff dropped in almost every day ("I just happened to have a bit of free time," they would say). Elvira also spent four to five hours daily with us. She had been widowed for years. Aldó didn't allow her to touch the bedpan, either. He was grateful for her cooking, however... as long as he was able to eat.

When it reached the point where all I could do was to sit by his side for hours, he said: "As soon as I'm gone, stop watching my body. I'll be somewhere else by then. But always close to you. Should you call or ask me, I will respond. Believe me. I know. My loved ones do the same. Because they love me."

He left peacefully. Some of the others thought he hadn't suffered too much. I thought, however, that it was more than enough. He died two months before his sixtieth birthday. The last evening, he seemed more comfortable and could say a few sentences. "Remember, I'm leaving for a good place. The time has come for me."... And he added: "You promised to wait for the man I'll send you. You will, won't you?"

At dawn when he left I was alone with him. I kept talking to him for quite a while, I think. When Pepe—guided by his devilish intuition—and the morning nurse arrived, I was sobbing and allegedly sucking my thumb. I don't know.

Despite all of Pepe's and Ági's efforts, I spent two weeks in bed, without really eating or washing up. If somebody had told me that Aldó had left a message that he was waiting for me on the Moon, I would've headed straight to the Moon. But nobody said so. One day, however, Elvira turned up again—as I learned later, Aldó had asked her to take care of me—and by using all her military school skills, she managed to take me to Uncle Miklós. You know that his therapy got me back together again—even if not too rapidly—but with lasting results.

At first, I blamed Aldó for not doing a decent job up there. Years passed, although he had promised that I wouldn't have to wait too long. (Of course, it was Uncle Miklós who made me believe in a future again.) When you finally popped up, I scolded Aldó during my visit to the cemetery: Well, you are, indeed, suitable for being loved by me like mad, but for God's sake, he should stop joking and look at the birth certificates! He sent me a kid, I thought—while I'm anything but a kid anymore!

Of course, Aldó knows what he is doing. It's only my comprehension that's so slow! It took me quite a while to understand that those three years were needed for me to regain my composure and for you to reach a presentable age! Of course, it's you he's sent for me. Should he have moved into one half of a duplex up there, one day you will move into the other half of it with me!

Your Klára

A Brief History of Hungarian Jews

Jews have lived in Hungary since the Middle Ages. Recent excavations uncovered a 14th-century synagogue and a small Jewish quarter in the medieval city of Buda. Jewish presence in Roman Hungary, (Pannonia), is remembered by inscriptions on tombs and other monuments which show that most of the Jewish population had assimilated into the Roman civilization. This became a fairly general pattern in later times as well: many of the Jews on the Danube were often willing to integrate, or even assimilate, into the majority populations of the region. The early history of Hungarian Jews shows a vivid pattern of dynamic interchange between sovereign existence and assimilation.

The modern history of Jews in Hungary is also a story of this dynamic. When Hungary was part of the Habsburg Empire, some of the emperors enforced partial assimilation—such as Josef II (1780-1790), when his 1782 Edict of Tolerance extended religious freedom to the Jewish population. The Edict changed the use of the written Hebrew and spoken Yiddish, and replaced them with the national languages of the empire. Jews' Hebrew names had to be written in the vernacular, although official documents and school textbooks were still to be printed in Hebrew.

Most Jews were very active in the anti-Habsburg revolution of 1848 and the subsequent War of Liberation, when they enthusiastically fought for the freedom of the Hungarian nation. Liberal leaders of the revolution, such as Lajos Kossuth, thought of the Jewish population of Hungary as equals to the mainstream population.

A new era for the Jews of Hungary came after the Austro-Hungarian Compromise of 1867. Minister of Religion and Education Baron József Eötvös strongly encouraged the emancipation of the Jews by a new law, and was instrumental in convening the 1868-69 Jewish Congress in Hungary. The *Act of 1867:XVII,* one of the very first voted by the new Parliament of Hungary, explicitly gave rights to "the Israelite inhabitants of the country" "to the practice of all civil and political rights (equal to those of) the Christian inhabitants."

The huge Moorish Revival synagogue in the middle of (Buda)Pest, arguably the biggest in Europe, became a symbol of the growing presence of Jews in Hungary. The new legislation brought about what seemed for some time a "honeymoon of Jews and Gentiles," though regularly interrupted by periodic outbreaks of antisemitism. With more and more Jews entering Hungary, mostly from Galicia (today's southern Poland), Hungary was viewed as a safe haven for East European Jews. Poorer Jews lived the life of an underclass, while the rich and educated had lives similar to the Hungarian upper classes, and were often ennobled, and even elevated into the Hungarian aristocracy.

The golden age of Hungarian Jewry, between 1867 and 1916 under the Habsburg Emperor-King Franz Josef I, was followed by the first World War and a series of tragic changes in the size, political structure, and social composition of the country. Two revolutions followed, including the Bolshevik-type Republic of Councils, headed by many secular Jewish politicians under the leadership of the journalist Béla Kun, a former prisoner of war in Bolshevik Russia. These 133 days in 1919 were considered, and are widely remembered, as a largely Jewish political intermezzo—which helped to put the blame for generations on the Jews of Hungary.

In 1920 the Peace Treaty of Trianon cut the country into pieces, and gave roughly two-thirds of its territory to the neighboring countries, such as Romania and the newly created Czechoslovakia and Yugoslavia. A large chunk of the population was also transferred to those countries, including some 3.5 million ethnic Hungarians. The Jews of Hungary were to become scapegoats, held responsible for World War I, the revolution of 1918, the Republic of Councils, and Trianon. They were severely punished by the savage and bloodthirsty White Terror of 1919-1920, and by the Numerus Clausus law of 1920, which drastically cut the number of Jewish students allowed to enter the universities of Hungary. Some of the most promising young Jewish talents left Hungary permanently, among them scientists such as future Nobel-laureates Eugene Wigner and Dennis Gabor, as well as John von Neumann, Michael Polanyi, Leo Szilard, Edward Teller; and conductors Antal Dorati, Eugene Ormandy, Fritz Reiner, Sir Georg Solti, and George Szell. Most of them developed their careers in the United States.

For many Jews in Hungary, this was the beginning of a long antisemitic era under the regency of Adm. Miklós Horthy, which climaxed before and during World War II. The anti-Jewish laws of 1938, 1939, 1941 and 1942 were a long journey that ended in the Holocaust, an industrial-style murder of some 600,000 Hungarian Jews in concentration camps, in territories then under German occupation. Remarkably, many Jews had come to Hungary from different Central European countries during the war years, mistakenly thinking it would be a safe haven again. Most perished, although foreign diplomats such as the Spanish Ángel Sanz Briz, the Swiss Carl Lutz, the Italian Giorgio Perlasca, the Apostolic Nuncio Angelo Rotta and the Swedish Raoul Wallenberg did their best to save them.

Post-World War II Hungary saw only a small fraction of its huge pre-War Jewry. Supported by the Soviet Union, the Communist Party, with a mostly Jewish leadership, became the leading political force in Hungary. The top ten party leaders were all secular Jews, igniting a new wave of antisemitic sentiment. The national revolution of 1956 released further antisemitic sentiments. Many of the 200,000 who emigrated were young and Jewish.

After 1956, politics under the long leadership of János Kádár, was no longer antisemitic, and became increasingly liberal. The experiences of 1919, the Holocaust and post-War politics and thinking, however, had linked 20th century Hungarian history with antisemitism, past and present, and a way of thinking which the country is still not quite free of.

Today's Hungarian Jews, typically secular, make up about 1 percent of the total population, which is close to some 10 million people.

Tibor Frank
Em. Professor of History,
Eötvös Loránd University, Budapest;
Member, Hungarian Academy of Sciences

Discussion with the Author

Q: Is the life of the characters in your novel typical of Hungarian Jews for that period of time?

ZV: In their ways of being frightened and cautious vis-à-vis every aspect of the outside world, most of them seemed typical. Also, losing faith in God after "experiencing Him abandoning His people in the Shoah" was a typical choice for many Jews, even though they may have observed some of the Jewish rituals, especially at crucial points in their life.

Q: Is your story autobiographical?

ZV: Not really. First of all because the main character of the story was already 16 years old when I was born. My family situation was also different from hers. The main characters however, are a compilation of two or three real people in my early life. Klára shows many characteristics that resembled me at her age, except that her courage to reach out to people she badly needed is something I never dared to do.

The general atmosphere, the general mood and the small but telling details of everyday life described in the book are "autobiographical."

Q: Was it typical for Jewish parents after the war not to talk about the Holocaust with their children?

ZV: Discussing the real-life details of the wartime events was absolutely taboo—not only for their children's sake, I think, but also to save themselves from reliving the terrible pain they had suffered. No word was said about those who disappeared in a concentration camp or were shot into the River Danube, as happened to probably thousands in

Budapest. (My family may have had just average losses with 32 members having disappeared.)

Some parents went further and made a taboo even about being Jewish. They avoided even the words Jew and Jewish. Their children had to face a dramatic moment when finally, somehow, in their teens, they understood that they were Jewish—after hearing dubious or frightful connotations of the very word.

Thanks to my mother, we belonged to a group where neither the horrifying details nor the taboos paralyzed us. We heard that we, being Jews, were persecuted during the war, "but survived somehow." As far as I can remember, we had the gut feeling that asking about details wouldn't be a good idea. My Jewish friends who talked about this topic later said something similar.

Q: Why did you write this novel many decades after its actual timeframe?

ZV: In this respect, it seems to me, I made a typical choice. Most flashback novels, films or other artforms about the persecution of the Jews came out typically in or after the 1990s only. For a long time I had a similar answer to why our mid-war or postwar generation was mostly taught in Europe to keep silent or at least low-profile "about the whole issue." Still, as soon as we realized (around the '90s) that our time might be up soon, many of us decided, despite all earlier warnings, that we should break the taboo and not leave this world without telling the story of our ancestors. Books by two Nobel-Laureates, Imre Kertész's *Fatelessness* and Elfriede Jelinek's *The Children of the Dead,* as well as some dramatic films such as *Schindler's List* and *Life is Beautiful* paved the way—they all came out rather late. Clearly, we all wanted to be sure that the message we wanted to leave behind would survive.

Discussion Questions

1. Aldó and Klára meet because Olgi is seeking a medical opinion about Klára's physical and emotional maturity. Explain how you see the relationship between Klára and Aldó develop. Does it seem realistic?

2. What accounts for Aldó's ability to connect with Klára, despite her apparent apathy?

3. How does Olgi's willingness to let Klára stay with Aldó affect her own life?

4. Why is Aldó willing to have Klára translate his medical journals? How effective is it in winning her trust?

5. What role do Klára's letters to her parents play in her healing process?

6. Klára and Aldó's relationship becomes a "marriage of sorts." How does their bond affect each one's ability to develop relationships with future partners?

7. Describe the emotional development that Klára experiences, that enables her to visit Mr. Wagner's grave.

8. Elvira, Klára and Olgi all take special care of Aldó when he seems to be ill and must stay away from work due to the political climate. How does this affect each person's development?

9. How would you characterize the dreams that Aldó and Klára have during the novel?

10. When Mr. Bauer is taken away by the communists, how does Aldó's behavior toward Klára affect how you view him as the story goes forward?

11. What attracts Klára to Pepe, despite her awareness of his faults?

12. How do the celebrations—Olgi's and Aldó's birthdays, Klára's new work position and Aldó's promotion—enhance your view of life in Hungary during this period?

13. Reflect on the losses experienced by Aldó, Klára, Olgi and Erzsi in the Holocaust. How do these losses impact their lives post-Holocaust?

About The Author

Zsuzsa Várkonyi
Photo courtesy of the author

Sixteen years younger than her heroine Klára, Zsuzsa F. Várkonyi was born into a secular Jewish family in Budapest. As a teenager, she spent three years in Vienna, where she went to high school. She then studied psychology in Budapest, at Eötvös Loránd University, between 1967 and 1972, and received her doctorate in 1975. Her first book on psychology, *Tájékozottság és kompetencia (Information and Competence)*, was based on her doctoral dissertation.

Dr. Várkonyi had the great honor to co-author *Felnőttek között (Among Adults)*, a book on child psychology, with Ferenc Mérei, the foremost Hungarian mind in psychology in those years. Mérei had an adventurous and near-tragic life. A sparkling intellect with thoroughly ethical beliefs but a weak sense of political realities, he studied in Paris, but remained an outsider in his profession for most of his life. Many young students like the author, however, were attracted to his personality, and learned great ideas and insights from him.

After finishing her own psychoanalysis, Dr. Várkonyi worked for five years as a child psychologist for a Budapest Counselling Center. Her next book, *Már 100x megmondtam (I've Told You a Hundred Times)* was conceived in those years, partly based on her experiences at work. First published in 1986, the book reached its 12th edition this year (2021).

In 1982, she received a copy of Thomas Gordon's revolutionary book *Parent Effectiveness Training*, and the author started to introduce his model of human relations for encounter groups, translated his book for Hungarian readers, and adopted his concept in her books in order to eliminate psychological games.

She taught psychology in the Teachers' College of Eötvös Loránd University from 1984 through 1987.

The years between late 1987 and mid-1991 were spent in the United States, where her husband, historian Tibor Frank, was a Fulbright Visiting Professor at the University of California, Santa Barbara—a great intellectual adventure, with a chance to compare two cultures, finding distinct positive features on both sides.

Returning home, Dr. Várkonyi continued her professional service as a psychotherapist, and also became a trainer for self-awareness groups. The number of groups was well above 100 when, a few years ago, she gradually handed the groups over to younger colleagues.

She was a guest-expert of a series of performances on psychological topics made by the improv-theater "Momentán" of Budapest, saying a touching farewell after the 100th evening.

She also broadcast a weekly chat on different psychological issues on Hungarian Klub Rádió for six years.

Zsuzsa Várkonyi remains active as a psychotherapist and has frequent invitations from various discussion and lecture forums on a variety of research and practical topics.

In addition to the above books, she has authored eight books on psychology.

As an acknowledgement for her work in the field of adult education, both as an author and a trainer, she has been named an honorary professor at Eötvös Loránd University.

Acknowledgements

Since I've never written a formal section of acknowledgments—as is customary in English language books—before, I started to think about whom I should render my thanks to: first of all to my mother. Every bit of my courage to present myself in front of others came from her. She was the single source of my self-confidence in any field where I do have self-confidence—like in speaking and writing. I might not even be aware of how much I owe to her sparkling eyes while she listened to me! The story you read in this book is not her story, but it shows partly the way she used to see things and people, partly the way she allowed me to see differently.

The second person on my "timetable of life" who I owe great thanks to for his constant support is my husband, Tibor Frank. I never came up with any idea whatsoever during our marriage of 47 years by now, that he hasn't supported and helped bring to fruition. (Being a historian, by the way, he is the author of the brief summary of the history of Hungarian Jews you can read in the preceding pages.)

And if I keep looking around within my family, I should render great thanks to our dear son, Ben, as well, who keeps offering instant assistance for his "over-age" parents in any digital problems we bump into (quite frequently).

In acknowledging the professionals whom I owe a lot of gratitude to for their help in implementing this English edition, the first to be mentioned are my two wonderful

American friends, Peter Czipott and Patty Howell. They made an easy-to-read, authentic English text of my precise but stuttering translation. I'm not only grateful for their work of literary quality but also for showing genuine signs of their love of my story indicated through their contributions.

I also have to mention Barnabás Tóth, the director of the film based on my book, *Akik Maradtak (Those Who Remained)*, shortlisted for the Academy Awards in 2020) for providing a new arc to the career of my story. Barnabás kindly made it possible for Joel Alpert to contact me.

Joel, his wife Nancy Lefkowitz, and Nina Schwartz are my great supporters in this edition. Joel—initiating the idea to have JewishGen publish the English edition—is actually more of a mentor of this undertaking, while Nina is not only the technical guru but also a most devoted proofreader of the text. Nancy contributed the Reader Discussion Questions and her knowledge of American book groups. I am grateful to be able to work with all of them.

Zsuzsa F. Várkonyi
Budapest, Hungary

Books by Zsuzsa F. Várkonyi

On Popular Psychology (in Hungarian)

Tájékozottság és kompetencia (Information and Competence)
Budapest: Akadémiai Kiadó, 1978

Felnőttek között (Among Adults) (co-author Ferenc Mérei)
Budapest: Minerva Kiadó, 1980

Már 100x megmondtam (I've Told You a Hundred Times)
12th Edition, Budapest: Kulcslyuk Kiadó, 2021

Tanulom magam (Learning Myself)
8th Edition, Budapest: Kulcslyuk Kiadó, 2020

Sors és sérülés (Fate and Injury)
3rd Edition, Budapest: Háttér Kiadó, 2015

Milyen nő lesz lányodból? Milyen férfi lesz fiadból?
(How Would Our Daughters and Sons Become Adults?)
5th Edition, Budapest: Csodasuli Kiadó, 2019

Amire felnövünk (Growing Up for What?)
Budapest: Háttér Kiadó, 2019

Hoztam, kaptam, átszabtam (Acquired, Received, and Changed)
Budapest: Kulcslyuk Kiadó, 2018

Novel

Férfiidők lányregénye (Girl In a Man's World)
4th edition, Budapest: Libri, 2020)

German Edition: *Für wen du lebst (Whom You Live For)*
Konstanz: Hartung-Gorre Verlag, 2005

English Edition: *Those Who Remained*
JewishGen Press, New York, 2021

JewishGen Press, JewishGen, and the Yizkor Book Project

This book is a publication of **JewishGen Press**, a part of **JewishGen, Inc.**

JewishGen, Inc. is a nonprofit organization founded in 1987 as a resource for Jewish genealogy. Its website (**www.JewishGen.org**) serves as an international clearinghouse and resource center to assist individuals in researching the history of their Jewish families and the places where they lived. JewishGen provides databases, facilitates discussion groups, and coordinates projects relating to Jewish genealogy and the history of the Jewish people. In 2003, JewishGen became an affiliate of the **Museum of Jewish Heritage–A Living Memorial to the Holocaust** in New York City.

JewishGen Press was created in 2021 to publish material of interest to the national and worldwide Jewish community. Print On Demand technology allows JewishGen to publish at much lower costs than the offset printing used by larger publishers. Production work, such as formatting, indexing, creating covers, etc., is done by volunteers, minimizing costs to allow books to reach the widest possible audience.

Hence **JewishGen Press** can publish, as a public service, important material of interest that may not have the profitability required by large publishers.

JewishGen Press includes the **Yizkor Books in Print Project** (see below).

The **Yizkor Book Project** was organized to publicize the existence of Yizkor (Memorial) Books written by survivors and former residents of Jewish communities throughout the world that were affected by the Holocaust. Volunteers connected to these communities began cooperating to have the books translated from their original language—usually Hebrew or Yiddish—into English, giving a wider audience access to the valuable information in them. As each chapter of these books is translated, it is posted on the Yizkor Books website and made freely available to the general public.

The **Yizkor Books in Print Project** prints and publishes Yizkor Books that have been translated into English by the Yizkor Books Project, making hard copies available for purchase by the descendants of these communities, as well as scholars, universities, synagogues, libraries, and museums.

JewishGen Press also publishes Holocaust memoirs, compilations of material from Yizkor Books, fiction, biographies, history books, cookbooks, art books, children's books, Haggadot, Megillot, and other books of Jewish interest.

A list of all publications of JewishGen Press, with prices and ordering information, can be found at:

www.JewishGen.org/Press/press.html

Lance Ackerfeld
Yizkor Book Project Manager

Joel Alpert
JewishGen Press Project Manager

Avraham Groll
JewishGen Executive Director

CPSIA information can be obtained
at www.ICGtesting.com
Printed in the USA
JSRC011231310521
15276JS00014B/15

9 781954 176089